SERMONS AND ADDRESSES

George Smeaton (1814–1889)

SERMONS AND ADDRESSES

GEORGE SMEATON

Edited by

John W. Keddie

THE BANNER OF TRUTH TRUST

THE BANNER OF TRUTH TRUST

Head Office
3 Murrayfield Road
Edinburgh, EH12 6EL
UK

North America Office
PO Box 621
Carlisle, PA 17013
USA

banneroftruth.org

First Published 2022

*

ISBN
Print: 978 1 80040 119 8
Epub: 978 1 80040 120 4
Kindle: 978 1 80040 121 1

*

Typeset in 11/14 Adobe Garamond Pro at
The Banner of Truth Trust, Edinburgh

Printed in the USA by
Versa Press Inc.,
East Peoria, IL

Contents

Biographical Sketch

1. Introduction

To this writer, the two most outstanding Reformed Theologians in Scotland in the nineteenth century were William Cunningham and George Smeaton. Through a voluminous biography by James Mackenzie and Robert Rainy published in 1871, much is known about Cunningham. Not much is known about George Smeaton. In 1939, in a lecture at Westminster Seminary, Principal John Macleod said that 'his work as a theologian still awaits a worthy appraisement.'[1] Since the 1950s there have been several doctoral theses produced in Scottish divinity faculties on aspects of Smeaton and his work, though none has appeared in print. Smeaton is still largely unknown despite some prominence being given in the post-Second World War period through the reprinting of his major works on the *Atonement* and the *Holy Spirit*. To my mind these are the finest orthodox conservative exegetical works to be produced in the nineteenth century. George Smeaton and Patrick Fairbairn, arguably, stand as the high-water mark of conservative Reformed exegetical theology in

[1] John Macleod, *Scottish Theology in Relation to Church History since the Reformation* (Edinburgh: Free Church of Scotland, 1946), p. 289.

that period and in the old Free Church of Scotland. As Macleod commented on Smeaton: 'Next to Cunningham he stood as our foremost student of the history of the Reformed Theology.'[1] The neglect of Smeaton has been sad but perhaps not surprising, given that the tide was against him in the second part of the nineteenth century in which the once orthodox Free Church experienced such serious downgrade in Bible studies and theology.

2. Family Background

George Smeaton was born and brought up in the borders of Scotland. His father, also George, was a farmer in Hume, near Greenlaw, where George Jr was born in 1814. There were, it seems, two well-known forebears. There was a cousin of his grandfather, one John Smeaton, possibly the finest engineer of his day (1724–92) and the constructor of the fourth Eddystone Lighthouse off the south coast of England, along with other bridges and canals and the like.[2] These Smeatons were, apparently, descended from Thomas Smeton (or Smeaton) (1536–83) who became a leading light in the Scottish Reformation, not least as successor to Andrew

[1] Macleod, *Scottish Theology*, p. 288.

[2] In the *Fasti Ecclesiae Scoticanae* George Smeaton is said to be a 'grand-nephew' of John Smeaton. This, however, has been disputed. See www.bordersancestry.co.uk/blog/archives/11-2018. Accessed 10 January 2019. There was clearly a strong family tradition of a relationship and, if there is a family connection, it is most likely to be at the cousin level; that is, 'JS was a cousin of GS's grandfather'.

Melville as Principal of Glasgow University (1580–3). Thomas Smeton became a Protestant in Geneva in 1571. He returned to Scotland in 1577 as minister of Paisley Abbey and was Moderator of the General Assembly in 1579.[1]

3. Early Years

George Smeaton was brought up in a God-fearing home and early in his life confessed his faith in Christ as his Saviour. Apparently 'his pious mother having, contrary to her own expectation and that of others, survived his birth, in her heart consecrated him to God, and resolved to train him for the work of the ministry.'[2] Of Smeaton's spiritual experience a colleague was later to remark that 'as to the particulars of the beginning and early progress of his spiritual life, I know nothing. But I know that it was in his boyhood; while from the tenor of his conversation and his preaching in after years, I have no doubt that his acceptance of Christ and of His salvation was a very definite act.'[3]

Smeaton went up to Edinburgh for Arts and Divinity as a sixteen-year-old in 1830. These were days of a great recovery of Biblical Evangelical religion in Scotland. The

[1] On Thomas Smeaton, see H. M. B. Reid, *The Divinity Principals in the University of Glasgow, 1545–1654* (Glasgow: J. Maclehose and Sons, 1917), pp. 83-105.

[2] Thomas Smith, in *In Memoriam: Sermons Preached in Buccleuch Free Church, Sabbath, April 21st 1889 on the death of the Rev. George Smeaton, D.D.* (Edinburgh: T&T Clark, 1889), p. 35.

[3] Smith, *In Memoriam*, p. 35.

principal moving light was Thomas Chalmers (1780–1847). What a galaxy of outstanding gifted and godly men were raised up in Scotland at that time of revival in the 10 years up to 1843! It was said that George Smeaton was a favourite student of Chalmers. He excelled in his theological studies. Apparently in his time at Edinburgh University, he committed to memory every word in a great folio Greek lexicon! John Macleod reminds us that Smeaton was 'the most eminent scholar of the set of young men who with M'Cheyne and the Bonars sat at the feet of Chalmers.'[1]

4. Preacher

The few examples of Smeaton's sermons that survive show him to have been a preacher in a distinctly experimental Calvinistic mould. It was said that 'his preaching set forth the great evangelical doctrines with rare power and unction.'[2] And another testified that 'his sermons were full of Christian fervour, and were characterised alike by purity of diction and breadth of scholarship.'[3]

In a sermon on Psalm 89, verses 30-33, entitled, 'The Lord's Jealousy against Backsliders Consistent with His Unchanging Love,' Smeaton speaks of indwelling sin and its dangers:

[1] Macleod, *Scottish Theology*, p. 287.

[2] Extract from the minutes of the Committee Meeting of the New College Senate, Edinburgh, 16 April 1889 (handwritten).

[3] 'Tribute to the Memory of the Late Professor Smeaton, D.D.' (handwritten tribute from the Free Church Defence Association, A5, 1889), p. 3.

> The sin that dwells in us comes on with noiseless step, disarming all suspicion, it may be under the guise of weariness, or suggesting delay in spiritual service, and it is little suspected, nay, spiritual slumber is accounted sweet. Indwelling sin is of dreadful strength; and if we cannot trace out all its windings and deceitfulness, if it is a friend within to every temptation from without, and wars in every power of the soul with the Most High, is not the most unwary soul most sure to fall?[1]

A sermon on Acts 1:5-8 entitled 'A Witnessing Church — A Church Baptized with the Holy Ghost' preached in 1846,[2] is also a powerful and challenging sermon. To the Church he says: 'A Church is only so far a witnessing Church as it is thus baptized with the Holy Ghost.' As to the preacher: 'Can he be a witness of the Lord's abiding with his people to the end of the world, who knows not in his heart a daily intercourse with Jesus — who has not the witness of the Spirit that he is a child of God?' And as to believers in general, 'nothing, it seems to me, will strike the heart of this callous age, but new holiness in believers' lives — the awe-inspiring spectacle of men glowing with love to their Lord, openly separating from the world.' 'Say

[1] George Smeaton, 'The Lord's Jealousy against Backsliders Consistent with His Unchanging Love', in *The Free Church Pulpit*. Vol. 1. (Perth: James Dewar & Son, 1845), pp. 587-97.

[2] Preached before the Free Synod of Perth, 21 April 1846, and published in compliance with their request. Perth: James Dewar & Son, 1846.

not,' he says, 'O that a dead world were quickened; but, O that I myself were quickened.'

George Smeaton became a missionary in the parish of North Leith, before being ordained and inducted at a new Charge in Morningside, Edinburgh, in 1839. When he was at Morningside he had Dr Thomas Chalmers as one of his congregation. Smeaton, however, was not in Morningside long, as he was translated in September 1840 to Falkland in central Fife at the foot of the Lomond Hills. It was said that the Parish had been, like so many others in Scotland, 'blighted by a cold and unevangelical ministry for a long season.' It seems that 'he set himself bravely but quietly to his work, notwithstanding the difficulties which the laxity of discipline under his predecessors, and a general prejudice against distinctively evangelical preaching placed in his way; and God largely owned his faithful labours.'[1]

5. Family Life

Shortly after he went to Falkland, Smeaton was married to Janet Helen Goold (born 19 January 1814). Janet was the youngest daughter of Rev. William Goold (1776–1844), the Reformed Presbyterian (Covenanter) minister in Edinburgh. The bride's father married the couple. Janet's younger brother, William Henry Goold (1815–97) became a Reformed Presbyterian minister and was among the group that entered the Free Church

[1] J. G. Cunningham, 'Professor Smeaton, D.D.', in *The Free Church of Scotland Monthly* (Sept. 1889), p. 279.

in 1876. He was particularly well known through his editorship of the *Works of John Owen*, reprinted in recent times by the Banner of Truth Trust.

George and Janet Smeaton had the first two of their five children whilst at Falkland, George being born there in 1841, and Isabella in 1843. Two daughters did not survive infancy, though a son, William Henry Oliphant, was later born to them in Aberdeen in 1856.[1]

6. Free Church Ministry (1843–54)

Smeaton 'came out' at the Disruption of 1843 and was instrumental in forming a Free Church congregation in Falkland. He was soon called, however, to the emerging Free Church congregation in Auchterarder, a village about thirteen miles south west of Perth, and to Auchterarder he removed towards the end of 1843. For 10 years, Smeaton devoted himself there 'with unwearied energy to every part of pastoral duty.'[2] At that time there was a profound spiritual awakening in the district. It is recorded that in 1848, half way through Smeaton's ministry in Auchterarder, the membership of the Free Church congregation there amounted to 770 souls.

7. Professor in Aberdeen (1854–7)

In 1853 the Church appointed George Smeaton as assistant in divinity to Patrick Fairbairn in the fledgling Aberdeen Free Church divinity faculty, whilst he

[1] Cunningham, 'Professor Smeaton, D.D.', p. 279.

[2] *Ibid.*, p. 279.

was still in his charge at Auchterarder. The following year, however, Fairbairn and Smeaton were appointed full professors. Whilst in Aberdeen George Smeaton attached himself to the West Free Church, then under the excellent ministry of Alexander Dyce Davidson (1807–72). He became an elder in the congregation.

8. Professor in Edinburgh (1857–89)

Having a considerable reputation as a good Greek scholar and excellent theologian, when a vacancy arose in the Free Church College — New College — in Edinburgh, his name carried the day in the Assembly of 1857. The man who nominated Smeaton had very distinct views about the abilities necessary for the task: 'Was it enough to say that a man aspiring to this office had the ancient languages?' No, it was not enough. He needed more than the acquaintance with them acquired through High School, Academy or College: 'He must ... not only ... know Hebrew, Chaldee, Syriac, and several other languages with whose barbaric names he would not disturb the ears of the Assembly, but he ought to be intimately acquainted with the Hebrew Scriptures, and familiar with the Septuagint version ... in order to supply the science of exegesis to the New Testament.' He went on to say: 'As for the Greek Testament itself, he ought to be able to take it in his hand and read it off fluently in English. He must also be able, not at second-hand, but for himself, to make use of the Syriac, and other ancient versions for determining many nice points as to the true reading of the original text, and in many cases, also, the true rendering. Unless possessed of these' — we wait for this with bated breath! — 'and other peculiar qualifications which he shortly enumerated, he could not vote for any man as a fit person to fill an Exegetical Chair.'[1] The fact that he supported the appointment of George Smeaton speaks volumes of his regard for that man's linguistic attainments. Smeaton took up the teaching of New Testament Exegesis at New College in the Autumn of 1857. The divinity course covered four years in the course of which students would have two years with Smeaton — a Junior and a Senior class. Four main areas were addressed:

- Introduction to the New Testament, including questions of the Canon;
- Principles of Hermeneutics;
- Exegetical Study of the Gospels, including a view to the synoptic questions and commentary proper;
- Regular commentary on one or other of the Epistles, with constant reference to the Acts of the Apostles as an historical basis.

Smeaton kept himself abreast of the literature in his field. In his last Statement at a Quinquennial Visitation (1885) he said: 'My object is to keep my classes as much

[1] The Free Church of Scotland General Assembly, *Proceedings and Debates of the General Assembly of the Free Church of Scotland, 26 May 1857* (Edinburgh: James Nichol, 1857), pp. 88-9.

as possible acquainted with the true Interpretation of the New Testament Scriptures, and abreast of the best literature on the subject, and to aid them in forming a proper estimate of its value.'

Smeaton's view of the canon and text of Scripture and its interpretation were throughout soundly conservative and evangelical. This is perfectly clear from his own volumes on the Atonement and the Holy Spirit which are models of sound Exegetical Theology. At New College, Smeaton joined William Cunningham, John Duncan, James Bannerman and James Buchanan. This constituted the Great Senatus of the College in its best days.

'George Smeaton was a scholarly devout soul,' said one former student, 'whose earnest prayers in the class brought the heavens near. He knew his subject, New Testament Exegesis, thoroughly. His students would have prized the slightest suggestion of heresy such as they found in his successor [Dr Marcus Dods]. But Dr Smeaton held on like a full moon slicing its way through the clouds. His lectures were like golden paths which his students found richly monotonous. ... Dr Smeaton never marched his men into the land of surprises.'[1]

Another student recalled that, 'We well remember the zeal and hope with which the students of our day welcomed the new professor, and entered eagerly under

[1] Norman C. Macfarlane, *Rev. Donald John Martin: Preacher, Soul Winner, Social Reformer* (Edinburgh: Oliphant Anderson & Ferrier, 1914), p. 34.

his able guidance on the exegesis of the New Testament, a department of theological research which had then only begun to be valued and cultivated as it deserved. For our own part we found in the work of the class and in the sympathetic fellowship of the professor an intellectual impulse and a spiritual impression of the most helpful and useful kind.'[1]

George Smeaton always had a positive concern for the promotion of the gospel through men properly grounded in the truth. The tide of course was against him and there was no clearer indication of this than in the appointment of Dr Marcus Dods as his successor in 1889. Dods took the Free Church further along the line of a broad and liberal understanding of the New Testament Scriptures which showed little regard for the plenary and verbal inspiration of the documents — a death-wish to any Church as a spiritual power. Consistent good health and the retention of his basic faculties had enabled Smeaton to complete all but thirty-two years in the work at New College.

9. Involvement in Church Affairs

George Smeaton was not a prominent figure in Church Courts. Rarely did he take part in General Assemblies even when he was entitled to do so. A search through the records indicates that of the eleven General Assemblies he might have attended between 1854 and 1885, he only

[1] J. G. Cunningham in *The Free Church of Scotland Monthly* (Sept. 1889), p. 279.

took part in three! There were matters, however, which arose in the last twenty-five years of his life which were to exercise his soul greatly and bring him, reluctantly, into the arena of controversy. I want to mention three areas in particular:

1. *The Union Controversy*. Barely twenty years had passed since the Disruption, when the Free Church was consumed by an issue which threatened to tear the Church in pieces. The controversy rumbled on with various degrees of heat and light over 10 years from 1863 to 1873. It concerned a proposed Union with another main line Scottish Presbyterian denomination, the United Presbyterian Church. The United Presbyterian Church had arisen in 1847 from a Union of two Secession groups: the 'Relief Church' and the United Associate Synod of the Secession Church. A distinctive tenet of the United Presbyterian Church was what was known as *Voluntarism* which denied the rightness of the establishment of a national Church and the support of it by the State authorities. This was not the position of the Free Church, which held to the *Establishment Principle* that maintained the responsibility of the State authorities to uphold and advance true Christian faith. Those, like Smeaton and many of the other men of Disruption times, in holding to what is called the Establishment Principle — admittedly rather alien to the American Church scene — did so from the conviction that it was not necessary for the State to be

secular. And as long as there were sufficient safeguards as to the Church's spiritual independence the State for its part should acknowledge the true Christian religion and support it. This is a principle these men saw being worked out in the Old Testament, though they did not hold to the direct application of the civil and ceremonial laws of the Old Testament except in so far as the general equity made it evidently sound and sensible. At any rate, on this Church/State relations issue there was a fundamental difference between these Presbyterian Churches. Wrote Smeaton: 'the two larger Churches, judging by their public documents, are separated by a wide, yawning and impassable gulf.'[1] He for one could not consent to the denial of the State's responsibility to maintain the true religion in acknowledgement of the Headship of Christ over nations. So, he was 'anti-union.' But that was not the only issue. There was also the serious suspicion that the United Presbyterians were less than orthodox in their view of the atonement. It was felt that there was a tendency among them to deny limited atonement and to accept a sort of universal redemption. Wrote Smeaton on this subject: 'As to the other great doctrine — the doctrine of the Atonement ... I am ready to prove at any one moment that the United Presbyterian Church ... not merely allows, but adopts the doctrine of universal atonement, irrespective

[1] The Free Church of Scotland General Assembly, *Proceedings and Debates of the General Assembly of the Free Church of Scotland, 28 May 1873* (Edinburgh: Ballantyne), p. 154.

of any distinction between elect and non-elect … an error fatal to all Calvinistic Churches, because operating backwards and forwards in the most subverting way — backwards upon election, and forwards on all sound views of conversion. I never will consent to legalise this error in the Church.'[1] Smeaton was in the anti-union party which was in a minority in the debate. Nevertheless because of the significance of the minority the majority decided to discontinue the union negotiations with the United Presbyterians in 1873. Worthies like Andrew and Horatius Bonar, Alexander Moody Stuart and Hugh Martin were one with Smeaton on this issue.

2. *Biblical Criticism.* On the back of the Union controversy was one of perhaps even more far-reaching significance for the health and strength of the Church as a spiritual force. It had to do with Bible Criticism which among other things questioned the historicity and trustworthiness of the books which comprised the accepted canon of Old Testament Scripture. Such views had crept into the Free Church almost unawares through the teaching of A. B. Davidson (1831–1902). He was appointed as lecturer/assistant to the saintly John Duncan in 1863. He subsequently became Professor in 1870. It was he, says Principal John Macleod, who became 'an alien infusion in Old Testament studies in Scotland.' Macleod adds, tellingly, 'Robertson Smith

[1] For the whole speech see: The Free Church, *Proceedings and Debates, 1873*, pp. 154-7.

caught the infection and spread the plague.'[1] The catalyst in this matter was an article on 'Bible' by Smith in *Encyclopaedia Britannica* [1876] in which the young scholar maintained radical Higher Critical views. From this point the issue of Biblical Criticism and the nature of divine inspiration convulsed the Free Church till in 1881, when, after the appearance of an even more offensive article on 'Hebrew Language and Literature,' he was removed from the Old Testament chair at the Aberdeen Free Church College (though not as a Free Church minister) on grounds, essentially, of expediency. Smith's critical views were generally in line with the Graf-Keunen-Wellhausen scheme. Smith made no reference to the supernatural origin of the Bible. He accepted the 'Documentary Hypothesis' as far as the first four books of the Bible were concerned, treating them as being pieced together from various sources (JEP) and not at all the work of Moses. As to the book of Deuteronomy (D), this he considered to be a post-Mosaic 'personation' of Moses. He played down the prophetic element in the Prophets. In relation to the New Testament, he denied that the Synoptic Gospels were written by those whose names they bear, they were, rather, 'non-apostolic digests of spoken and written apostolic tradition.'

Smeaton took a strong stand against this. He wrote to the younger man. 'I would beseech you to pause, to take counsel with your father and your seniors before

[1] Macleod, *Scottish Theology*, p. 288.

committing yourself to positions from which you will find it every day more difficult to recede. Who has not been drawn — if he has thought at all into speculations and opinions on which he now looks back with contempt and grief? The peril is in a public committal to crude notions. I wish I could do something to rescue a gifted young mind and save it for the future usefulness which we all fondly anticipated. … Are not the theories without any basis of solid historical fact? and what is the worth of such theories where the basis is mere conjecture or petty internal criticism leaping to arbitrary conclusions? I hope your mind will soon revolt from this castle-building in the clouds. … We, as professors, [he went on to say] are not appointed by the Church to teach what tends to shake the faith of any, or to advocate a criticism which is not legitimate.'[1]

Generally speaking, the older orthodox professors and ministers were simply discounted by the 'progressive' scholars. These men were impatient with the confessional theology and conservative approach to the Scriptures. Smeaton was part of the College Committee which met from 1876 onwards to deal with the matters raised by Smith's writings. The Committee examined the article 'Bible' and also an article on 'Angels' which was found objectionable (by conservative men at least). The opinion prevailed among the majority on the committee that there was no *prima facie* case for heresy

[1] J. S. Black and G. W. Chrystal, *The Life of William Robertson Smith* (London: Adam and Charles Black, 1912), p. 200.

against the Professor though it felt that his critical opinions were scarcely compatible with his position as a teacher of divinity students. Smeaton objected to this. He had maintained that *judicial* action was appropriate. He recorded his dissent from the Report. He thought the conclusion of the Report inadequate. Here is part of Smeaton's dissent in this very vital issue: 'An attack on the genuineness and authority of the Scripture, whether dignified by the title of the higher criticism or prompted by the lower scepticism, ought never to be permitted within the Church on the part of any office-bearer. We can keep criticism within its proper limits, and this occasion may have been permitted to occur that we may show to other churches how we can act in the exercise of our independent jurisdiction.'[1] Summing up his position he was very clear: 'I hold that the doctrine of inspiration and Professor Smith's views are irreconcilable.'[2]

Though Robertson Smith was eventually removed from the Chair in 1881, there had been a revolution, and for all the 'promise' expected, it would sound the death-knell for much of Church life in Scotland (and elsewhere in the West) in the twentieth century: the bitter fruit of a denial of Scripture's authority and trustworthiness which had come in under the guise of

[1] The Free Church of Scotland General Assembly, *Proceedings and Debates of the General Assembly of the Free Church of Scotland, May 1877*, Report V A, Appendix IV (Edinburgh: Ballantyne, 1877), p. 37.

[2] Free Church, *Proceedings and Debates, 1877*, p. 39.

evangelical terminology. It is a sad irony that Smeaton was followed in his Chair by the liberal Marcus Dods (1834–1909). As John Macleod curtly put it: 'between the two men there was a yawning gulf.'[1]

3. *Hymns and Instruments.* George Smeaton did not become involved in any direct way with the controversy over the expansion of praise in the Free Church beyond the Psalms. Discussions took place in the Church and hymns were allowed from 1872. The legislation was permissive and so the use of the hymns was patchy. However, in Smeaton's own congregation, Grange Free Church, which he had been largely instrumental in founding in the early 1860s, there was no move to introduce the Hymn Book until 1883. Horatius Bonar (1808–89) was the minister of that congregation. He was the writer of many lovely hymns, yet he clearly did not push the hymns question at the Grange till 1883. When the matter was forced, by Bonar and other elders in the autumn of 1883, Smeaton and a number of other elders issued a *Statement* indicating that they were not prepared to sanction the use of the Free Church Hymn Book in congregational worship. The majority of the Session went ahead despite this and as a consequence George Smeaton, with others, resigned from the eldership of the congregation he had been instrumental in planting twenty years earlier.

[1] Macleod, *Scottish Theology*, p. 289.

As it happens Smeaton was also clearly unhappy about the permissive allowance of instrumental music for the accompaniment of praise in the Free Church after 1883. Smeaton concurred with these arguments against the adoption of instrumental music. [He would have concurred with J. L. Girardeau's *Instrumental Music in Public Worship* (1888)]. 'I deplore the disturbance of the unity, peace and spiritual prosperity of the Church [he said in one place on this issue], by the introduction of new elements in worship, which are not in keeping with the genius of Scottish Presbyterianism. I trust that all wise men will do what in them lies to guard the Church from such experiments as these. The truth is, that organs, and organ recitals, artistic execution, and fine performances, are vain appliances, and do not touch the real disease. Enlightened Christians know what is awanting, and what alone will take off the load from the heavy heart. Certainly instrumental music will not yield that result.'[1]

10. Writings

Without question the enduring legacy of George Smeaton lies in his writings. The strength of Smeaton's writings lay in the fact that they were such positive statements of truth. His greatest works, on the *Atone-*

[1] George Smeaton, 'Preface', in Rev. John McEwan, *Instrumental Music: a consideration of the Arguments for and against its Introduction into the worship of the Free Church of Scotland. With a Preparatory note by the Rev. George Smeaton DD, New College, Edinburgh* (Edinburgh: James Gemmell, 1883).

ment and the *Holy Spirit* have thus become classics of Reformed Theology.

Interestingly, for the greater part, Smeaton's writings were produced in his mature years (i.e. after 1868). He was 54 years old when his first volume on *The Doctrine of the Atonement as taught by Christ Himself* appeared (1868, 460pp.). The second volume *The Doctrine of the Atonement as taught by the Apostles* (1870, 548pp.) came out two years later. As far as the volumes on the Atonement were concerned Smeaton's aim was to survey the entire New Testament teaching on the subject. The works are therefore exegetical and expository rather than dogmatic. 'I have endeavoured,' he says, 'to bring out the results of exegetical investigation, not the process, and to put these within the reach of the educated English reader, to aid him in the great work of making himself acquainted with the Lord's mind, through the medium of the language of revelation.' In his Preface to the second volume Smeaton states that 'The work is rather biblical than formally dogmatic or polemical, and intended to embody positive truth according to the setting in which the doctrine is placed in the apostolic documents.' This, no doubt, is the strength of both volumes. They are clearly the result of mature reflection and ripe scholarship. His conclusions are entirely orthodox, as, for example, on the question of the extent of the atonement.

George Smeaton's other major work was his superb Cunningham lectures of 1882 on *The Doctrine of the*

Holy Spirit. The work must stand as one of the finest produced in the nineteenth century. The author's thinking behind the volume is clear. He says: 'Except where Puritan influences are still at work, we may safely affirm that the doctrine of the Spirit is almost entirely ignored. The representatives of modern theology, it is well known, have almost wholly abandoned it.' It was Smeaton's aim to rectify this deficiency and keep before men's minds and hearts Scripture's great truths concerning the personality and work of the Holy Spirit. 'The distinctive feature of Christianity, as it addresses itself to man's experience, is the work of the Spirit, which not only elevates it far above all philosophical speculation, but also above every other form of religion.' In *A Reader's Guide to Reformed Literature* (1999), Dr Joel Beeke writes: 'Begin with George Smeaton. His work on the Spirit is readable, thorough, and edifying.'

The other area of special interest for Smeaton was in Church/State relations, or the place and position of the Civil Magistrate in supporting the Christian religion. In 1871, at the height of the Union controversy in the Free Church he made two distinct contributions in that area. First of all, there was his *National Christianity and Scriptural Union* (Edinburgh, 1871). John Macleod describes this book fulsomely as 'one of the fullest and most luminous expositions one can see of the historic Scottish Reformed view of Church and State or of National Religion.'[1] In addition, there was his published lecture

[1] Macleod, *Scottish Theology*, p. 289.

on *The Scottish Theory of Ecclesiastical Establishments* (Glasgow, 1875), an address to a Conservative Association in Glasgow on the 'antidisestablishmentarian' side of the political argument.

11. Family Sadness

In their time in Edinburgh, George and Janet Smeaton had the sadness of losing their eldest two children. Their daughter Isabella died in 1862, aged 19 and their oldest son George on his way back from India at the end of 1870. The Smeatons' youngest son, who became popularly known as Oliphant Smeaton, pursued a career in teaching and journalism in New Zealand and then Australia, but returned to Scotland after his mother's death in 1893. He became a well-known figure in the literary circles of the day and is perhaps best known as editor of the 'Famous Scots' series, produced around the turn of the century.

Oliphant Smeaton associated with the congregation of Grange Free Church (subsequently Grange United Free Church, after 1900) and he became an elder in 1909. The history of that Congregation records that, 'He was the last survivor of the company who first met in his father's dining room for worship before the Church was formed. As a boy he had played with his companions among the piles of materials gathered for the building of the church. He had a great love for the church all his days. He lived abroad for some years and when he returned, he renewed his association with the

Grange. Appointed Session Clerk, he was involved in all its interests and activities.'[1] He died 31 March 1914 and was survived by his wife, Wilhelmine (1859–1931) and one daughter. He was buried in the family plot in the Grange Cemetery.

12. Eventide

After 1884 Smeaton moved to Buccleuch Free Church, where the minister, Robert Gordon (1823–1909), and most of the congregation, did not go into the union of the Free and United Presbyterian Churches in 1900. In February 1889 the second edition of his work on the Holy Spirit came out, but suddenly, on Lord's day, 14 April that year, just after the close of Session in New College and having reached his Jubilee in the ministry the previous month, he passed into the presence of his Lord. His friend and colleague at New College, Thomas Smith, described the circumstances:

> After spending the last day of his life in the discharge of important professorial duty, writing kindly letters to a student, to a former student and friend, and to his colleague, Dr Duns, enjoying the converse of the beloved one who had shared his joys and sorrows for well-nigh half a century, after sleeping apparently through the night the sleep which God gives to His beloved, on Sabbath morning he uttered a great shriek of momentary bodily pain, and ere it had ceased to pierce the ear of her who heard it, the earthly note

[1] Thomas Maxwell, *St Catherine's in Grange: A Centenary History 1866–1966* (Edinburgh: Bishop & Sons, 1966), pp. 50-51.

> of anguish was transmuted into the strain of the heavenly Hallelujah!

Smith movingly ends his funeral oration with these words: 'In contemplation of such a scene each one of us may well say, "Let me die the death of the righteous, and let my last end be like his!"'[1]

For his part, Robert Gordon concludes his appreciation of Smeaton with these moving words:

> He pointed many souls to heaven, and he has led the way. And while we thank God for his life and labours, may the remembrance of them quicken us to follow in his footsteps, even as he followed Christ's.[2]

George Smeaton's mortal remains were laid to rest in the Grange Cemetery in Edinburgh. Janet Smeaton survived her husband by just four years. She passed away in March 1893 and her remains were also laid to rest in the family plot.

13. Testimonials

George Smeaton was an outstanding scholar. He was widely read. Apparently, when he died, Dr Smeaton left

[1] Smith, in *In Memoriam*, p. 42. Thomas Smith (1817–1906) was Professor of Evangelistic Theology (Missions) at New College (1880–92). John Duns (1820–1909) was Professor of Natural Science in New College, Edinburgh (1864–1903).

[2] Robert Gordon, *In Memoriam*, p. 16. Robert Gordon (1823–1909) was the minister of Buccleuch Free Church in which George Smeaton was a member.

a personal library of above 13,000 books, many of which found their way into the New College library. He was a divine of the old School. A thorough Calvinist, and one who held the high doctrine of Biblical Inspiration in a day when the Churches were wilting in the face of the attacks of the critics. A colleague said this of him:

> I do not know that in this country there is, or ever has been, a man more accurately conversant with all the great theological schools, the Patristic, the Mediaeval, the Reformation, the Puritan, the Dutch and the Modern German. It was said to me the other day by one well qualified to judge, that the erudition of the late Dr Cunningham might be more minute in regards to the third of these schools ... but was far inferior to Dr Smeaton's with regard to the others.[1]

Above all, perhaps, Dr Smeaton was highly regarded for his piety. The Kirk Session of Newington Free Church recorded this tribute after his passing:

> Professor Smeaton was a man ... of singular benevolence and sweetness of disposition, universally beloved for his goodness, as well as highly esteemed for his work's sake, and respected for his moral worth and the constancy of his life and character. He was eminently distinguished for genuine piety, and for following after peace with all men, and personal holiness ... as a pastor and preacher of the gospel he was highly appreciated, especially by the most spiritually-minded of his hearers, for the earnest

[1] Smith, *In Memoriam*, pp. 39-40.

> simplicity and solemnity of his manner, the force of his teaching, the clearness of his spiritual discernment, the soundness of his views, the vigour and valour of his defence of the truth, and the richness of his Christian experience.[1]

He was 'a man of God,' said one tribute 'and one who had much sweet communion with Jesus. He had a deeply spiritual mind. He seemed to look upon all things in the light of Eternity, in the relation they bore to the glory of God and the good of immortal souls.'[2]

The obituary notice by the Rev. J. G. Cunningham summed up Smeaton's life as a minister of Christ in terms of the verse: 'We will give ourselves to prayer, and to the ministry of the word.' 'The direct, earnest, and varied requests which flowed from his lips in public prayer were manifestly the utterances of one who was accustomed to be much alone with God.'[3] Stewart and Cameron justly wrote of George Smeaton that he 'was perhaps the most learned theologian in the Free Church, and a man of deep and unaffected godliness.'[4]

[1] Extract from the Records of the Kirk Session of Newington Free Church, 8 May 1889 (handwritten).

[2] 'Tribute to the Memory of the Late Professor Smeaton, D.D.' (handwritten tribute from the Free Church Defence Association, A5, 1889), p. 4.

[3] Free Church of Scotland, *The Free Church of Scotland Monthly*, (Sept. 1889), p. 279.

[4] Alexander Stewart & J. Kennedy Cameron, *The Free Church of Scotland: The Crisis of 1900* (Edinburgh: Knox Press, 1989 [1910]), p. 31.

Introduction

George Smeaton is especially well known in Reformed Christian circles through the reprinting of his major works on the *Atonement* and the *Holy Spirit*, as mentioned elsewhere. The following pieces comprise various printed sermons, lectures, and other shorter writings gleaned from various sources and covering the whole period of his ministry and professorial work.

The earliest piece is a discourse on 'Immanuel' which appeared in *The Scottish Christian Herald* in 1840. He was then minister in the Church of Scotland congregation at Falkland in Fifeshire. The last piece is a moving sermon preached in Newington Free Church, Edinburgh after the death of his friend, the Rev. James Begg, in 1883. Several of the examples of his sermons in this volume are sermons preached after the passing of colleagues in the ministry. Though the individuals in question may be unknown to the modern Church, the expository gift and passionate applications in these sermons are there for all to see. They are models for any generation of preachers concerned to preach Christ and plead with sinners to receive Him as Saviour.

The items included in these 'Sermons and Addresses' are wide-ranging in their content and in one respect or another reveal the characteristics of an exercised man, whether speaking, or writing, for ministers, divinity students, or the general reader. The rare tract on 'The Improvement of a Revival Time' is not to be found in any university library in Scotland. It was clearly written in the context of the revivals of 1859–60 which touched many parts of Scotland. The article on 'Faith' constituted his one contribution to *The Imperial Bible Dictionary* [1864–6] and reveals his theological acumen. In 'The Necessary Harmony between Doctrine and Spiritual Life' — his first lecture at the Aberdeen Free Church College — and in 'The True Preacher,' he shows his concern for the exercise of faithful ministry. His sermons reprinted here show the passion of a pastor, the soundness of a theologian and the earnestness of an evangelist. In his thinking Smeaton clearly shows a high view of the inspiration and authority of the Bible as the word of God. He is concerned throughout with the *application* of truth, and with faithfulness to the person of Christ as King and Lord.

Also included here is Smeaton's classic defence of the Establishment Principle as a biblical principle. His 1875 address on *The Scottish Theory of Ecclesiastical Establishments* was given in the context of agitation in Scottish Presbyterianism and politics for disestablishment. The issue seems to be a rather redundant one today, and yet Smeaton's exposition will sharpen the thinking of Christians in the contemporary scene in which secularism has replaced the Church as an 'Established Principle' of the modern State.

The editing of the material has been largely confined to corrections and some revision of punctuation. There has also been some standardisation of section headings. In cases where names of people or places are referred to in the text some basic information has been provided about them by way of footnotes.

May the publication of these Sermons and Addresses, under God, be blessed to readers. May they be as edifying, challenging and stimulating to this present generation as they were to Smeaton's own.

> *Whose faith follow, considering the end of their conversation, Jesus Christ the same yesterday, and to-day, and for ever* (Heb. 13:7, 8).

JOHN W. KEDDIE
June, 2020

I

Immanuel[1]

And shall call his name Immanuel.—Isaiah 7:14.

They shall call his name Immanuel, which, being interpreted is, God with us.—Matthew 1:23.

'GREAT,' exclaims Paul, 'is the mystery of godliness; God was manifest in the flesh' [1 Tim. 3:16]. The Godhead of Christ is the greatest truth of the gospel. Without this, it has neither value nor importance. The Evil One puts forth his every effort to obscure it. In the early spread of Christianity it was this truth on which he made his fiercest blast. For five hundred years after the apostolic age the Church was troubled by various forms of its denial. Though much evil overspread the Church on account of these heresies, and though the African and Asiatic Churches were submerged by a deluge of Mohammedanism, yet the doctrine shall stand and be established. 'On this rock,' says Christ, 'I will build my Church, and the gates of hell shall not prevail against it' [Matt. 16:18]. The Evil One seems now to have altered

[1] Reprinted from *The Scottish Christian Herald. Conducted under the Superintendence of Ministers and Members of the Established Church; January 4–December 26, 1840*, vol. 2, Second Series (Edinburgh: John Johnstone, 1840), pp. 617-22.—Ed.

his attack, allowing it to stand as a speculative mystery in the movements of the Church. It was the practical avowal of this truth which stained the wild moors of Scotland with martyr-blood. It was the ignorant unbelief of it that led to persecution.

The same ignorance prevailed when Christ appeared. When the Mighty One bent his own heavens, and came down, there was none to pay him reverence. The dark earth was shrouded in the primeval curse, and men, as insensate as the trodden earth, were unconscious of their visitant. But in other regions of the universe, the announcement — 'Lo, I come!' [Heb. 10:7, 9; Psa. 40:7] — did not fall upon unheeding ears. Though men discovered not their Lord, the hosts of heaven, who heralded his advent to the plains of Bethlehem, exulted with all the rapture of augmented knowledge. To them was revealed the manifold wisdom of God and higher views of the Infinite Mind. Their song was, 'Glory to God in the highest; on earth, peace — goodwill to the children of men' [Luke 2:14]. If they rejoiced at God's love and wisdom, let us, too, with minds unruffled and full of holy awe, approach this greatest of the miracles of God.

We do not here set ourselves to prove that Christ is God. The truth of that is written in the text. In many passages of Scripture there is not only the express ascription to him of the term God, but also various attributes of supreme divinity, and the tribute of adoration, praise, and prayer. We shall proceed on this as true, and devoutly believed by all.

If this doctrine is so clearly written in Scripture, let faith triumph over the doubts of fallen reason. If it is in Scripture, let not the spirit of a false philosophy stumble at a mystery in a revelation from the throne. Had reason been able to discover truth, nothing would need to have been revealed. But when a revelation is imparted, in the grace of God, reason must become a learner, not a judge. The mystery is not in the words of Holy Scripture, but in the stupendous fact. At this, even angels bend down and adore.

From these words, then, I mean to contemplate, with you, *the divinity of Christ*, from two points of view, *first*, as it is connected with the Divine procedure towards us; and, *secondly*, as it directly affects ourselves.

1. *The significance of the Incarnation of Christ in God's dealings with sinners.*

Let us consider this subject in reference to the Divine procedure. It is this that warrants all God's dealings with us. Why the Son assumed our nature, and not the Father or the Holy Spirit, it is not for us to speculate. This is among the secret, not the revealed, things of God. But had this incarnation never been, we should have been for ever exiled from the fountain of life, estranged from all communion with Deity, and without prospect of relief.

In the boundless love of God, an agreement was made between the Father and the Son to deliver from ruin the creatures of his hand. A council of peace was formed between them both (Zech. 6). By this the Father receives the obedience of the Son and the Son becomes the servant. The Father is glorified in receiving the sacrifice and the Son is glorified in finishing the work that was given him to do and in the Holy Spirit in applying that work to us. This is the 'mystery hid from ages and generations' [Col. 1:26; cf. Eph. 3:9], revealed in these last times to us. A Trinity of persons in the Godhead is disclosed, in a council of unutterable wisdom as well as condescension. Who would have imagined that the Creator would stoop in person to redeem us? Who, even if they are aware of a distinction in the Godhead, understands the nature of the unity of the Godhead? Who is to say how far they act in one, or so understand the peculiarity of the distinctions in the Godhead, so as to say how the salvation of our race could be secured on it? Who is to say that the Father might be greater than the Son, and the Son become his servant? 'O the depths of the riches, both of the wisdom and knowledge of God! How unsearchable are his judgments, and his ways past finding out!' [Rom. 11:13].

From the moment of the Fall, this counsel, hid in the bosom of God, began to be disclosed and shed upon our fallen world the dawn of a better day. Then it was that a scheme was prepared to defeat the hopes of hell, a scheme to maintain untarnished the Creator's glory in his works, to restore the order and beauty of creation, and to bring back a company of new-born creatures to their pristine image, even the image of God. This is not effected like his other works by the mere exercise of power, or by his creative word, as when he said, 'Let there be light,' and there was light [Gen. 1:3]. Rather, he came down from on high to save that race whom he could have magnified his glory in destroying by a word. And, 'though he was rich, yet for our sakes he became poor!' [2 Cor. 8:9]. If any can coldly ponder such a mystery, or set above its inexplicable wonders either the results of vain philosophy, or the wild dreams of fallen man, what does it argue, but a soul alienated from the life of God, engrossed by earth's trifling objects, which will disappear like smoke among the general conflagration? This covenant of God will evermore unroll, to the enraptured spirits of the just, fresh and undiscovered wonders. But, placed upon the mount of vision, as now we are, let it be ours to explore and trace the manifold wisdom of our God. I think it proper to call your attention to these two points in the development of this mystery:

(1) *The person of the Mediator.* — The Mediator entered on his office at the moment of the fall. He suspended the consuming curse that followed on the violation of the law, saying, 'Lo, I come'; 'I will repay it all.' A mediator between God and man must be competent to effect a reconciliation. He must both vindicate the claims of God, and execute the duties of our race. He must have a divine knowledge of our amount of disobedience, and a nature fit to expiate it. He must both take hold of the nature that was injured, and yet be of a nature to obey and

suffer; in a word, he must be God and man. God could not obey his own law, nor die for sin — mere man could not obey for millions — a God-man Saviour could do both. To deliver us from sin and death, then, the Infinite One became finite — the Eternal was made in time — the Immortal became mortal—the mighty God became the child born—the Ancient of Days became the babe of Bethlehem. The Son is equal to the Father, but became economically less; for a little, lower than the angels. He was not a servant, but became a servant when he took the flesh. The Lord Jesus possesses a divine nature and a human nature, a divine will and a human will, each complete and perfect, but not confounded — always in harmony, but each entire. No change took place upon his manhood, and none did or could take place upon his Godhead. None of his eternal attributes are, or can be, laid aside. His power, which called us into being, still works all in all; and without it, we, like a bubble in water, should melt into the blank of nothingness. His omniscience is the same — his omnipresence is the same — his attributes are all the same. When it is said, that he emptied himself — that he became poor — it is only meant that he did not appear in all the glory he had with the Father before the world was, and which he now has reassumed. It is only meant that he became *economically* inferior to the Father, yea, lower than the angels. The distance between the two natures is infinite; it is free grace that formed the union. 'Who is this that engageth his heart to approach unto me, saith the Lord?' (Jer.

30:21). If it were a fallen creature, he could not answer for himself; if a creature unfallen, an infinite curse from every region would bury him amid the crash of a dissolving universe, which a hand so weak, and a capacity of suffering so limited, could not uphold. He is the being on whom the whole order of the world hangs, attracting to him every eye — to whom God looks for satisfaction, and man for aid — with whom God declared himself well-pleased — and with whom we, too, should be well-pleased. That toil-worn Jesus, who trod the plains of Palestine, is the God in whom we live and move, and who, when he appears again, will bid the heavens pass away. He came to his own, but was not welcomed. His footsteps trod the world he had made, and poised upon the vault of space. Does this not give assurance that is perfect, because God hath done it? Whatever the Son did was pleasing to the Father. He was daily the delight of the Father from eternity, so, when he stood on Jordan's banks, a voice from heaven through a fissure in the clouds, announced, 'This is my beloved Son, in whom I am well-pleased' [Matt. 3:17; Mark 1:11; Luke 3:22]. This was given forth when the Son entered on the mediatorial economy. Hear this, you scoffing worldlings, and dare to scoff again. Hear this, you unstable professors; and can you trust a rending world, which may disappear tomorrow? — can you trust an arm of flesh, and not more firmly trust the Mediator's everlasting arms?

(2) *Consider the Mediator's work.* — He came to obey the law, and make his obedience count. 'Behold,' says

the Father, 'my servant whom I uphold' [Isa. 42:1]. It is this obedience of the willing servant, in every part of duty and of penalty incumbent on us, that he came to render as the ground for our salvation. The law demanded death, — Christ's death is our propitiation. He endured the pressure of the world's guilt; but being infinite, he sunk not under it. What he did had infinite value, for he was God. His sacrifice satisfied the law, but the demand was not abated. He redeemed us from the curse of the law, but he was made a curse for us. The very curse which will overwhelm the lost for ever, the utmost penalty and obligation which the world's sin contracted, all — except the gnawing and remorse of an awakened conscience — all fell on him, and fell without reserve in his hour of agony. In the place of woe, indeed, sin incurs wrath without end or respite; and the penalty will be ever paying, and never paid; and an indefinite lapse of ages (to speak of time where there is none) will find the obligation as stern and unabated as at first: but in Christ's atonement the sufferings were not eternal, although the satisfaction was a full equivalent; and why? The atonement of a God-man Saviour was equal to the debt which, in a fathomless eternity, the lost shall never discharge.

But he not only expiated all iniquity by his death, but fulfilled all righteousness in his life — meeting the law's demand, 'Do this, and thou shalt live' [Lev. 18:5]. Behold him bending his own heavens, and coming down to magnify the law! Behold him, as he trod this earth, bearing with him the utmost of its claims, and realizing a perfect satisfaction to it in his every step! Here we see what never previously appeared upon a fallen world: the living spirit of the law embodied, not in Sinai's cold and frowning tables of stone — not in the dead letter — but in a living soul. Is it freedom from iniquity that is required? He challenges his enemies, 'Which of you convinces me of sin?' [John 8:46]. Is it love to God that is required? It was his meat and drink: 'yea,' said he, 'thy law I have within my heart' [Psa. 40:8]. Is it love to man that is required? He went about doing good—he loved us to the end. All, all is fulfilled. 'Heaven and earth shall pass away,' we are informed, 'but one jot or one tittle shall in no wise pass from the law, till all is fulfilled' [Matt. 5:18]; and now, all is fulfilled. What was it, at the fall of Adam, that brought a distracted world to a solemn pause, arresting on the wing the bolts of vengeance? What was it that upheld the world so long in being, and to which the movements of providence converged? What was it that maintained such breathless expectation? Nothing but Immanuel's coming righteousness. And what else but this same righteousness that magnified the law, prolongs to us this light of heaven, that we have forfeited this day, this day of grace—this offer of salvation — all our great and precious privileges? Jesus was the righteous servant — the well-beloved of the Father. When his obedience closed, and he uttered his expiring cry before he bowed his head, 'It is finished,' [John 19:30] heaven and earth were not separated, as before, by an impassable gulf. The fallen creature was restored to favour, and regarded with more than pristine love. Our heavenly Father rejoices over us, as the father of the prodigal, to do us good.

This righteousness we must connect with the person of our incarnate Mediator. It is nothing else but his obedience. But we must not assign it to the Godhead nature of Immanuel, for God could not obey his own law. The obedience must be of the very same sort that Adam should have yielded, that is, in the nature and the form of man. Hence the suitableness of the parallel condition: — 'As by one man's disobedience many were made sinners, so by the obedience of one shall many be made righteous' [Rom 5:19; cf. Isa. 53:11]. But while we carefully assign this obedience to the *manhood* of the Saviour, it was his glorious Godhead that gave it such immeasurable value, upholding and guiding him in his high career, and also making it so eminently meritorious, that it is adequate, and more than adequate, to all the wants of our united race. Such is the righteousness, for the acquirement of which the eternal Son prepared himself a body, in which he said, 'Lo, I come to do thy will, O God; yea, thy law I have within my heart' (Psa. 40:8). This obedience is not limited to his single person. He *owed* no obedience. It is boundless in merit as the nature of the Godhead. It is coextensive with the wants of all creation. It is offered to the very chief of sinners. It is this which covers heaven and earth with smiles. It is this that hides from our despondent eyes the frown of an offended God, and removes the day of darkness and gloominess. It is this which draws from us to God the calm of an unbroken trust, and from God to us the beaming of a Father's countenance. 'Glory to the Lamb' [Rev. 5:12, 13]. 'Lo, it is our God, we have waited for him, and he will save us; this is the Lord, we have waited for him; we will be glad and rejoice in his salvation' [Isa. 25:9].

Such, then, is the ground of God's procedure, by which he can be just, and the justifier of the sinner. Christ took our place, and he gives us the merit of his own. There has passed between us an exchange of place. This is the ground on which God deals with sinners. He can give the sinner an investiture of all the Saviour's purchase. In our guilt, he can throw around us the Saviour's righteousness. To our weakness he can give almighty strength. On our darkness he can cause to arise the day-star of everlasting life. From a state of slavery he can make us sons, because Christ is the only begotten Son. In a word, 'all things are yours,' saith Paul, 'for ye are Christ's and Christ is God's' [1 Cor. 3:21-23].

2. *How the doctrine of the Incarnation affects ourselves.*

But we now come to consider how this doctrine affects ourselves — how it bears upon the human heart. Every doctrine of the gospel produces, as its fruit, a corresponding frame of mind. From this truth should flow new supplies of holy joy and wonder, strength and peace, faith and love. All the spiritual graces are refreshed by it, and cheerfully expand, like the full-blown flower, to the sunshine of its fostering influences. But here we shall trace the effect only on these two — faith and love.

(1) *It is on this truth alone that faith steadfastly rests.* A dead faith looks but to one of Christ's two natures. Hence the Jew blasphemes, and the superstitious tremble. Unbelievers virtually deny the incarnation, and have respect to one or other of his natures, but not to both. To the spiritual man, the incarnation never ceases to be wonderful, yet it is a faithful saying. It is plainly necessary to look to *both* Christ's natures, inasmuch as the manhood is not singly all-sufficient, and the absolute Godhead confounds a fallen spirit, but gives no rest or hope. Hence as the Lord said to the blind man, 'dost thou believe on the Son of God?' [John 9:35]. As the eunuch said to Philip, 'I believe that Jesus is the Son of God' [Acts 8:34-39]. And as Paul preached Christ, that he is the Son of God. If this great truth is not the ground of our faith, then *ichabod*, the glory is departed. A Socinian's or Unitarian's view of Christ can never be a ground for faith. An Arian's view can give no peace. Faith consists only in a reliance on that God who appeared as the babe of Bethlehem, over whom the angels sang. It is not flesh and blood, indeed, that reveals this doctrine to us, — it is the Father in heaven. But this is the truth on which the Church is built. 'On this rock,' on this confession of the Godhead, the Lord declares, 'I will build my Church' [Matt. 16:18], and who does not perceive, that, according to the neglect or steady maintenance of this,

the character of Christianity declines or flourishes? O, if in all the Churches this great truth of God becoming man were animated with a vital energy, would it not throw off the adventitious embarrassment that age and superstition have wreathed around religion? Will it not also impart both principles of action and a glow of piety worthy of a better time? Of other principles, the unfailing issue is, that something different than the distinctive doctrines of the faith, whether the whispers of a legal spirit, or the abatement of the amount of guilt, or a full denial of the fall, constitutes the dark retreat. What thus appears the sad issue in those who have reasoned out a system of belief without the recognition of Christ's Godhead, holds true of all who do not embrace the doctrine with a real faith. They cannot have a steady hold of any doctrine. On this truth the Church is built, and two millennia have already established the truth of the Redeemer's prophecy, 'that the gates of hell shall not prevail against it.' 'Blessed art thou, Simon Bar-Jona' [Matt 16:17, 18], said the Lord, when Peter made the confession; and blessed are all they who still make it with Peter's faith.

Having thus established the fact, that faith contemplates only a divine Saviour, we shall briefly illustrate this in the actual operations of faith. The degree of trust of which we are susceptible, is in direct proportion to the ability and fitness of him who is its object. Who would lean upon a broken reed? Who would trust his all, or even could do so with confidence, to one who had neither the sanctuary nor protection under his command? Were a parent cut down in the vigour of manhood by the hand of ruthless violence, and left spent and prostrate on the lonely highway, the efforts of his child might be unwearied in his behalf. Could that languid eye expect efficient aid in all the resources of his feeble child, that could only gaze upon a parent's face, and relax his efforts in its tears? And neither will the mind surrender its self-sufficiency, unless in one whose resources amply meet our wants. His faith could not be reposed even in an angel. Had we not a Saviour, omnipotent and of divine perfections, nothing could give our heavy-laden spirits rest. Nothing could fix the heart, or compose its fluctuations. In point of right, our faith ought to be given to none but God, and, *in effect*, it *can* be given to none but him alone. Every truth of Scripture that secures a sinner's safety, concentres on Christ's person. Without him there is no refuge, no secure footing, no rest for a troubled conscience. A man is only mocked and baffled with visions of relief, till Christ is relied on as the Son of God. 'God is my salvation,' saith Isaiah [Isa. 12:2]. Faith cannot be strong if our succour is not ample. A faltering confidence follows a precarious aid. But if Christ is thy king, believer, who shall dethrone him from his eternal glory? 'Go,' you may exclaim to every enemy, 'ye can no more prevail against me, than ye can supplant my Sovereign from his throne upon eternity.' Yes. Earth may roll an eclipsed and cheerless thing upon infinitude, or may disappear in the solitude from which it sprung, but the believer shall mount up into the presence of his Lord, to see him as he is. 'Who is he (saith John) that overcometh the world; but he that believeth that Jesus is the Son of God' [1 John 5:5].

But faith views Christ's *willingness* as well as his power. Mere power may destroy us as well as save us. There can be no faith without an assurance of the Saviour's ready will to help us — if the soul rests not on his love. The carnal mind dreads God's presence. It hides from it, like our guilty forefather, and views all power as hurled against him by an angry Judge. Before him whose presence is around us, and whose dread visitation is inevitable, the sin-burdened spirit stands appalled, and would fain that there were 'no God.' And why? Because it cannot be denied that, with every advance of the career of sin, with every repetition of allowed rebellion, men have only a higher disrelish of God, and a hatred of him too, because he has been injured and offended. This enormity of crime, in returning malignity for love, in showing hatred because we have done the wrong, may almost appear incredible. Where is the unreconciled offender whose evil conscience, hurrying from a broken law to a formidable Avenger, from the scenes of guilt to the lightnings of the judgment-seat, does not attest the truth of it, and, as it were, repeats, 'Hast thou found me, O mine enemy?' [1 Kings 21:20]. To reduce us into obedience to the faith is what no sanctions, no threats of retribution, could effect. For what, though Sinai's thunders, and its voice of words, and terrible accompaniments, were at every step under the scope of all the senses? What though at the rise of every sinful purpose, the earth were wrapt in gloom, or heaved beneath our feet, or the menace echoed around us, 'Thou shalt surely die' [Gen. 2:17]? These might overcome the paralysed and nerveless arm, but they could not subdue the stubborn heart, which would still distrust and fear him as before. From this down-hill career we are rescued by a new attraction. We trust in God only because he manifests his love, and grace, and mercy. And have we not the amplest warrant for our faith, in the incarnation of the Mighty One? May we not be more than conquerors over all our guilty fears and weakness of purpose? The distance that sin has interposed between us and God we see already overcome, when we behold our nature united to his own. The assurance that he is willing to be reconciled, is confirmed by the most stupendous pledge. We are afraid by nature, and think God altogether such an one as ourselves — as vindictive and implacable. Yet how much is this jealousy disarmed when we behold the Deity descend and walk among his creatures! This may go far to reassure our trustless hearts; but how much more, when we know that both the bodily and mental fabric we inherit are united indivisibly, and shall throughout eternity belong, to the incarnate Son! O it is too great, and too good! And well may we admire, as we ever shall, its unfathomable condescension; but who should stagger at the promises through unbelief, or show despair or instability of faith when this is revealed? 'I know one,' you may exclaim in the hour of heaviness, 'who bears my own flesh and blood, and yet regulates the movement of the universe, who has vouchsafed to call me friend, and say, "my Father and your Father, my God and your God"' [John 20:17].

I might dwell upon the human feelings of the Lord Jesus, to show his willingness, and furnish a ground for faith. But I shall only touch on this. With tenfold greater tenderness than one man loves another, does the Saviour's heart beat for his brethren. Never is there a discordance between the human feelings and the divine, and that eye which wept on earth is still full of pity, — a pity never separated for a moment from unbounded power. Can we expect love in a human heart and not be far more certain here? The absolute Godhead terrifies us, — but Christ is man as well as God. And while the frail human bosom recoils from an absolute God in dismay, it can lean with unruffled serenity on him who bears a human bosom amid all the overpowering glories of the throne. Can there be doubt or irresolution in the most desponding, when the Saviour's love and pity beat warmly toward sinful man?

(2) *Let us now trace the influence of this doctrine on the affections.* Nothing can reduce us to the love of God, but the satisfactory assurance, that he first loveth us, — 'we love him because he first loveth us' [1 John 4:19]. And in what form is this expression of his love presented? Not in the audible announcement from the skies, not

in an inaudible sign from heaven, but by the most stupendous act, by condescending to assume our flesh. Conceive the mighty God united to our nature, — the Creator to a portion of his own creation, the everlasting Father become a child born. We may conceive ourselves united to a loathsome worm or toad. What were that but the connection of one creature with another, of one clod of the valley with its fellow. But this assumption of our nature into a personal subsistence with Deity. This, 'O Lord God, we can only admire and adore.' 'What is man that thou art mindful of him, or the son of man that thou visited him?' [Psa. 8:4]. To this, there were obstacles all but insurmountable opposed: our obstinate neglect, our haughty independence, and our resolute rebellion. Above them all, his grace arose and swelled, till the tidings, 'lo, I come' [Heb. 10:7], proclaimed that sin was now condemned, and yet the sinner saved. That the Son of God should come at all, — that he should come over every obstacle and insult — disappoints at once our preconceived ideas of his nature. It is, however, that overpowering condescension in which he will for ever be admired in all them that believe. He came to save a fallen world. He came to save the guiltiest transgressor.

As nothing can check suspicion or disarm hostility but the experience of affection, what higher proof can be given of love, than that the Son should disrobe himself of his glory, that God should humble himself, that we might be redeemed? This is language which none would be warranted to utter unless it were revealed in Scripture.

Blessed be God that it is true. This is the most transcendent evidence of love. Should it not subdue every heart? Who can admit it as a truth, or realize the fact, as unexpected as it is undeserved, without the melting of affection, awakened as a fresh and new-born feeling? In the sympathies of human fellowship, there are daily instances in which welcome kindness, alleviating wants, will overpower the manly bosom, and unlock, even in the hardened and depraved, the tears of overflowing sensibility. How, then, in reference to this, can our hearts continue the monument of rocky ingratitude, and not become the well-spring of an everlasting love? O, when Simeon stood within the temple of Jerusalem, bearing in his arms the greatest birth of time, in whom time, indeed, and all events, and the continuance of the world centred, what a tide of grateful love, what irrepressible emotions filled him of profound abasement, as well as overpowering tenderness, when he reflected that this was he who rides in his excellency on the sky, by whose word, himself and all creation were upheld in being, and who yet became the Lord his Redeemer [Luke 2:25-35]. If prophets and righteous men desired to see his day, and were not permitted [Luke 10:24], may we now, when the desire of all nations is come, receive him with indifference, as if the charm of novelty were gone? Not to mention, that that is repaying love with ingratitude and scorn. Not to mention, that above this is a subject ever new; let every bosom be persuaded, that if it can succeed in defeating this most powerful argument and motive to the love of God, it will stand for ever impregnable and proof against assault. For if we are reduced to the love of God, not by fear of punishment, but by the experience of love toward us, then this is its highest evidence and most constraining demonstration, 'God so loved the world' [John 3:16]. Nothing else will raise our prostrate affections.

This represents the Deity as near and dwelling among us. This unfolds his compassionate and amiable nature; and we can delight ourselves in him, as our portion and defence. The excited fears, as well as the malignant hatred, of the carnal bosom now give place to love. The gloomy prospect of sin and doubt, of dreaded punishment, and of a wrathful Judge, are now withdrawn. In its place, our spirits are refreshed by God manifest in love alone, assuming on his incarnate person all the causes of our distance and rebellion and reconciling us to himself, not imputing unto men their trespasses. When all that made him formidable is removed, and all that fostered our resentment is effaced, then free scope is given for an unruffled meditation of his excellence. Who can realize this love to himself, and not be lost in deep amazement at so unexpected a deliverance from such a hand? When standing on the margin of the precipice from which he has been rescued, and reflecting that for his deliverance the invisible world opened on his puny insignificance, and the Creator issued from eternity, and, by no second cause but by immediate miracle, outstretched a saving hand in his mid-way descent, is not the transport of security mixed with wonder, as he beholds himself the monument of such compassion? He is apt to utter: 'Can my God have humbled himself so low? Can his love to me be so unbounded?' This is uttered not with the unbelief which pronounces it impossible, but as the expression of overflowing gratitude, and on a reflex view of personal unworthiness which wonders as it gazes on its incomprehensible mysteriousness. It should be our prayer, as it was Paul's, 'that we may comprehend, with all saints, what is the breadth, and length, and height, and depth, and to know the love of Christ, which passeth knowledge' and, when understanding falters and comprehension is at a stand, still to be absorbed in holy admiration. From this, as from an islet, we may gaze on the profound expanse of Divine love, and see mirrored there every relation that connects our wellbeing in time and in eternity: the marvels of redemption, the condescension shown, the obstacles overcome, the source of every present emotion and future prospect; in a word, our all in all. And blessed be God that, beyond our circumscribed field of vision, there spreads an unsurveyed infinitude of love, a scope for ever-new investigation, where all our doubts and natural fears may for ever be absorbed. If this love were bounded, we should apprehend defect, but it is a 'love which passeth knowledge.'

One word in conclusion. Can you, dear friends, say, some of you, that you are made nigh to God? Is your natural antipathy removed? Can you bear to be alone with God? Are you composed and delighted in his presence? Can you love him who first loved you? Rejoice, then, in God your Saviour, and let this be the ceaseless theme of wonder. Or, again, who of you, still in an unrenewed state, dare not approach and call God your friend, and you see no constraining motive here? And is this to be the gratitude displayed? Is this to be the new obedience given? O the sin of this contempt, the enormity of treading underfoot this love, far outbalances all other guilt. Do you never think, 'I am in the hands of One for every breath I draw, who, if not my Saviour, is yet the eternal God, and who will be my Judge whether I consent or no?' And do you never ask, 'How shall I find him a Redeemer, whom I cannot elude as a Judge?' But the day of terror is reserved till the judgment-morn. This is still the reign of grace. Why, then, are you a blot on God's creation, when he is not only willing, — when he has come, to save you? Take this entreaty. Reflect continually on the man Christ Jesus — on his deeds and on his sufferings. Connect the whole with his Godhead nature; and never cease your contemplations, till your hearts are melted into love to 'him who first loved you' [1 John 4:19]. Amen.

2

The Lord's Jealousy against Backsliders Consistent with His Unchanging Love[1]

If his children forsake my law, and walk not in my judgments; if they break my statutes, and keep not my commandments, then will I visit their transgressions with the rod, and their iniquity with stripes. Nevertheless, my loving-kindness will I not utterly take from him.—Psalm 89:30-33

WHAT a triumph Satan will obtain in Scotland, if we lose sight of the Redeemer's reign in the heart, after all our declarations that he is a King! And the very same temptation, if at first resisted, is usually brought to bear upon us in a form more subtle and more captivating. I believe the text is in no common sense addressed to Scotland; and he that hath an ear let him hear.

In the context, the Covenant between the Father and the Son is at large unfolded. The Eternal Son undertakes to come down to this world to put on our sin and our wrath, that God may love us as he loveth him. On this Mighty One our help is laid (ver. 19), and when he comes, he is strengthened for the work given him to do.

[1] Reprinted from *The Free Church Pulpit*, vol. 1 (Perth: James Dewar & Son, 1845), pp. 587-97.—Ed.

His Sonship is discovered when he cries, 'Thou art my father' [ver. 26]; and his every step in doing and in dying is taken in the room of all and every man whose person he sustained and for whom he acted as a surety; for they were given him by the Father. The believer, realizing this oneness with his Lord, says, I am Christ's righteousness, yea, as Christ, the well-beloved before the Father; and evermore he hears the Mediator saying, I am yonder sinner's guilt and sin, for I bore him on my person on the tree. It is then taken for granted (ver. 30), that the seed of the Messiah shall go astray; but their sins, it is added, do not break the Covenant, which stands fast for ever more; for it was not made with us, but with the Son for us. For evermore the savour of Christ's sacrifice is as fresh as ever, and he ever cries, on behalf of all his own, Let them be brought back again white as ever — whiter than the snow. But we shall now, by God's help, analyse and open up the words as simply as we can. Notice,

1. *The seed of the Messiah stand in his relation to the Father, sons by Grace because he is the Son by Nature.*

His children. The full meaning, we take it, is, they are children in him; for the expressions *his children* and *his brethren* are interchangeably used — 'He is not ashamed to call them *brethren*, saying, Behold I and the *children* which God hath given me' (Heb. 2:11-13). He raises all whom the Father hath given him as near himself as possible, to the rank of sons in the family of God, with a title to the heavenly glory. The foundation of our being children is, that Christ is God's only begotten Son in a sense peculiarly his own before the world was; and we find the order of the Covenant, when he said — 'I ascend unto my Father and your Father, and to my God and your God' [John 20:17], not to *our* Father, for there is no such equality, but to my Father by nature, and yours by being found in me. This relationship is Christ's of right, it is ours of grace through him — an undeserved boon; and God becomes our Father only because he is the Father of one so near and dear to us.

Christ's Sonship is not a mere official Sonship, beginning when he took the flesh. The relationship is from everlasting founded in nature and not arbitrary; and in like manner the love involved in it had no beginning, and can have no end. The Son dwelt in the Father's bosom before the world was, dear to him as his own soul. Had the Sonship begun in time, as some men vainly speak, we could imbibe but little comfort; for there might be constant fear, that what had a beginning might also have an end. But when we see that the Sonship is founded in the very nature of the Godhead, and can no more change than God can change, a joy unspeakable is derived from the discovery. And is not the thought an overwhelming one, that to us it should be given to stand within this bond between the Father and the Son — to be taken up, as far as may be, into this relationship, and remembered in inseparable connection with God's dear Son?

Do we look at the act of power put forth in calling us into the fellowship of his Son, Jesus Christ our Lord?

We are redeemed by power, as well as price, from being children of the evil one; and if Jesus, by his cross, made Satan's title but an empty name, the question now is simply one of power — who is strongest; and in the word of the gospel, Jesus goes throughout the world to claim his own, and by a mighty hand to dispossess the strong man armed of his lawful captive.

Do we look at the change in our relation to the Lord the Judge, in passing into the family of God? When the Most High has seen the sinner consenting to be righteous in the Saviour's righteousness — to be saved in God's own way — sentence of acquittal is given forth by the holy Judge the very moment we believe on Jesus, and there is joy in heaven on account of it. It is passed even now in the court of heaven, and the judgment-day will but proclaim it to all worlds, but not make it more perfect than it is now. It is passed, moreover, in a man's own conscience, and then there is assurance, peace, and joy unspeakable, the glorious liberty of children in the family of God.

Do we look at the frame of soul with which the joint-heirs are imbued? Though the Lord Jesus is in heaven till the times of the restitution of all things, yet is he ever with his children by his spiritual presence, till the end of the world. Their experience is not a mere dim resemblance of his own, but the very same in the measure in which they apprehend him. His peace is our peace — his joy is our joy, though he has an oil of gladness above his fellows — his spirit is ours, one spirit with him his life is our life; we live, yet not we, he liveth in us in a word, there is not one feeling or emotion that pervades the holy soul of the man Christ Jesus in the sanctuary on high, but vibrates in a greater or less degree through all the ranks of the redeemed, whether in the bliss above, or in their lowly dwelling place below — 'I in them and thou in me' [John 17:23].

Do we look at the love within which Messiah's seed are taken? They are more precious in God's sight than all the universe, and he loves them with a real father's love. It is not different love the Father bears to Christ's people from what he bears to him: 'Thou hast loved them as thou hast loved me' (John 17:23). Our capacity, indeed, is limited, but if we are Christ's we are loved with the very same love in kind, yea taken within the bond of that very love that from eternal ages has knit the Father to his only Son. Lift up your heads you drooping saints. The more you taste God's glory and desire him, will it not ravish your soul, that this God loves you, and has set the very love on you that he has set upon his Son?

Or do we look to the standard, the image after which God's children are to be conformed? They are to be conformed to that loveliest of holy scenes, the life, the character, the mind of Jesus — conformed to the image of God's dear Son. As they have borne the image of the earthy, they shall also bear the image of the heavenly; and at last they shall be like him, when they see him as he is. Yet a little while and the reviled sons of God shall shine brighter than the sun in a glory that will make kings and great men wonder.

2. *The Lord narrowly observes the new obedience of his children, and whether they will go astray.*

Allusion is made to that declension as proceeding step by step. When God says, '*If his children forsake my law*' [ver. 30], he names the first step when they lose a relish for his presence and his holy will; when he adds, '*and walk not in my judgments*' [ver. 30], he names the next step when they walk no more with him, and lose the fear of God upon their hearts; when he adds, '*if they break my statutes*' [ver. 31], he shows that all comes to open highhanded sin at last, although the first step was but a loss of secret delight in God. Perhaps we may, with more advantage, advert here to the first commencement than to the open fruits of declension.

The sin that dwells in us comes on with noiseless step, disarming all suspicion, it may be under guise of weariness, or suggesting delay in spiritual service, and it is little suspected, nay, spiritual slumber is accounted sweet. Indwelling sin is of dreadful strength; and if we cannot trace out all its windings and deceitfulness, if it is a friend within to every temptation from without, and wars in every power of the soul with the Most High, is not the unwary soul most sure to fall? Never did men occupy such an awakening position as the disciples in the garden. The three were honoured out of all the sons of men to be with Christ in the crowning act of his obedience, when he formed his high and final act of choice to drink the cup which the Father gave him. He had often been with them in Gethsemane's quiet retreat, as if he loved the scene of his future trial; and now, when he was to gaze on the eternal hell not too great for one sin when he was called to the highest act of his obedience, to choose, as man, whether he would be cast into the wrath of God as far as it could kindle on the Lord of glory — he wished to be refreshed by his disciples' fellowship and surely they will watch and keep him company. Ah, no! thrice that suffering one came back to get comfort in their fellowship, and his sweat was great drops of blood falling from his every pore upon the frozen ground, and they are fast asleep. If it was his gentle complaint, 'What, can ye not watch with me one hour?' [Matt. 26:40; Mark 14:37]. O how many an occasion shall we trace as we look down from the heights of future glory, when we, too, enjoyed the same forbearance of Almighty love on our way to Zion. We have begun this departure, if our thoughts turn not naturally and habitually unto God as the needle to the pole, or if less drawn by the cords of his constraining love than in other days. We have entered on a path of declension, if, like the slumbering virgins, we have lost transforming views of the glory yet to be revealed in the presence of the Lord at his coming—if we press forward the less and not the more when accepted in the beloved.

O declining soul, you are not in *the same earnest effort*! The day was when you ever saw some new perfection in the Son of God, and sought some new occasion to commend him. Where is the happiness you spake of? You abuse the doctrine of conversion, if it is made a resting place for sloth, as if you might on that account be less in prayer, less in awe of God. The almighty power of God on dead souls at first conversion — the very power by which the Saviour rose — must be as much as ever put forth on us from hour to hour; and if God is waiting to carry on the work, are you unwilling to be the subjects of the same Almighty change?

You have ceased to seek *the same blessings*, although they are designed to be revealed from faith to faith till we are ever with the Lord. When light from heaven first shone on you, you were eager to *win Christ himself*; now, though you feel your loneliness, you do not desire so much to apprehend him. O how different is it now! You once mourned over your thick darkness, and were not content with doctrines, without more glowing discoveries of heavenly things; but now you seek not *heavenly light* so much as you did then. As to *pardon*, again, through the imputed righteousness of God, the very highest attainment any child of God shall know on this side of heaven, is to wash daily in the fountain, and yet hate sin as much as ever; but in your pride you will not daily be indebted to forgiving love, and in your unbelief you will not rely upon its freeness as you once did. Remember whence you are fallen. And if we speak of *strength for hourly duty*, the day was when you saw no reason why you should be weak when Christ is strong, or empty when it has pleased the Father that all fullness should dwell in him; but now, because God tries you whether you will labour for every blessing, and contend for it, you fall back discouraged.

Nor do you pursue the *same spiritual exercises.* As to private *prayer*, excuses multiply as years roll on. Every company and pursuit is not abandoned that unfits you for it, and the form is very irksome. If we ask how far you war with your *corruptions*, are you not weary of doing constant violence to your sinful nature, bolder now with little sins, less tender in your walk before the Holy One, and more careless in draining off corruptions daily, by slow degrees? And as to the measure in which you cherish *implanted graces*, time was when you strove to have them in the highest exercise, and were most of all afraid to have less of God and of his presence than on the day before. How different is it now!

You pillow your soul upon a time when your tears were turned into joy, your fears into peace, your sighs into songs of praise. You trust to past experience, to past recourse to Christ, and not upon himself as the refuge from the tempest now. What if you repose on a delusion, on an awakening which was but the savour of death unto death? It matters not what you once were, what are you now?

But notice here, again, that when the Lord so narrowly watches if we walk in *his law and judgments* he means the law of liberty written on the heart, which neither can condemn nor justify a child of God. The children of

God do not obey to be put among the children, for they are sons already, and they obey both in the rest above and here below with a love that casteth out the fear to which the law appeals. Obedience is heaven begun, and the sons of God rejoice to see him take his honour, and call all worlds around him to esteem and love him, as most worthy. They are not under the law in whole or part, so far as it has sanctions, threats, or promises. But let us bear in mind — for there may be ere long another Antinomian outbreak — that in the measure in which we win Christ, it will be our meat to do the Father's will as it was his beforehand. Our willingness to obey just shows how far we have tasted the sweetness of the promises, how far we have apprehended Christ.

Let us bear in mind that every child of God is under high and holy discipline, and that true grace is certain to be tried and sifted. If Jesus learned obedience by the things he suffered, though he were a Son, good cause there is that we too should be sifted. Remember that the Lord tried Israel for forty years, to prove what was in their hearts; and if he cross our will, it is to try our faith and patience — if heresy come in to deceive if it were possible the very elect, it is to make manifest them that are approved. Let us labour that, whether present or absent, we may be accepted of him, and count it all joy to meet the trials which strengthen faith.

3. *God, jealous of his honour, cannot pass over the transgressions of his children without chastisement.*

Then will I visit their transgressions with the rod, and their iniquity with stripes. This rod — these stripes — may come in many a form, in personal affliction or bereavement, in sorrow or reviling, in the buffetings of Satan or the hiding of the Father's face. These visitations come not as the curse of the law, for believers are not under the law, nor does their Father disinherit them. God distinguishes between the persons of his children whom he loves and their faults which he punishes. 'Thou wast a God that forgavest them, though thou tookest vengeance of their inventions' (Psa. 99:8).

The afflictions which God sends to prove and try his people come when they most ardently grow up into him, who is the Head in all things; but of these God speaks not here. The cross we are to bear in following Jesus is felt most keenly when we are most alive to *God*, for we must do violence at every point to the natural aversion of our evil hearts, and to a world in open arms against our God; but of that God speaks not here. The afflictions which he speaks of here are punishments, and may be easily distinguished from the other, because they come in seasons of departure from the Lord. Upon these occasions, and even for sins of omission in which *we* live more readily, the Lord allots, as his messages to Israel show, a just recompense of reward. Have we to do with a God less jealous now? If a holy God could not pass over one offence in Moses, without making him bear the mark of his displeasure, we have to do with one the same yesterday, today, and for ever; for *our* God is a consuming fire. The Lord, who will not be mocked, inflicts fit punishment for every declension, for all distrust of him. Do you make light of small departures from the Lord, because it is a day of grace? Do you wink at decays of grace in yourselves, at sloth or unbelief or a defiled conscience, at lukewarmness in prayer or in holy love, as if God winked at them too? You shall suffer loss though you may be saved so as by fire. Though God is at peace with us as Judge, his jealousy as the Holy One burneth with fire. It is told of a holy minister that he died imploring pardon, especially for his sins of omission. But more affecting than even the testimony of a dying hour, is the frown with which a God of love must visit them; and, if it be by spiritual judgments mainly that God now visits sin, the blighted religion in these souls of ours, the pointless sermons falling half-way to the heart, and the ease in Zion, may just prove that God is jealous. If any think that backsliding is a light matter because it is a day of grace, hold up the sin to the holy light of the Redeemer's countenance as he speaketh to the Seven Churches, and you will cry, who may abide the day of his coming? and who shall stand when he appeareth? for he is like a refiner's fire and like fuller's soap.

We have said that there is nothing properly penal in these frowning visitations of a heavenly Father, for they have their source in his grace, and for their aim a return to himself. They are not from a Judge, but from a Father. The Lord has no pleasure in the sufferings of his children, but there is a glory in the connection between sin and punishment which never can be broken, and he will show that sin is an evil thing and bitter. When the warnings of Jesus in the garden could not keep the disciples awake, his rebuke was, Sleep on now and take your rest — he is at hand that doth betray me, implying, that the awakening providence of God would now compel their watchfulness. Alas! how many are never aroused till startled by tremendous judgments and alarming providences! God will deal in love with us if we can be drawn by the cords of love. But if kindness will not allure, the trials of a severer discipline will compel us to live near him, to cry unto the Lord in our distress.

Look at Israel, on entering the land of promise. Unmindful, after first success, of their work of vengeance on the doomed nations round them, they neither work *for* God nor *in* God; and when the angel tells them in Bochim, for their punishment, that they should not drive out those nations any more, such a day of weeping followed — such a day of repentance — as has seldom been in this dark world. But why did they not return to their first works? It seems that the courage once given them was not given again — the Lord was not with them in such measure any more. Is this a new thing in the earth? Ah! it is common to lose first love, but all do not regain their former place. Many are but blasted trees — melancholy monuments of what they were, or might have been. Some all zeal once are now lame in every effort, and what time is lost if ever they recover!

Could I reach some young convert, ready to take a little slumber when the Sun of Righteousness has chased away the darkness of the night, as if the keen edge might be abated and all be well again, I would say, no quarter can be given in this warfare, till we see Jerusalem and the Lamb face to face. O, if any live as if they might safely be ever sinning and repenting, can you dread no danger? — is it only after a fall that you will stand in awe, when our God is a consuming fire?

The Holy One can let alone men of the earth till the great day; but the Church, which is the only holy house in which he dwells — the renewed soul which is his temple — may not be left polluted. 'You only have I known of all the families of the earth; therefore will I punish you for all your iniquities' (Amos 3:2). The jealousy of our God smokes on all sides of his chosen ones. What he can bear with for the present in the children of the wicked one, he cannot bear in those who are a people near him. Judgment begins at the house of God, on those who bear his image; for more heinous in God's account, and more ruinous to souls around them, is sin in God's people than in others.

By doubts and fears in a hesitating bosom, the Lord oft-times chastens his people, who once had joy unspeakable and full of glory. Satan is allowed to cast his fiery darts, and setting forth a long train of decays, with all their circumstances, takes occasion by some sickness greatly to terrify them, saying, What have such to do — the guiltiest among men to do — with life to come or with Jesus here. Their hands hang down — their songs in the night are silent. Is it not so with *many at this day*, as if wisdom's ways were not ways of pleasantness, and her paths the paths of peace? And in most cases — I say not in all — is it not because they have sinned away their light, and peace, and strength, and now they weep as they remember Zion. They would not keep awake when they might, and now they cannot imbibe the holy joy they fain would know again. They would not leave their spiritual sloth or worldliness when they might, and now they cannot let them go when they would. Who can stand before this holy Lord God? Oh! you who live as if the Christ within were not to be the same holy image of the Father as the Christ without — who rather would be safe than holy — when put into the refiner's fire of James or of the prophets, what but dross is left behind, after the wood, the hay, the stubble are burned up? Oh you who think that free grace will cover another and another sin, instead of labouring to depart from all iniquity, call to mind with whom you have to do; for the Lord is not mocked. Will you provoke the Lord to jealousy? You who think it legal to take a single glance at your unweeded hearts — who will hear that Christ is *for* you, but who will not ruffle self-complacency by the thought that he is *in* you except you be reprobates, you cannot serve the Lord, said Joshua to such a people; 'for he is an holy God — he is a jealous God — he will not forgive you your transgressions nor your sins' [Josh. 24:19]. Lose not Israel-views of God — Old Testament views of God, for they are not to be forgotten, but carried with you when you think of God in Christ.

4. *Our declensions do not utterly remove God's loving-kindness, because it is not founded on ourselves, but on another.*

It is striking to observe (ver. 33), that the Lord changes the person, and when we expected to read, '*nevertheless my loving-kindness will I not utterly take from them*,' he drops all mention of the sinner, and, reverting to the covenant, says, '*my loving-kindness will I not utterly take from him*.'

The Father's love to the Son is the very foundation of the gospel. The Father cannot be an enemy to him who is his very heart. To show that the Father cannot cease to love him, let us bear in mind that, when he came forth as Mediator, it was not a new affection that the Father bore to him, but the very same that had been borne to him before the world was. When he put off his glory and appeared eclipsed, self-emptied, humbled, the Father said of him, what had been upon his heart before time began, 'This is my beloved Son, in whom I am well pleased' [Matt. 3:17; 17:5; Mark 1:11; Luke 3:22; 2 Pet. 1:17]. When he put on his people's sin, he met the anger of an offended Judge, not the enmity of an offended Father. Even when his God forsook him, as he hung surrounded with the terrific garment of our sin, and his human soul wanted all sensible comfort, he was the object, amid all his woe, on whom Eternal love was resting. The great triumph of the cross is, that he who hung there was more pleasing in the Father's sight than even sin was hateful — *that the sin could be consumed, and yet the love remain entire.* Had this love not been as full as ever, as high as ever — had there been an interruption of it but a moment — our salvation had been hopeless. But while Christ took on him what was due to us, he did not lose, he could not lose, what was eternally his own: the light of everlasting love did not forsake, and could not forsake, the temple where it ever dwelt.

If then, the Father's love was not abated when Jesus bore the garment of our guilt, and if a time shall never come when that love shall cool toward him or be withdrawn, never shall it cool toward his seed, who are taken within the bond of such a love. The love they enjoy is not different, but the same. At all times alike, and in all conditions alike — even in times of dreariest declension, God's love for ever rests on all who are joint-heirs with Christ, though at the time they do not feel it shed abroad upon them. Even then they are as much beloved as ever, and Jesus is to be heard saying, 'Thou hast loved them as thou hast loved me' [John 17:23].

These words, 'My loving-kindness will I not utterly take from him' [ver. 33], show us, we believe, the *proper motive to be brought to bear on sad backsliders, and the Lord's way of restoring them.* While the mind of God is here revealed, it is not as if he kept the secret to himself; he designs to give a spring of action unto us, to forestall undue despondency, lest the spirit fail before him. If any presume on such words of tenderness — halt! they are not spoken unto you, but to the downcast child of God, at a loss to know how God can love him with so little that is pure and lovely — ready to doubt how a worm, a rebel, an enemy, can be endeared to God. When the declining soul is grieved with his own distempered heart, and his backslidings have reproved him, the Lord removes the cloudy day, by showing that the only cause of the Divine favour is that, without a claim on our part, everlasting love rests on us because it rests upon the Son. When sin is on the soul, we are prone to think that God is turned against us, and we dare not look again to his holy temple; and to counteract this, God announces that he is unchanged — the very same he was at first. God's voice at first was, This is my beloved Son, in whom I am so well pleased, that by him the guiltiest may come from wrath to grace — from sin to holiness — from death to life; — in whom I am so well pleased, that in him all guilt is swallowed up, all wrath for ever hushed, and condemnation rolled away — all controversy between God and you forgiven and forgotten, — a heaven of light and glory is open over you, and the unveiled countenance of a friendly Father smiling on you with inexpressible complacency. You then put on the Lord Jesus; you become most dear in God's sight, as free from wrath as he is free, and partakers of a love which no creature can fathom. What made you rest so sweetly under the refreshing beams of the Father's love to firmly anchor here, when nothing amiable in you drew forth the Divine complacency? For his dear Son's sake alone, the sunshine of the Father's love first rested on your soul, and it is the same view of his unfathomable love in Christ that leads the downcast backslider to return.

The Eternal Father calls you, O backsliders, to look up from the depths to him who giveth you his Son, and your warrant to embrace him now is not that you received him formerly, but God's present gift, as if you never heard that blessed name before. Seek to be one with Jesus by receiving him afresh from day to day, if you would inherit God's love; for it is by cleaving to God's dear Son anew, and not by leaning upon past experience, that you find, to your soul's joy, no wrath upon his countenance, nor vengeance in his heart, but the very heavens and the skies raining down love. The declining child of God is prone to think that God is turned against him as unworthy, and he is unworthy more than he ever dreamed of; but in the holy of holies the merits of the Lamb are as fragrant as ever. We are ever to realize that Christ puts in his righteousness to adjust the balance between God and us. The Father never removes his loving-kindness from him, and there is no propitiation necessary between the Lamb and us. O, if you think that your sins are higher than the grace of God, that you cannot again be rendered amiable even by God's dear Son, what is this but unmortified pride, because not beloved for what you *are*, or may have done? If a backslider refuses to lean his guilty *soul* on what he leaned at first, he will only pierce himself through with farther sorrow. However near we live to God, there is no other way of pleasing God, no other way of coming under the warm beams of the Father's love, than the plea from hour to hour to hour which is founded on his Son. And, after going backward, if you doubt whether the Father's smile again can settle on you — if you question whether God can again be pacified by what is laid up in Christ — you cast contempt as much upon the treasures of his grace, as if you hoped to be forgiven because your sins are small. Begin at the beginning, as if you never knew the truth. Believe with all your heart that God has been more glorified by Christ than dishonoured by you — that the law is more magnified by the obedience of the greatest Being in the universe, than even violated by you; and look upon yourself as *in him* when he died, as *in him* when he rose, putting off our curse. Behold him, then, acquitted, and that you too were acquitted in him. Draw not your comfort or your confidence *from anything wrought in you* as a ground of faith, but look simply to God giving you his Son, and all the fullness of his Son, in the precious promises. Cast yourself on God's *self-moving grace without you*, and peace will fill your soul, *within.* Faith is the simplest act of leaning on the obedience of another — on Christ himself, our righteousness; it is the opposite of leaning upon aught within. Hear him saying to the Father, for you, 'I have glorified thee on the earth' [John 17:4]. It is when you thus look, expecting the Spirit to reveal the Son in you, to glorify the Lamb in your eyes, that you regain the joy you long for.

3

A Witnessing Church — A Church Baptized with the Holy Spirit[1]

For John truly baptized with water; but ye shall be baptized with the Holy Ghost, not many days hence. When they therefore were come together, they asked of him saying, Lord, wilt thou at this time restore the kingdom to Israel; and he said unto them, it is not for you to know the times or the seasons which the Father hath put in his own power. But ye shall receive power after that the Holy Ghost is come upon you; and ye shall be witnesses unto me, both in Jerusalem, and in Judea, and in Samaria, and unto the uttermost part of the earth.—Acts 1:5-8

THE last interview with a dear friend, and his last words, are wont to be embalmed in fragrant remembrance; and when Jesus, about to enter on his glory, stands before our eye, promising the Spirit, with his last recorded words, should not this holy image be indelibly portrayed on our hearts, and ever recur, in the multitude of our

[1] Preached before the Free Synod of Perth, 21 April 1846, and published in compliance with their request: *A Witnessing Church—A Church Baptized with the Holy Ghost* (Perth: James Dewar and Son, 1846).—Ed.

thoughts within us, to delight our souls? The baptism of the Spirit was not alone for early times, nor confined to miraculous gifts, but is as lasting and extends widely as the duty of bearing witness unto Christ.

Omitting the question raised by the disciples in the sixth verse, a comparison is made between the baptism with the Holy Spirit, and John's baptism of repentance for the remission of sins. Such as truly turned from sin to God, whose hearts were prepared as a dwelling for the Spirit, were, at a later day, baptized with the Holy Spirt as with fire. The first — repentance from dead works went before — the new unction from above came after — and this is not to be explained away.

Notice also the time — not many days hence. God is sovereign in fixing a fullness of time, and we may not ask why that time was appointed to reveal his arm. But on our part, also, it is necessary to know our want of the Spirit, and to feel it, that we may welcome him with the more delight to testify of Jesus. Had the disciples not continued with one accord in prayer and supplication till the Spirit came — or had they begun to testify of Jesus without child-like compliance with his word and will — their labour would have been in vain. And, in like manner nothing but bitter disappointment can await us, if we go forth to proclaim the tidings of great joy, not clothed with power from on high — with lips not touched with a live coal from the altar of our God. Often, alas! have we returned with nothing but the toil for our pains, because we did not wait to pray down the

Spirit. How often do we run in vain, and labour in vain, when we presume on a sufficient message, and a sufficient preparation to declare it, though not glowing with the love of Jesus, nor with the savour of the heavenly things we testify?

The doctrine then we shall examine is, a church is only so far a witnessing church as it is baptized with the Holy Spirit. For while no fitness can be found in any instrument to procure the Spirit by intrinsic excellence, or to move the sovereign Lord to reveal his arm, neither does God pour out his Spirit to any large extent without fitting for the work the instruments whom it shall please him mainly to employ. In opening up the doctrine, consider: —

1. *The nature of this Baptism, its marks, and on what occasions it is conferred.*

That somewhat more is meant than renewing in the spirit of our minds, is plain from this, that the disciples were already found in Christ. The baptism of the Spirit is the great promise of New Testament times to all the Israel of God. Before Pentecost, God's children were not wholly exempt from the spirit of bondage, nor were the saints of old; but in the days of the apostles, the saints in general seem to have enjoyed the promise of the Spirit through faith. The Holy Spirit is the first fruits of glory; and the complete inheritance, when sin shall be found no more, is just a fullness of the spirit. Let us take whatever measure of the Spirit we enjoy below as but a foretaste of those joys, a spark of that glory, a part of that fullness of holiness, a drop of that ocean of bliss. To undervalue this baptism of the Spirit, is the beginning of all declension. Are we baptized with the Holy Spirit? — then not only condemnation ceases in the conscience, but also the refreshing from the presence of the Lord, for which we longed, is in good part realized. Are we baptized with the Holy Spirit? — then, forgiven much, we love much, and give ourselves to him who gave himself for us, heart for heart, surrender for surrender. Thus, being ravished with the excellency of our Lord, and glowing with a high esteem for him, our heart is full of love, and our mouth of praise. It is the nature of fire to send forth light; and when the Spirit comes to baptize us as with fire, truth is shed abroad upon our hearts as part of ourselves, and Christ is set before our eye in the bright image of his dying obedience and of his glorious reign. It is of the nature of fire to warm us, and when the Spirit comes in this fiery baptism, he comes to kindle our cold souls into a flame of love to God and man. The approach of this genial spring to the barren winter of our hearts, opens the blossoms of new life, of humility, and godliness. Not only does he confer the Divine seal of a peace that passeth understanding, but he leads us to yield ourselves for evermore to the Redeemer as his dear-bought property, and to walk with God. It might be thought that the heavenly joy of this baptism would make a man secure; but, on the contrary, he now renounces all claim to himself. A believer, anew baptized by the Spirit, is like the springing fields glistening under the rains of heaven; he revives as the corn, and grows as the vine; and, feeling that he is not his own, he lives alone for his Redeemer. They who are content without this boon are just content without partaking of God's holiness. It is the nature of fire, moreover, to spread abroad. I am come, said Jesus, to send fire upon the earth, and what will I, if it be already kindled? And, when the Spirit comes in this fiery baptism, the words of Jesus spread like a conflagration from mouth to mouth. In the early days, when the apostles were under this fresh baptism, and also in the days of the Reformers, the burning words spread from home to home, from land to land.

If we would know to what extent we share in this heavenly baptism, let us ask, how far does the unction of heavenly knowledge, the self-denied humility, the boldness, the decision of the first disciples, imbue our minds? The comparison will furnish matter for deep humiliation.

I said the unction of heavenly knowledge, whereby we know all things — for no sooner did the Spirit come upon them, than they penetrated into the inmost nature of the revelation of God. They who a few days before scarcely understood the Saviour, whom he often reproved as slow of understanding, who had well-nigh forgotten what they learned for three years, in his company, came, in the twinkling of an eye, to a clear, vivid understanding of the things of God. Every faint remembrance of the words of Jesus and of his office stood fresh before their eye, as if bathed in light, and they spoke with an authority no less overpowering than had been stamped on the burning words of the prophets. Would we learn how far this baptism with fire is ours? Let us ask, is the word as a fire shut up in our bones, opened up to us with living power, with spirit and life? The Spirit, in his blessed errand, comes only in the word which he inspired at first. Is the truth, then, shed abroad with such brightness, with such an overpowering flood of light, that every promise is joyously sealed upon the soul, and the word is taken up into the heart as part of ourselves? In so far is this baptism ours.

I said their self-denied humility: for however envy and a proud thirst for honour held possession of their minds before, they now discover a single eye to the Redeemer's glory. They were only awed by what they saw of Christ's humility, in whose soul no self-seeking wish found a place, but now they no more seek the highest place. They no more betray a restless craving for sitting, one upon the right hand, and the other on the left. Nor do they make Christ a servant to their wish for pre-eminence; but they longed to decrease that Christ might increase. Inflamed by a different spirit, their previous desire to stand forth as the greatest was laid in the dust. Would we learn how far this spiritual baptism has been shed upon our Church, our ministers, our people? If filled with self-complacency, as if we stood in need of nothing — if we cannot bear to be wholly laid in the dust, we have not seen the Spirit, neither know him. No church in Christendom is more exposed than ours to self-complacency for its sacrifices, its devotedness, its self-denial — more liable to be elated with unexpected success — more prone to glory in its ministers, its means, its numbers, in its contributions, in its schemes, in its prominent position before the world's eye. Let us watch and pray against the snare, and learn to glory in the Lord. Are we still full of self-complacency — of the fond opinion that we possess peculiar claims on God for the self-denial in his service? Do we squander time, talents, reading, speaking upon self, while Christ's honour is not habitually our highest aim — while our absorbing desire is to enjoy distinction above others? Do we betray our self-sufficiency by censorious judgments upon other saints instead of thinking others better than ourselves? Do we betray our pride by embittered feeling against such as thwart us, as neglect our own or our Church's fancied merits, not trembling like Paul, lest men should think of us above what they see us to be, or that they hear of us. The disciples would be great, and the Redeemer tells them, that they must be as humble as the little child he placed among them; and are we still as they before Pentecost? The Lord will not give his glory to another, and severely visited this sin upon a Nebuchadnezzar, a Herod, and even on his own beloved Moses; and are we still over-weaning, self-seeking, proud? To that extent we have sinned away the Holy Spirit, and lack this fiery baptism.

I said their boldness: for however timid before, the disciples no sooner receive the Spirit than they come forth like different men, to speak the word without fear. They who durst not speak a word for Christ, became of a sudden so undaunted, that they charged home their heinous sin upon the Jews; and he who, but a little while before, had trembled in the presence of a servant maid, could not but tell thousands to their face, that Jesus whom they crucified with wicked hands, is now Lord and Christ; and so far as we too are baptized with the Holy Spirit as with fire, we shall summon the world to submit to Christ as Lord of all. But do we sit side by side with the impenitent, and not quit ourselves as witnesses for God, as living epistles of Christ, as the salt of the earth? Are we a comfort to the world by conforming to its ways? Are we the cause of evil to unconverted men by our worldly spirit, by our flattering words? Does the fear of man prevent us from openly walking in Christ and Christ in us, so that he may be set in us for the fall and rising again of many? So far we sink into inaction, content to live in friendly neighbourhood to a world lying in the wicked one, content without further aggression, do we show we want that fiery baptism that made the disciples feel they could not without blood-guiltiness let men alone? O, if we can sit as a church or as individuals, in easy fellowship with sinners, not seeking to save souls, not daring to encounter the adversary, face to face, we show that we are not baptized as with fire!

I said their decision: for however the disciples might be diverted from prayer and the work of Christ before, no sooner did the Spirit come upon them than they gave themselves wholly to these things. They who vacillated to and fro, who changed like the tide, had now one all-absorbing motive, and were borne along in the work of Christ, turning neither to the right or to the left; they continued daily with one accord in the temple. How can we then have received the heavenly baptism, if we are without the habit of religion, if our earnest efforts are but fitful, if we neglect present duty, and yet cherish the romantic hope of future service in a post which God has not required us to fill? If slothful in seeking God in prayer, in cultivating a holy relish for the things of God, if we never pray unless peculiarly helped, if we never put forth any activity in holiness unless God give us victorious aid, can we have this fiery baptism? So intensely occupied in one pursuit were the apostles, that public business was handed over to others, that they might give themselves to prayer and to the ministry of the word. If, as a church, or as individuals, we can afford time for work of a distracting nature, to lead us from prayer and from the word — if business of a public nature holds a loftier place in our esteem, so far we show that we have not the disciples' baptism. I might mention other things in the disciples, as a willingness to suffer for the Lord, their cordial love, and unanimity; but how shall we obtain this baptism, and on what occasions is it given? I do not say that a gracious God has bound himself by any promise to the impenitent in all the scriptures of heaven — that means employed by them has power with a sovereign God or prevails; but I do say, from the word, that such as already enjoy the baptism of repentance for the remission of sins, may obtain supplies of the Spirit a thousand-fold greater than any they have ever known.

Are we faithful in a little? God's rule is, To him that hath shall be given, and he shall have abundantly. Small at first were the faith, the hope, the love of the apostles; but yet a little while and the spark became a flame — the mustard seed became a tree. We, too, may yet have small delight in holiness, in prayer, in the word — we, too, may yet be of little faith, of wavering love, of flickering hope; but be faithful in a little, and a larger measure shall be given. The least breathing of the Spirit is worth a thousand worlds; and only as we are faithful in a little is this fiery baptism shed upon a church, a minister, a follower of Christ.

This heavenly unction is conferred when we keep the Lord's word, and show a humble, penitent compliance with his will. Behold this in the hundred and twenty disciples who were enjoined by their Lord to tarry in Jerusalem till the Spirit came — who were neither to return home to Galilee, nor to distract their minds with worldly cares. They continued through those fifty days to wait as they were told. And, if we would receive the Spirit's special presence to enlighten what is dark; to inflame what is cold, to strengthen what is weak and ready to perish, we must emerge from cold indifference to a simple compliance with the Lord's word and will. The world cannot receive him, cannot see him, neither know him. But, said the Saviour, If a man keep my words, we — that is, my Father and I, by the baptism of the Spirit — will come to him and make our abode with him. Repent, said Peter, again, to the awakened multitudes, and you shall receive the Holy Spirit. And we, too, shall be filled with the Spirit, if we discover their godly sorrow and contrition — their penitent compliance with the will of Christ. Let him who was addicted to the lusts of the flesh — who could not receive the Spirit or become his temple — daily learn more and more to abandon all fellowship with darkness, and he shall receive the Holy Spirit. Let him who was addicted to the lust of the eye, daily learn farther to give up his worldliness, his covetousness, his unmerciful hard-heartedness to others, and he shall receive the Holy Spirit. Let him who was addicted to the pride of life, learn daily to think more meanly of himself, and to take the lowest place, and he shall receive the Holy Spirit.

Another occasion is, when some heavy trial, some arduous duty, is laid upon us for the sake of Christ. Witness John in the Spirit amid the wilds of Patmos, or Paul glowing with the love of Christ, and singing praises in the inner prison. A special presence of the Lord, a better and more ample unction from on high, awaits us as a gracious reward for every dutiful compliance with suffering for Jesus. For the honour of the Lord, it becomes us to bear in mind that, in the history of this Free Church we have felt, and our brethren in Switzerland seem to experience at this hour, that a fresh baptism of the Spirit follows every step of faithfulness to our Lord. This is a new gale to fill our sails, and sent by him who is not forgetful of our labour of love — to waft us forward to fresh devotedness, spirituality, and success. Let us seek, then, new fields of self-denial; for we know that there is laid up for us on high the Spirit's rich communications — the full supplies of the gracious Saviour as a present reward. But as a solemn warning to take heed lest we fall, how seldom, if ever, do we see a Church rising above its first tone — how common for all Churches to fall far below it?

Another occasion, and a rule with God in reference to this baptism, is our unceasing prayer of faith. Ten days had the disciples continued with one accord in prayer, when, of a sudden, the Spirit came to give spiritual eyes, and a joy which no man could take from them. But the prayer which brings down the Holy Spirit, is not that which ceases if not heard at once, or if the heart is out of tune — that is content to stop with praying out some little savour or enjoyment of God's presence. The prayer which prevails with him who gives the Holy Spirit to them that ask him, is that which will not let him go without a blessing. Might not every day be a Pentecost — might not we receive the Spirit daily — if, using what we have in all faithfulness, and pleading in faith for what we have not, we feared to grieve him by unholy passions, or by slighting his presence? Every day would be a Pentecost if we prayed like a Cornelius — if we heard the word like the three thousand, and prized it like the eunuch.

2. *A Church is only so far a witnessing Church as it is thus baptized with the Holy Spirit.*

The connection between the two is plainly pointed out in the text: 'Ye shall receive power *after that the Holy Ghost is come* upon you, *and ye shall be witnesses* unto me.' The Redeemer does not send skilful orators, but witnesses, such as have seen with spiritual eyes and heard with spiritual ears. A witness must know what he testifies, and he has little liberty to speak of what the Lord has not wrought in him; he believes, and therefore speaks. Witnesses shall testify, while the world stands, of the love of God in Christ — of redemption through his blood, and of the forgiveness of sins according to the riches of his grace. Their sound must go into all the earth; but they do not testify what they have heard, or read, or thought out upon the things of God, for the Holy Spirit gives them a savoury experience of the tidings of great joy which they proclaim to others. Many called ministers have nothing they can testify; for can he be a witness unto Christ, whose heart is not filled with the presence, the love, the life, the Spirit of Christ? Can he be a witness of the cross of Christ, who does not daily look to the dying Lamb for pardon, peace, and cleansing? Can he be a witness of the Lord's abiding with his people to the end of the world, who knows not in his heart a daily intercourse with Jesus — who has not the witness of the Spirit that he is a child of God?

They who have Christ in them, therefore, can alone bring men into living contact with God. Christ makes it plain that a new unction must visit his followers before the blessing spreads to the impenitent; and to look for an awakening, therefore, before we ourselves receive that baptism as with fire, is to expect the end without the means. A Church cannot long continue to display a living testimony, unless this fresh holy baptism is repeatedly renewed; and to hold forth, like many declining Churches of the Reformation, a form of sound words, when the Spirit is sinned away, is but like a removed sign-post carried down a swollen river. For it is not protests, or creeds, or formularies, but living souls under the baptism of the Spirit, that make a witnessing Church. However, not apostles alone, but every believer waited for the Spirit before Pentecost. And nothing, it seems to me, will strike the heart of this callous age, but new holiness in believers' lives — the awe-inspiring spectacle of men glowing with love to their Lord, openly separating from the world. But can those believers be witnesses for Christ, who trifle with the Spirit's presence, who tremble not at decays in holy communion with God, who do not hourly rekindle their torch in God's own presence? Can those believers be really witnesses for Christ, whose life savours of the spirit of the world more than of God — who lie in doubts and fears, with no peace within and no zeal for God? May they not tremble to see how many, by their worldliness, they keep at ease on the brink of eternal hell?

Why do we so seldom see a Pentecost, a day of the Lord's right hand, when Jesus still lives as Lord, and the Spirit is waiting to descend? Times there are, indeed, when believers are anew baptized with glowing first love, and continue pleading for the salvation of the Christless, as if this were their only work, when breathless assemblies are hushed in death-like stillness before the felt presence of the Lord Jesus; and the awe on every soul is only chequered by the bright joy of reconciled countenances. Times there are when the sharp arrow of the King pierces many hearts — when heaven and hell seem to open before our face; compelling many to decide amid all men's overwhelming earnestness — when the general feeling is, the Lord is here, and a wide spread fear prevails lest others should be taken and they left. But why, O why, are such times so rare? Is it because our desires are so slender, our expectations so narrow? Is it because we too much select the post in which we choose to serve? Is it that, without being hourly led by Jesus as a child is led — without waiting for the Lord's direction — without following his guidance and complying with his Spirit, we trust to our own wisdom and to our own power — alas! found unavailing in the kingdom of God? 'Awake, awake, O arm of the Lord' — awake as in the ancient days, for our toil and study end in nothing.

We may yet be far from testifying with the Holy Spirit sent down from heaven, but who, in reviewing the past, will not exclaim, Had I given the same proportion of my days and nights to prayer which I give to toil, to other pursuits, or even to study — had I fallen down at the feet of Jesus, pleading for the Holy Spirit, till my lips were touched with fire, and my heart with love — till he showed me how to do this work, it might have pleased him to make use of me. Had I not run without this unction from on high — had prevailing prayer for the Spirit gone before all my work and followed it, I should not have spent my strength for nought. The review of the past shows what our present course should be; but let us not faint or be discouraged. The disciples were not to testify at all before they were anointed. They would not have succeeded in awakening a soul had they not waited for the shower from heaven. And can we succeed without the precious method that the Saviour has enjoined? Without this fiery unction the disciples were not to go forth; and with child-like dependence on Christ's grace and power, we too are to follow the same rule. O if we would take him at his word, and let him act! If we waited for the Spirit, should we toil in vain? They only who are chosen vessels, themselves baptized with the Spirit, can preach the gospel with the Holy Spirit sent down from heaven — can be unto God a sweet savour of Jesus Christ in them that are saved, and in them that perish. This coming of the Spirit with unction and power, with light and life, made the word quick and powerful, piercing to the dividing of soul and spirit, and discerning the thoughts and intents of the heart. No sooner were the disciples replenished, than others, yea, thousands, were inflamed. It was said by the holy Livingstone, 'There is sometime somewhat in preaching that cannot be ascribed either to the matter or expression, and cannot be described what it is, or from whence it cometh, but with a sweet violence it pierceth into the heart and affections, and cometh immediately from the Lord. But if there be any way to attain to any such thing, it is by the heavenly disposition of the speaker.'

To the same purpose said the heavenly-minded Brainerd, 'When ministers feel these special gracious influences on their hearts, it wonderfully assists them to come at the consciences of men, and as it were to handle them. Whereas without them, whatever reason or oratory we make use of, we do but make use of stumps and not of hands.'

Fathers and Brethren, in fulfilling our testimony, this church is in special danger of settling down upon its lees. Is there no danger lest we take the wonderful prosperity of this Church as a compensation for the spiritual glory of a church? Is there no temptation to be less dependent upon God amidst success — to say my mountain standeth strong — than when apprehensions of an unknown evil beset us on every side? The Lord breathes over Israel the affecting complaint, 'I remember thee, the kindness of thy love, the love of thine espousals, when thou wentest after me in the wilderness; what iniquity have your fathers found in me that they are gone far from me?' And is there no danger lest we too surrender ourselves to carnal slumber, content with past exertions, and enjoying an inglorious response before the rest of eternity arrives? Is there no risk of beginning in the Spirit, but seeking to be perfect in the flesh? If not watchful unto prayer, may we not ere long be surprised with sleep, and grow weary of well-doing, or give way to a reaction? The eminent Hooker, on embarking to New England with the pilgrim fathers, thus expressed his apprehensions, destined too soon to be realized: 'Farewell, England, I expect now no more to see that religious zeal and power of godliness which I have seen among professors in that land. Adversity has slain its thousands, but prosperity its ten thousands. I fear that those who have been zealous Christians in the fire of persecution, will become cold in the lap of peace.' May the Lord keep this Free Church awake at whatever cost!

But another temptation, no less perilous, is the expenditure of time and energy on thankless schemes and delusive enterprises. Should it not be the answer of this Church to every such allurement, I am engaged in a great work and cannot come down? Perhaps the most powerful temptation with which the enemy can ply this Church, is to cast ourselves down from the pinnacle of the temple, in the presumptuous hope, that, because protected in positions which our Master chose for us, we shall be equally protected in those chosen by ourselves. May we be kept from the seductive idea that we could render better service in some other post than in that in which the Omniscient Saviour bids us occupy. It is a blessed discharge from every kind of work that forces us back on this land for which we are especially responsible, till we see the reception of our message. Let schemes be as bright and captivating as they may which divert us from our post, which draw us off, I suspect them, and the quarter whence they come; and while we confess our readiness to fall asleep at our post, or to be seduced from it, let us at every interval afresh resume our work — let us ever and anon encourage one another to greater love, and zeal, and faith, and prayer — let us fall back afresh on the humiliation, the devotedness, the vows of other days, when we were most sensibly baptized with the Holy Spirit as with fire.

In sending forth this discourse, let me briefly add, that all who have the Spirit of Christ, ought equally with ministers to stand forth as witnesses, and feel that they are kept for a season on the earth to do a work for God, after their title to the heavenly joys is secured. Would not God's people tremble, if they saw how many their lukewarm lives embolden to abide in sin? God will be with us while we are with him, nor will he withdraw the Spirit till we sin him away. And what if God's own people themselves mar his glorious displays of grace and power in this dark age, because the salt is losing its savour when the land needs it most, and their love is waxing cold through abounding iniquity, when, if ever, it should burn most brightly? Say not, O that a dead world were quickened; but, O that I myself were quickened. Do not many grow weary and faint in their minds, because the example of those most eminent for gifts and graces tends not to encourage, but to dishearten them?

Nor can I omit a call to prayer. When an ardent desire is cherished for the Holy Spirit — when the spirit of extraordinary supplication is poured out from on high — the time to favour Zion, the set time, is come. But the prayer that breaks through the clouds, and opens heaven, asks on a scale no lower than according to God's riches in glory, and expects, with joyous confidence, such great things as Christ's great merits can procure, and as it is God-like and worthy of God to bestow. For all the persons of the Godhead are the more highly honoured by the greatness of the benefits conferred. While God's glory is the highest end in prayer, let us, with believing hearts, hold up the one-prevailing name of Jesus, neither expecting an answer for the inward peace, the enlargement, the fervour of the holiest frame; nor apprehending a denial for an uncomfortable frame, for the merits of that name that prevails with God is evermore the same. Let us look at the prayers in Scripture, and we find that God's glory, the Church's growth and welcome, her holiness and progress, were ever highest in the thoughts and breathings of the saints of God. And if we are animated with any other frame — if that weighs lightly with us that weighs most with God — if our aim does not harmonize with God's in seeking the glory of his name — neither can it be prayer taught by the Spirit, nor prayer offered up in the name of the Son. For the prayer which is of God maketh intercession according to the will of God (Rom. 8:27). The greatest work, perhaps, that some can do for God — and who does not long to do something for him? — is to give him no rest, and never to keep silence, till the Spirit is sent like floods upon the dry ground.

4

The Necessary Harmony between Doctrine and Spiritual Life[1]

GENTLEMEN, the study of Systematic Theology, which is to engage your attention, in that relation which we, for a season, occupy to each other, lays claim, in no ordinary way, to all your previous acquirements. It calls them into the fullest efflorescence. And if you come to the study with that high ardour and that generous enthusiasm with which the minds of youth are generally filled, and which this study is fitted to inspire, it is not too much to say that the subject, from its nature, affords materials that surpass your highest anticipations. There is no doubt that the richest images which you entertain of what Bacon[2] has fitly termed the 'transcendent science,' and 'the queen of sciences,' fall short of the results which will be reaped when the study is conducted in the proper spirit, that is — *in the fear of God.*

[1] *An Introductory Lecture delivered on 9 November 1853, to the Free Church Students attending the Divinity Hall in Aberdeen* (Aberdeen: A. Brown & Co., 1853).—Ed.

[2] Sir Francis Bacon (1561–1626) was an English philosopher and statesman. He served as Attorney General, and as Lord Chancellor of England. His works are credited with developing the scientific method.—Ed.

Nor, if we glance at the position which we occupy in the world's history, ought you to be insensible, as Students of Theology, to the impulse imparted by the peculiarities of the age you live in an age of violent intellectual fermentation. You have fallen on times which on this account lay claim incessantly to the highest culture, and to the greatest mental effort. But, furthermore, you have fallen on times of religious effervescence and of conflicting tendencies on spiritual things on times of action and reaction to which, we may say, without exaggeration, no parallel, for at least two centuries, is to be found. We are ushered in the course of history into one of those periods of vehement action and inquiry which stir the minds of nations to their depths, which put an end to all stagnation of thought on Theological principles and doctrines, and which thrust mind into violent collision with mind on almost every dogma of importance. Whoever has gained a place of observation or a mount of eminence which enables him to survey the struggling elements of Theological opinion, agitating the Churches and society at large, in this land and in other lands, is well aware that the mind of Europe heaves with a strong excitement on religious things — that mental inactivity on doctrinal principles is now left far behind us, and that another order of things is coming on, by which we are compelled, from the very law of our position, to examine every thing anew. We have alighted on a period in the world's history, when much that seemed formed for perpetuity is again subjected to a fiery trial, when every doctrinal position must make good its rights in the face of many a challenge, and establish its authority by an appeal to the Bible, and the Bible alone; and knowing, what this one book is, the incorruptible word of God, which liveth and abideth for ever, we have no fear, and we need have no fear, as to the issue.

In this Preliminary Lecture, therefore, it may not be unseasonable, to single out for more particular notice one of the great conflicting tendencies, antinomies or contrasts, by which the times are moved, and which will front you in your progress at every step. One of the contrasts which will meet you at every turn is the one-sided and unnatural isolation into which theological dogmas and spiritual life are now put, as if either could stand alone. Dogma and life are in many quarters severed from their mutual dependence and connection. That which God hath joined together, as by a conjugal tie, is violently put asunder. Some lay all emphasis on the life, and disparage doctrine as of little weight in comparison. And, conversely, as one extreme just generates another, another school lays all emphasis on outward form as the whole hope of the Church. The former comprehend all who may be classed among the heterogeneous orders of modern spiritualists, intuitionalists, rationalists and mythists. The latter comprehend all who may be classed under the name of restorationists of what is merely old — with whom the form overshadows life, and, I may add, overlays life, and who have their representatives in the Restoration school abroad, and in the Puseyites[1] of this country. We have here indicated one of the most active antinomies or contrasts of the present day, which has thrown a surging commotion into the educated mind of Europe, and which is yet far remote from that adjustment which still awaits it in the future. Now, you at once perceive that both tendencies are incomplete, one-sided, partial, when taken singly and alone; and the further they go, they become the more erratic — they diverge into the most devious paths and into irreconcilable estrangement. It may be useful, therefore, to occupy the present hour in laying down a guiding principle applicable to many, nay, to almost all, the controversies of the present day, viz: — *the reciprocal dependence and mutual harmony which should obtain between orthodox doctrine, on the one hand, and spiritual life on the other*; and in order to render this principle, which we deduce from the conflicts of the time, the more clear and obvious, we shall take a closer view of these two diverging tendencies.

On the one side, then, we find the principle asserted in various ways, that ecclesiastical doctrine, as heretofore known, must either be anew constructed, or pass away among effete and exploded forms. Among the various modifications which are given to this principle in the

[1] This was the name given to the Anglo-Catholic party in the Church of England in the nineteenth century, derived from Edward Bouverie Pusey (1800–1882) who adopted sacramental views akin to Roman Catholicism.—Ed.

present day, we may mention *three* — and, without subjecting them to very minute analysis, we put them in due gradation.

1. *First of all, then, one of the most seductive forms in which this principle appears, is in the demand for progress in doctrinal opinion.*

This is a sentiment which, as it is generally put, takes its colour from the political theories of the age, and which, to a large extent, implies that Christianity must be regarded as a speculative system. That there is a salutary progress, no one will gainsay. That new truths have been elicited through the whole course of centuries, by means of the collision of controversy, and from the position which the Church has occupied, is clear and palpable to every mind, by a comparison of the Confessions of the Reformation, with those cruder ideas which were entertained on many doctrines during previous centuries. But the only occasions on which it can be said that any progress in doctrinal opinion has been gained, deserve to be attentively considered. These were *either times when the Church made new and great attainments in the life of faith*, and, in consequence, received new light on many single departments of revealed truth, *or times when some great and fundamental errors emerged*, against which she was constrained to maintain the truth of her faith. These two occasions have usually coincided. The latter has frequently, indeed, been, at the same time, the occasion of the former. But, can it be said of the present times, as contrasted with the epoch of the Reformation, or as contrasted with the Puritan age, in which the doctrine of the Church received its latest form, that we have made such advances as truly warrant us to speak of progress, and that the Church has in modern times been sustained in a higher spiritual elevation than the men of those days ever reached? That new attainments will be made in faith and life by the Church, there is no room to doubt; and these advances will find their proper expression in natural and organic progress, on the field of doctrine. But that course is wide as the poles asunder from progress through a course of speculation. It may be said, in general, that those who speak most of progress in the latter way are the most remote from it. They have caught up an external idea of Christianity, and confine it to the speculative, as if it were a system merely to be known, or to exercise the mind by novel sentiments, by exciting theories, and by startling excursions into the realms of thought. They do not feel, at least to any adequate degree, that Christianity comes not as a system susceptible of reformation or amendment in our hands, but to achieve a reformation on us. It comes not to regale human ingenuity by new and daring speculations — though to those who surrender their minds to it as a heavenly system, it will constantly present fresh and undiscovered wonders — but to elevate and to ennoble our fallen natures. But these advocates of a self-made progress, adopting a merely external idea of the Christian faith, treat it as a theory, and not as a transforming life; and, having speedily learned all its doctrines, and finding themselves at the conclusion of their jejune idea, they see nothing to fill up the blank but the shifting visions of an uncertain and unsatisfying speculation.

2. *A second form in which the principle appears, is the disparagement of doctrine in comparison of the divine life.* This is the distinctive principle of the Schleiermacher[1] school of divines, which has its home in Germany, but its representatives and a wide spread influence in every Protestant country. According to this school, doctrine is transitory and widely diversified, while life is the same in all. Theological dogmas, it is said, grow old and antiquated, while the divine life is always young. Maurice[2] of London, and Morell[3] represent this school

[1] Friedrich Daniel Ernst Schleiermacher (1768–1834) was, ostensibly, a pastor in the German Reformed Church. In the course of time he became a moving influence in the development of Liberal Protestantism. To him the essence of religion was to be found in subjective experiences of individuals and not on the objective truths of Scripture as a revelation from God.—Ed.

[2] John Frederick Denison Maurice (1805–72) was an Anglican minister who became a co-founder of a 'Christian Socialist' movement. He was notably heterodox in maintaining baptismal regeneration and the denial of eternal punishment.—Ed.

[3] John Daniel Morell (1816–91) was a Congregational minister. In 1845 however, he gave up the ministry in favour of philosophy. It appears that he ended his days as a Unitarian.—Ed.

in this country, Schérer[1] in Geneva; Park[2] of Andover, and many others, in America. According to this school, perfect doctrine, conformed to the truth of the spiritual life, is declared to be an impossibility. It is held that little weight must be attached to any attempt to reach the absolutely true in doctrine, and that faith is so little dependent on definite doctrine, that it can exist and flourish in a mystic element without it. The spiritual life, it is said, is one, while doctrine is manifold. To undermine more completely the attachment due to doctrine, and the importance assigned to it, they set forth, with great apparent warmth of religious feeling, that Son of God came[3] not to inculcate a

[1] Edmond Henri Adolphe Schérer (1815–89) was a Frenchman who became Professor of Exegesis in the Evangelical Church at Geneva in 1843. He was to become a notable advocate of Liberal Protestantism.—Ed.

[2] Edwards Amasa Park (1808–1900) was an American Congregational minister who became a Professor in Andover Theological Seminary. There is some ambivalence about his position in theology, some considering him to be inadequately conservative and others insufficiently liberal!—Ed.

[3] One of the great errors of Schleiermacher's theology is, that, instead of acknowledging man's entire spiritual ruin, and presenting the gospel as a remedial economy, he tells us of natural faculties, still existing, that need only to be developed. Though he makes Christ 'the Life', yet Christ becomes, in his system, rather the perfecter of the imperfect, than the restorer of the lost. Chalmers is the great antithesis to all this; and his method of theology, based on a remedial economy, and making the doctrine of sin the centre around which the whole circumference of his system is drawn, is the inheritance which Scotland should prize.

didactic system, but to give eternal life — not to furnish dogmas, but to bestow life. As against dead orthodoxy, such a view vindicates for itself a certain right: dead orthodoxy cannot maintain its position before this assailant; and that it is a *reaction from dead orthodoxy* is, to a large extent, unfortunately true. This mystical view, proceeding on a principle which is, in substance, identical with that of Quakerism, attends almost wholly to subjective emotions, and to dark feelings, or to the spirit within, rather than to the word without. It asserts that the spiritual life is the same in all, while doctrine on the other hand varies, because it is merely an individual view derived from individual experience, and gathered from a process of self-reflection. It is held to be impossible to conceive accurately of the infinite and of the eternal. Now, it is obvious that such a principle, though hitherto held in check by the restraints of a public opinion widely different, has its birth-place only in an erroneous view of inspiration; that it has a native tendency to excess; and that, if left alone, it would rush into irregular extremes. The learning of the men by whom it has hitherto been propounded, together with that sobriety which must attach to the scholar and the thinker, have hitherto kept it from developing all the germs which it contains, and all the consequences with which it is fraught. But these dangers are not concealed by the Christian dress in which it is arrayed. The Lord of the Church, however, we find from his word, has not left his Church to the direction of blind feelings, he has furnished a clear and certain scheme of truth on which her faith is to be fed. The Church's faith is fed by sound doctrine, and announces itself through sound doctrine, and is recognized through sound doctrine.

3. *A third form of opposition to doctrine is given out by the negative and destructive criticism, the extreme section of which pays only the most distant homage, and, in some instances, no homage at all, to Christianity.*

They openly avow their desire to break loose from doctrine altogether. They insist on a Pantheistic religion, without doctrinal opinions, without *dogmas* of any kind — they plead, where they plead at all, for the worship of God without forms — they enforce practical life without theories, without creeds, without forms of doctrine in any shape. The 'Nemesis of Faith' for instance, the work which recently made such a harrowing impression on the public mind — the writings of Carlyle — the school of free-thinkers; who take the *Westminster Review* as their organ,[1] supply illustrations of this form of opposition to doctrine. Looking down from a fancied elevation, with feelings of unmingled contempt for everything approximating to proper doctrine, they direct attention to the ills of life, and exhibit a fervid earnestness, and an intense aspiration after an idea which is confessedly

[1] Thomas Carlyle (1795–1881) was a Scottish historian, essayist and social commentator. Though from orthodox Secession roots, he came to repudiate Christianity and adopt a sort of deism. The *Westminster Review* (1824–1914) was in its day a quarterly magazine of a radical sort.—Ed.

sometimes goodly to behold; but they know not how to make the ideal a reality. *Mentors of that description, and they are numerous, now read lectures to the Church of Christ on her decay of activity, and benevolence, and vital earnestness.* They, in this respect, resemble Julian[1] in his scheme of restoring Heathenism to the splendour of its early days. He proceeded on the vain attempt to array the heathen faith with the moral beauty of the Christian life, and to produce similar effects without an efficient cause. He concerted the scheme of making the religion of Jupiter no less distinguished than the religion of Jesus for its moral virtue, for its domestic beauty, and for its self-denied benevolence. He planned the effect, but he omitted the consideration of the cause. He wished the fruits, but he could not plant the tree. *For how could that ideal become a reality on a heathen stem?* In like manner, the school in question, who repudiate doctrine with unmitigated scorn, and who wish to light up the moral glory of a pure and happy society, of a loving and earnest life, forget whence these fruits are to be derived, and how they are to flourish in a heathen soil. The ethical part of Christianity, which these writers seize on, and which they display without acknowledgment, is a mere plagiarism of which they ought to be ashamed. They borrow the earnest ethics of the gospel, dissociated from

[1] Julian (331/2–363) was Roman Emperor between 361 and 363. He rejected Christianity and consequently was known by the church as Julian the Apostate.—Ed.

its doctrines, just as Lord Herbert[1] and the Deists of a former age borrowed, without acknowledgment, their religion of nature from the Bible. But the ethics cannot exist without the faith; and yet they disclaim the faith, and seek only to enforce the ethics.

Such is one side of the conflicting tendencies to which we adverted at the outset. But it is always found in theology that one extreme generates another. The demand for progress, on the one side, with its watch-word 'forward,' induces others to proclaim, with equal vehemence, on the other side, a return to the way of the Fathers. The disparagement of doctrine, on the part of one school, produces a reaction on the part of others, who draw all their hopes from a rigidly reinstated orthodoxy. The ardour with which one side hails the creation of the new stimulates the activity of those who seek only the restoration of the old. While some lay all emphasis on the life, to the neglect of dogma, others, taking an alarm for which there is only too good occasion in many quarters, lay emphasis exclusively on definitions, and on nothing beyond the limits of accurately defined dogmas. While some dissever life from form, an equal number begin to cling to dead forms as the last plank of safety; and the more powerful Rationalism becomes, on the one hand, the more resolute, as we see in the Restoration School of

[1] Edward Herbert of Cherbury (1583–1648) was a diplomat, historian and poet, widely considered to be 'the father of English deism.'—Ed.

Germany, and in the Puseyite movement of this country, becomes the adherence of others to ancient forms and to ancient orthodoxy, for their own sake; and this spirit grows till they persuade themselves that they find something good even in the dead forms of the Greek and Romish Churches, from which the spirit of life has fled; and they foster hopes of a resuscitation, merely because the outward husk remains. They look on these mere forms with similar feelings to the Egyptians, who carefully preserved their dead in the form of mummies, and who entertained the hope that, though after the lapse of three thousand years, the soul would re-enter and reanimate them. But the mere revival of ancient forms, or of orthodox definitions, will, of themselves, accomplish nothing — they will bring back no spiritual life apart from living faith, and apart from a reliance on the person of the Son of God, who alone is the life, and who alone, in wise and glorious sovereignty, makes all things new.

Such, then, are the conflicting forces before you. Such are the two sides of that antinomy, of that contrast, with which I thought it useful to commence your studies in Systematic Theology. Nor will such a condition of things take you by surprise, if you embark upon this study in the spirit which it presupposes; for theology takes for granted, on the part of all who aright engage in it, that they set out in faith, and not in doubt; and, in that spirit, you are not only free from all uncertainty as to the truth, but perfectly tranquil as to the issue of the most conflicting views. The violence of those counteracting forces, which are called into activity, sometimes startles the timid, and sometimes takes the inexperienced by surprise. But to those who have gathered skill in tracing the historic path of theology, they appear but as the regular and usual track along which the kingdom of God advances in its path. The controversies excited on the most sacred subjects, the attraction and repulsion created by the truth, the collision of mind with mind, just evince that the truth is going forward. These controversies are just what the prophet says concerning the clouds: — 'The clouds are the dust of his feet' and we may say that controversies are just the dust of his feet as the Redeemer moves forward in his kingdom. Luther said, with his usual indomitable faith, when he saw the tumults occasioned by his doctrines: — '*Nisi hos tumultus vidissem, Christum esse in mundo non crederem.*'[1] He was right. It is the gospel that sends this fire on the earth. It is the reappearance of spiritual life in greater power among the nations, that gives rise to all this mental and spiritual effervescence. When a chemical action, for example, has disengaged a chemical agent, the very effervescence, that often ensues, serves only to indicate the fact that a substance is set free; and when the truth of God is set free, the disengagement is only indicated by the action or commotion which follows as a thing of course. Vital truth, in these recent times, has

[1] 'Did he not see those tumults, he would not believe that Christ was come forth into the world.'—Ed.

been sent forth anew by the Church's everlasting Head; and it will not return empty, but continue in incessant action till its work is done; and the commotions of the present day, as we may safely infer from the course of all previous ages, will only encircle the truth with still greater glory. And, moreover, the truth will reach its full development amid those mental and spiritual sorrows — amid those sorrows as in travail — which always usher in its triumphs among the nations of the earth.

Having thus viewed these two diverging tendencies, with a view to render more clear and obvious the principle which we deduce from the conflicts of the time, we revert to the guiding principle which we laid down, viz., *the reciprocal dependence and mutual harmony which should obtain between orthodox doctrine, on the one hand, and spiritual life, on the other*. We have seen their isolation, and, as resulting from that isolation, the risk of consequences from which our minds recoil. For our own part, we have the most profound conviction that the great problem before theology, in this age, is to place them in perfect harmony, — to watch with diligence their mutual action, — and never to suffer any invasion, even when wearing a favourable aspect, to dispossess them of their inalienable rights. They are formed for harmony. They are the complement of one another. And it is fraught with perilous consequences when any disturbance in their mutual relation disorganizes their connection, or when they are allowed to quench or to mar each other. If there is one thought more important than another in the general bearing of theology it is this. If there is one principle more important in my eyes than another, or one which I am more particularly anxious to place, or to see placed, as a moving spring of action in the minds of our rising ministry, it is just the highest cultivation of the spiritual life, in combination with the highest appreciation of orthodox doctrine. And these principles must be lived before they can be taught. They must breathe in the ministerial experience before they can leaven and pervade the Church. They must be a living unity in the teacher before they can lend their beautiful consistency, their energy, their elevation to the Church. It is impossible to carry these too far, if they go hand in hand. It is impossible to be too eager in the advancement of the spiritual life, on the one hand; and it is impossible to cultivate too ardently that holy doctrine, the study of which properly arises from the spiritual life, and which tends to nourish and to invigorate that life in all its parts. But if they are put out of their connection and dependence, the effect can only be compared to the crash or the collision of a piece of intricate machinery deranged. There is no harmonious action to a useful end, and only a violent abrasion of the disordered parts upon each other. But to make this more evident, let us, for a little, direct attention separately to both these elements.

As to theological doctrine, on the one hand, the importance of cultivating sacred science to the highest possible extent will readily appear, if we consider that, as Christianity apprehends the whole man, so provision must be made for the necessary exercise of profound thought. The practical department, it is true, is the end to which all else is but a preparation. But even for the successful prosecution of the practical, a fresh impulse must be constantly received from the field of what is more elaborate, and more profound or scientific. And, if the mind is not taught to range over the domain of theological enquiry, and to receive its invigorating food and nourishment from deep thought, you will soon find a languishing and contracting effect spreading over the most practical departments of the Church's life. The whole must be refreshed from the perennial fountains of theological investigation; and, on this account, I, for my part, never cease to value the Confession of our Church for the very breadth and volume of its rich theology. If some, not of our communion, complain of its amplitude, I say, is it not, on that account, a richer inheritance, into the possession of which we have been ushered, and where we are to find ourselves at home in following up those walks of contemplation and enquiry which it opens up? If some, not of our communion, would wish a larger margin of debatable land round the domain, where they may exercise their intellects in the warfare or the tournament of noisy speculation, I say, should not we be rather thankful for so wide a field of achieved and certain truth, within the boundaries of which the uproar of controversy is no more heard, and where regions of enquiry stretch away on the right and on the left, as land to be possessed? It is an ampler provision to expand a Church's enquiries, and to lead to profound thought, than is elsewhere to be found.

But another consideration, showing the importance of cultivating sound and orthodox doctrine to the utmost possible extent, is, *mind will find its level.* Those nations and those churches which are most equipped in theological acquirement, come, by the very law of mind, to exercise a control, nay, an irresistible dominion, over others. Some Churches, such as Geneva, in the period of the Reformation, and the celebrated Universities of Holland, in the following century, long continued, from this cause, to exercise the most salutary sway. Others may be named which, with great theological equipment, exercise sometimes a doubtful, sometimes the most baneful influence; and that influence, it is obvious, can be held in check or counteracted only by an equal learning of an orthodox character. It is almost impossible, then, to over-estimate the importance of an incorrupt and sound doctrine.

Again — if we turn our attention to the course of history, we shall find that the everlasting Head of the Church has attached such value to doctrine at every step of her progress, that he has put very many of the revivals of the Church in close connection with the assertion of the truth. The records of the Church are so strewn with examples of this fact, that the difficulty is to make the selection. I shall instance three:

(1) *The Pelagian controversy*, which called forth the devoted Augustine to maintain the grace of God against every form of natural ability, and natural free will, raged long and widely; but the discussion deposited seeds which ripened to a plenteous harvest, and was accompanied with a revival that more or less pervaded the whole Western Church.[1] As to Augustine himself,[2] his whole life may be called a confession of the forgiveness of sin, a hymn of praise to saving grace, and a prayer for new and fresh communications of the spiritual life; and in him the Confession of the Church was so much a personal matter, that he may be regarded as the meeting place where the streams of the past were united, and whence they were sent forth anew to refresh and fertilize the future. Christianity reached its highest point on the Roman soil in connection with his labours, and streamed forth from his works to all who had intercourse with that highway of nations: — all that attained ecclesiastical or spiritual importance in the Western World, was in one way or other derived from the school of Augustine,

[1] Pelagius (*c.* 354–418) was a monk of British origin who denied the doctrines of original sin and the transmission of Adam's guilt. He advocated the doctrine of free will and denied the necessity of divine grace in salvation. For a thorough discussion of the teachings and implications of Pelagius see William Cunningham's *Historical Theology*, vol. 1 (1862; repr. London: Banner of Truth Trust, 1960), 321-358.—Ed.

[2] Augustine of Hippo (354–430) over against Pelagius emphasized the total inability of fallen man and the necessity for divine sovereign grace in salvation. His theology greatly influenced the Reformers and subsequent Reformed theology.—Ed.

and through the testimony which he raised for pure doctrine.

(2) A second example is *the Reformation*, which in one point of view was a marvellous revival of the spiritual life, but in another point of view a movement which went hand in hand with the maintenance of doctrine, and which took the form of testifying for pure and saving doctrine against all the corruptions and errors of Rome. We see here, again, the Confession of the Church embodied in the personal experience of a Luther, and finding its unity in him, as well as the historical connection of the past and future. The testimony which he raised was for imputed righteousness through faith in the one Mediator between God and man; and in all he uttered, we find a constant application of imputed righteousness to those vain and self-devised additions which Rome had made, and which now fell off as nugatory and superfluous, as well as dishonouring to the sole merits of Christ. The whole Reformation, which shed such moral glory on the world, and which conferred such inestimable blessings, was a revival of the Church, but a revival which moved forward along the channel of a testimony for the truth.

(3) A third example which we do not hesitate to put in connection with the two former, was *our own Disruption.*[1] It was in one respect a great revival of religion, and

[1] Smeaton is referring to the Disruption of the Church of Scotland

in another respect a testimony for the doctrine of the sole Headship of Christ. And to show the paramount importance of sound doctrine in connection with this truth, and the same thing of course holds good of every truth, all the three Reformations or Revivals which have successively dawned upon our native land have stood in indissoluble connection with the testimony, that Christ is Head over all things to the Church which is his body. These three instances may suffice to show the importance to be attached to doctrine. And the inference is obvious. If the Head of the Church has from century to century summoned his people to defend the truth and if the times of greatest blessing and revival coincided with the times when she testified to some present truth, and mustered to some rallying point of doctrine which had been assailed, the inference is *she must guard all truth with vigilance.* Her rising ministry must not abate their love of orthodoxy. In a latitudinarian age, like the present, they must keep themselves unspotted from the contagion of false doctrine. No one can read the publications of the present age, or attend to the peculiar tone which animates the Churches, without an anxious feeling in

---

which took place in May 1843 and from which the Free Church of Scotland emerged. Smeaton aligned himself to the Free Church. Around one-third of the ministry (481) left the Established Church to form the Free Church of Scotland. The majority of the Free Church united with the United Presbyterian Church of Scotland in 1900, though a minority remained out of that union and won a famous case in the House of Lords in 1904 in their claim to being regarded as the continuing Free Church of Scotland.—Ed.

reference to those lax and unsettled views which in too many quarters exist, and cannot be concealed. They give less heed than formerly to the precept 'Buy the truth and sell it not.' They are confounding what is old with what is exploded and worn out. They are listening to the siren voice which confounds orthodoxy with narrow-minded exclusiveness; and, forgetting that there is a far greater bigotry for error, and that the greatest of all intolerance is exhibited by those who are the advocates of laxity, many, in the present day, plume themselves upon their liberality in surrendering doctrine after doctrine of the truth. Among the many things included in the mission of this Free Church of Scotland, one is — and to my mind it is not the least important — to stand as the bulwark of all the truth of Christ, and to be very jealous for all the truth in a lax age. Hitherto she has continued uncorrupted; and her rising ministry, I confidently hope, will be preserved from the infection that surrounds them, and then the Church will be preserved from the weakness, the disunion, and the distraction which lax doctrine introduces, and which cannot be sufficiently deplored. Long may the Free Church stand, the witness of undefiled doctrine, and its bulwark against attack. And long may her rising ministry, as they succeed each other from age to age, adhere to settled truth, not indeed because it is old, but because it is true, and because the Spirit has sealed it with undoubting certainty upon their hearts.

But I now turn to the other element, which is equally important, and which is indispensably necessary to balance the element of doctrine, to the element of life already mentioned. Theology is not all doctrine. Man's nature is not all intellect. He is heart as well as head; and, while we plead for orthodoxy with all earnestness, we mean living orthodoxy, or truth embosomed in the spiritual life. Dead orthodoxy is a tendency as calamitous, and a spectacle as painful, as that against which we have sought to erect a beacon of warning. The intellectual must not predominate to the exclusion of the spiritual. Dogma and life must be one organic whole, and be placed in perfect harmony. Christianity is not a mere system of opinions, but a renewing power to pervade the whole faculties from the inmost centre of man's being. It is not a mere doctrine, but a divine life, destined to transform humanity. It is not a mere theory, but a new relation to Father, Son, and Holy Spirit; and consequently when it is viewed only as a system of doctrines or of ideas which are to be canvassed, and argued, and discussed, this is a conception of Christianity little higher than that which puts it on a footing with a system of philosophy; and whether men fly off to the regions of speculation, or confine themselves to mere doctrines, they equally do violence to the organic unity of Christianity. In other words, they deal with Christianity, and not with Christ, with a system of notions and not with a personal Saviour. But as the great idea of the gospel is not exhausted by the revelation of a few special truths which may soon be learned — as it is developed in a spiritual kingdom, which is to apprehend the whole man, and to raise up his whole moral nature from ruin, *so Theology is neither to be taught, on the one hand, nor to be learned*, on the other, *as a complex system of notions*, doctrines, or opinions. Accordingly, if we cast our eye over the centuries of Church history, we find without exception that when the dialectic turn prevailed, when supreme attention was devoted to the accurate definition of doctrines, the spiritual life withered and decayed. Of the many periods that might be instanced, we shall mention three.

(1) The first shall be taken from *the Greek Church*, which became a mere petrifaction about the fifth century. Receiving the dead matter of tradition, and exhausting her energies upon the dialectic subtleties to which she had recourse in settling the great doctrines of the Trinity and of the Person of Christ, the balance between dogma and life was utterly subverted. It is not to be denied that after ages owe that Church a debt of gratitude, which cannot be over-estimated, for carrying out those doctrines to their full development. But then it must not be forgotten that the undue attention paid to nice distinctions and to accurate definitions, though necessary in the circumstances, because forced upon her by the subtleties employed in the Sabellian, the Arian, the Nestorian, the Eutychian controversies[1]

[1] For information about these controversies in the Early Church

in their chequered and ever-recurring forms, destroyed the harmony between doctrine and life, within her pale. Notions took the place of the animating life; and hence, without attending to the spiritual and ethical results, and content with formulas and accurate distinctions, the Oriental Church ceased to breathe the breath of life. She has lain accordingly, for twelve centuries, as a fossil remain amid the lapse of the Western revivals.

(2) A second example shall be taken from *the scholasticism of the Middle Ages*, which put forth so rich a blossom. Seldom indeed in the history of the human mind have more magnificent developments appeared, more vigorous and lively theology, greater dialectic power, or more varied mental gifts, than came to light in the great men, who shed a halo over the twelfth and thirteenth centuries — from a Lanfranc, and an Anselm, to an Aquinas, and a Scotus. But here again the harmony between dogma and life was not preserved, and that extraordinary efflorescence faded and passed away. Dogma overshadowed holiness; speculation quenched the spiritual life.

(3) A third example shall be taken from the times succeeding *the Reformation*. Scarcely had Luther left the stage when a new order of things appeared. The words of ardent testifying, the noble deeds of faith,

see Louis Berkhof, *The History of Christian Doctrines* (1937; repr. London: Banner of Truth Trust, 1969).—Ed.

the companies of bold evangelists, who sought only to proclaim the words of grace, disappeared, and were succeeded by an age of form. The harmony between dogma and life was dissolved. Life was quenched in dead form, and bitter controversy; and the noble efforts of an Arnt, of a Spener, and a Francke, of a more vital character, were only partially successful.[1] These instances may suffice to show the danger of disturbing the natural relation between doctrine and holiness. We long for the noble spectacle of living orthodoxy in all its amplitude, consistency, and vigour. But we tremble at the thought of a dead orthodoxy, which is the immediate precursor of Rationalism and of Neology, just as the withdrawal of the sun is the immediate precursor of the cold dews of night.

Such is the great regulating principle for your theological studies. You perceive, then, that all theological knowledge must be a spiritual knowledge, or a knowledge in the faith. You must begin, not from a principle of doubt, but from a principle of faith, understanding because you have believed. On the field of systematic theology, whatever it may be in other fields of knowledge, it is the certain conviction of religious truth that must lead us to thought. The great principle of Augustine — you will find it, for instance, among the

[1] Johann Arndt (1555–1621), Philipp Spener (1635–1705) and August Hermann Francke (1663–1727) were German Lutheran divines associated with the development of evangelical pietism in the devotional life.—Ed.

first of his *Sermons* — the great principle of Augustine, which we must carry with us to the whole of systematic theology, is *crede ut intelligas.*[1] For it is only through regeneration that the human spirit, obscured as it is by sin, can be raised to a right condition, and have a true eye for divine things, and regeneration has its true expression in the exercise of faith *credo ut intelligas*[2] was the motto of Augustine, and it made him the pre-eminent theologian he became. *Credo ut intelligam* was also the motto of Anselm,[3] who was honoured of God to lay the foundation of the true doctrine of the atonement established in the Church; and that principle, derived from Augustine, made him the theologian he became. The principle indeed that faith precedes a true understanding of divine things, or in other words, that a man must have a new sense before he can apprehend divine things, is a postulate in theology, and it has its confirmation in every other department of human knowledge. It is vain to discourse, for instance, on the science of music to one who has not an ear for music, or to descant on the beauty

[1] A Latin phrase, meaning, colloquially, 'seeing is believing'; or, more accurately, 'I believe so that I may understand.'—Ed.

[2] Augustine meant that spiritual knowledge leads to faith, and that the exercise of faith brings in a larger contribution of knowledge. — Colossians 1:9, 10.

[3] Anselm (*c.* 1033–1109) was an Italian who became Archbishop of Canterbury. His most famous contribution in theology was his work *Cur Deus Homo?* (Why did God become Man?) It is a study of the Incarnation of Christ and its necessity for atonement, for the death of Christ to accomplish redemption for sinners.—Ed.

of colour to the blind, for they want the sense which the subject presupposes. And, in like manner, the science of theology presupposes the new sense, presupposes regeneration, presupposes faith, without which it is not understood, and cannot be understood; and, therefore, I repeat, *crede ut intelligas*. A famous contemporary of Anselm — the well-known Abelard[1] — *reversed* the principle that faith precedes theological understanding, and asserted, that we must proceed from doubt, as the principle of all knowledge. He accordingly changed all doctrines into problems, which are to be demonstrated before they are believed. This is the principle of rationalism, the principle of scepticism; and it only leads astray. But believe, and then seek as far as possible to understand; for faith gives wings to theological intelligence; and then, where knowledge is attained, you are to render thanks; and where you cannot understand — and there are many points where we come to the limits of our knowledge — you will silently adore.

Such is the spirit in which you ought to enter on theology, and in this spirit your whole being finds full repose; for, unlike all other sciences or departments of science, where a certain measure of doubt is frequently found adhering to the results, the mind here finds the satisfaction of complete and perfect certainty. And the whole faculties must be submitted to the results of this sacred science. The whole man is to be moulded by it, and

[1] Peter Abelard (1079–1142) was a French Mediaeval philosopher and theologian.—Ed.

surrendered up to it; and here it is impossible to go too far. The great power of false systems, for example, lies confessedly in the number of faculties to which they appeal, and which they apprehend. The extraordinary power of Popery lies in the fact, that it lays hold of the entire man. And, in like manner, I may safely say, the more numerous the faculties which are surrendered up to the truth, and which are brought under the power of the truth, the more completely is that mind educated in Theology; and when a man learns in this manner, he will teach in this manner. And I do not forget that I address myself to future teachers, who are, I trust, to be the formers of opinion to others.

One word in conclusion. Endeavour to keep up the freshness of spiritual impressions on your own minds while engaged in the ardent and strenuous study of Theology. I need say nothing to convince you that *Theology* is the noblest study under heaven. I need say nothing to convince you that, in this high walk, the whole faculties receive the noblest consecration of which they are susceptible. But I may add a warning. It must not be concealed that students of Divinity, more than almost any other class, run the risk of growing irreverently familiar with solemn truths. They are too apt, from the circumstance that they are professionally connected with the daily discussion of sacred truths, to grow common-hackneyed in a round of thought about the truth. Many grow seared and secular, cold and withered, in their personal religion. Avoid this with the utmost vigilance. Live upon the truth you study; and the more you live upon the truth, the more vividly will you comprehend it. The closer your walk with God, the more full and unclouded will be your understanding of divine things.

One other remark may be allowed me, in reference to our intercourse together: for I am deeply sensible that my work is but half discharged if I only communicate a certain definite amount of information on sacred science. Cultivate a spirit of prayer, in reference to all your studies, and to all your exercises. The preparation for your high and holy calling, as future ministers, will never be successfully accomplished but in the spirit of prayer. That full panoply of theological equipment, in which I desire to see you arrayed, will never be put on except in one way — except through the spirit of prayer; and let the daily, hourly prayer of us all be, 'Open mine eyes that I may behold wondrous things out of thy law.'

5

The Real Presence of Christ in the Midst of His People[1]

These things saith he who walketh in the midst of the seven golden candlesticks.—Revelation 2:1

THESE epistles to the Seven Churches of Asia, to which, in our day, men's thoughts are forcibly directed, seem, in the course of events, not only to speak to the west with a new urgency, but to exhibit, as it were afresh to us, at once the grace and the holiness of the Mediatorial dominion. The sad doom of these oriental churches lifts a warning voice to western Christianity, not unlike that perpetual lesson which the fall of Israel reads to the various sections and territorial divisions of the Christian church. When we listen to these notes of warning to the seven churches, and then trace their literal fulfilment in the light of history, we cannot but behold the goodness and severity of God, on them that fell severity, as in the case of Israel, but toward us goodness, if we continue in that goodness. The Mosque of the Moslem erected on the ruins of churches once so flourishing and making

[1] *A Sermon Preached before the Free Provincial Synod of Aberdeen, on Tuesday, 8 April 1856, and Published at Their Request* (Aberdeen: George Davidson, 1856).—Ed.

manifest the savour of Christ's knowledge, is at once a striking commentary on the import of removing the candlestick out of its place, and seems to cry to us as with a voice 'be not high-minded but fear.' He under whose feet all times and centuries pass along, made the march of armies, and the fall of empires, subservient to the execution of these holy threatenings; and when the set time is come, such a reconstruction of empires as, at this moment, absorbs the thoughts of public men as an end, may be, in the divine counsels, only a means to a far more glorious end, in connection with a revival of Christianity on those favoured spots where it was so early planted, and where it shone, for a season, with such a steady light.

As to the text, the words must be considered as describing the spiritual presence of Christ in the church. When he is said to 'walk in the midst of the seven golden candlesticks,' the language implies that as the priests, in the old economy, had charge of the sacred candlestick, trimming it to shed its light by night, so the Redeemer is present to provide his people with all spiritual light, as the dispenser of all necessary grace to them, and the holy observer of their conduct. Though the language does not imply corporeal presence, for a ubiquitous humanity is impossible, and a supposition implying that he does not continue to be in all points made like unto his brethren, yet there is a sense in which the personal Redeemer is to be regarded as really present, — and enjoyed as really present by his people.

In the power of his Godhead, and also by the operation of his Spirit, which not only replenishes his own humanity but also cements an intercourse between him and his people, he may be said to be truly present: and the term Emmanuel, meaning *God with us*, — conveys the idea of a perpetual real presence.

In opening up the text, then, and with an exclusively practical end in view, let us consider: —

1. That the presence of Christ must be regarded as filling ordinances with all their attractive power, fragrance, and glory.

2. That Christ, as the minister of the sanctuary, is present to conduct the whole communications of God to man, and the whole worship of man to God.

3. That Christ is present as the holy scrutinizer of men's heart and conduct in the use of ordinances.

And may that Almighty Spirit who alone gives efficacy to the word spoken, be poured out from on high, that he may show us the goings of our God and King in the sanctuary!

1. *The presence of Christ must be regarded as filling ordinances with all their attractive power, fragrance, and glory.*

I need not expatiate in this place on the nature of that spiritual presence which the Redeemer condescends to impart, nor analyze the peculiar manifestations of that presence which may be enjoyed in the hidden life of his people, and which come to light in the habitual graces implanted in the soul, in the actings, the experiences and appetencies of the new creation in its connection with the living Head. I shall content myself with exhibiting the reality of such a presence in the church of our day as well as in the early days of the Christian church. Among the last words which our risen Lord uttered among his disciples previous to his ascension to the Father, was the assurance, 'Lo I am with you always' [Matt. 28:20]; and when they saw him depart, and the cloud that received him out of their sight intercepted their view, as they looked steadfastly toward heaven, they seem to have felt that, so far from being separated from his beloved presence, as their gloomy forebodings had led them to anticipate, he was nearer them than ever in the highest sense of nearness, and also better known than he had ever been before. This we may infer from the singular fact, recorded by Luke in the conclusion of his gospel, 'that they returned to Jerusalem with great joy' (Luke 24:52). Though taken up out of their sight, he was not removed beyond the reach of personal intercourse or of sensible communion. At the moment when he disappeared, it would appear that the Spirit entering at once, and in an ampler degree, into his great function as the revealer and the glorifier of Christ, evinced to them the expediency of his going away, and convinced them, by present experience, that what they wanted in sight was more than made up by the communications of his spiritual presence to the eye of faith. Every look of love — every glimpse of emotion which had beamed from the human form of the Incarnate One, as they saw his glory — every word of endearing tenderness or of instruction which they had found to be spirit and life, would now be embalmed in their memories, and written in their hearts with a joy, with which a stranger cannot intermeddle.

Now into all this enjoyment of the Redeemer's spiritual presence, the church of this day may enter no less really, and should endeavour to enter no less fully, than the disciples of old. And for all this the history of his life supplies us, and will supply the church of every successive age, with equal facility. But, in addition to this method of maintaining intercourse with the Redeemer through the medium of his word, it must be yet further noticed, for the fact is equally undoubted, that the presence of the Saviour is specially evinced by those who bear his image. He must be regarded as coming near us in his people, and hence it is that when two or three are assembled in his name, his nearness is then most sensibly enjoyed. It is this which makes ordinances such fragrant spots, whereas they would, without the Redeemer's presence, be no better than the unreclaimed and cheerless waste. It is this, which makes a minister's connection with his people so delightful and so replete with spiritual refreshment, as they go in and out and find pasture. They meet in ordinances which are fragrant while they last, and pleasant in the remembrance:

because there the glory of the Lord shines, and his presence is felt, and his stately goings are seen. Thus there is a coming of the Lord in ordinances which, in one aspect of the matter, must be regarded as a faint foretaste or shadow of that ultimate and glorious appearing, when he shall come to be glorified in his saints and admired in all them that believe. When he walks amid ordinances with peculiar power, by the effusion of his Spirit, there as well as in the hidden communion to which we have already adverted, he is said *to come to us*. Thus he says 'I will not leave you comfortless or orphans (*ορφανους* [*orphanous*]); I will come to you' — (John 14:18); and the corresponding passage where our Lord announces that he will come and make his abode with us — (John 14:23) — conveys a sufficiently clear intimation that, while he does not manifest himself to the world, he will manifest himself to those who see him with spiritual eyes and who hear him with spiritual ears.

But here it is incumbent on us to advert, though briefly, to the common charge advanced against us, and against the Reformed church in general, in reference to our views on this whole subject. Is it true, then, that, as contrasted with the Lutherans, the Reformed church ignores the real presence of Christ in the preaching of the word, and in the dispensation of the ordinances of his own appointment? Is it true that with us, the church does not assemble round an objectively present Lord, in order to meet with him in holy ordinances, and to receive of his spiritual supplies? Is it true that our whole view of ordinances virtually shuts up Christ in heaven? We answer, it is not true. The worship of the Reformed church takes for granted that Christ is present in ordinances, without which, indeed, they would be but an empty vessel. It is held by all who understand the subject, that as the path of the Redeemer was traced of old by miraculous displays of power on the blind, the maimed, the lame, the deaf, and the subjects of every malady, so may his goings be traced in ordinances by like displays of almighty grace, and that as he stood of old in the midst of sinners, so does he still stand, in the midst of them in those sacred meeting places, nay, nearer them than ever in all that constitutes proper nearness. To quote the words of Dr Merle d'Aubigné,[1] 'this is the grand doctrine of the real presence which is too much forgotten among us. I do not refer to the parody which the church of Rome has substituted for it. I mean a living, spiritual, and real presence of Jesus Christ — a presence; the token of which is the holy supper: for if Christ invites us to his table, he certainly does not intend to be absent from it himself. Yes, I believe in the real presence of Christ in the midst of his people.'[2]

[1] *Jean-Henri Merle d'Aubigné* (1794–1872) was a Swiss Protestant minister and historian of the Reformation. Merle d'Aubigné attended, and addressed, the Free Church Assembly at Tanfield Hall, Edinburgh, in May 1845. He was said to be an enthusiastic supporter of the Free Church.—Ed.

[2] Merle d'Aubigné, Disc., 3 Oct. r, 1844, 'On the Character essential to the Theologians and Christians in general in the present day.'

If such a presence, then, inhabits ordinances, a *corresponding obligation devolves upon the worshipper.* The expectation to see the glorious power of the Redeemer ought to be a sustained and not a fitful expectation. That the want of this is one main reason why the divine power displayed in ordinances so little corresponds with the present plentiful supply of spiritual preaching, there is little room to doubt. The proper theory of ordinances implies that the whole body of the faithful are, equally with the pastor, acting faith on God for the success, and that they come together, when they statedly assemble in ordinances, to behold Christ's power and glory. But the proper idea of prayerful co-operation with the pastor is, we fear, practically carried out by but a very few! Nay, we have often doubted whether, at the best periods of our history, sufficient pains were taken to call into activity the manifold capabilities with which the church, as an organic body, is endowed, and whether far more might not have been done, on the ground of a common agreement and of a united faith, when we have met in sacred ordinances, to constrain the Redeemer to abide among us. 'What went ye out for to see?' is a question that would certainly startle many, as they meet in the place of our solemnities, in that city of God of which such glorious things are spoken. Many, doubtless, will persuade themselves that, if an appointed place were named, where they could hold direct and personal intercourse with the Redeemer, they would not shrink from going to the ends of the earth, just as pilgrims to what are called the holy places, do not grudge the length of the way, nor the toil of the journey, that they may tread where Christ once stood, and behold the spot where that sacred body, in which he accomplished our redemption, once lay. That vain toil, however, is a search for the living among the dead, and the whole mood of mind from which it emanates is exploded and disappears the moment men acquire a true idea of ordinances, as furnishing to them facilities for holding personal communion with a present living Lord. He is in the midst of two or three assembled in his name; and where will a Christian be but where his Lord is to be found?

But if so, a farther question solicits our attention: are those meeting places with the Lord made available for the purpose, and used to the extent, that they are intended to subserve? Though they are designated a glass in which, as compared with future vision, we see but darkly, are we, as a church, using them as a medium to see the King in his beauty? Are we, in that church capacity in which we must be regarded as having a collective unity, and in which we occupy a responsible position, employing ordinances both with a general impression of the great account hereafter, and with a conviction that the enjoyment of them may be forfeited even here, and that the glory may depart? One of the most affecting things connected with the history of Israel, as recorded in the visions of Ezekiel, is the final departure of the glory of the God of Israel from the temple. It did not depart all at once: it lingered as if loath to go: but, at last, after hovering over different spots, and casting a last lustre over its long-frequented habitation, it winged its flight from the defiled and polluted city, to return no more. We see, in like manner, the glory of the Lord departing from these seven churches of Asia; and it was in the same or in a similar way. He would linger as if loath to go; and abandoned his much-loved habitation only by slow and insensible degrees. He warned and allured them, as if he would wait till they returned to appreciate the privilege which they enjoyed — till they should constrain him to abide among them, like the two disciples in Emmaus, as their glory and their joy. In both these cases, a firm persuasion took possession of men's minds that the whole security predicated of the city of God, and her guaranteed immunity from dissolution belonged to them, and would for ever belong, by inalienable right. And, confessedly, one of the greatest and most perilous errors connected with the kingdom of God, into which the minds of men have, in all ages, been precipitated when sitting under the shade of ordinances, has been the impression that the church is indefectible in those regions where it has been planted. This was Israel's boast in the depth of her degeneracy, when she gloried in the possession of ordinances, though she neither sought nor found the God of ordinances. This is Rome's conviction to this day, under the deep darkness of that apostasy that has settled down upon her as a funeral pall. It is true that the church as such is indefectible, and that the gates of hell shall not prevail against her; but while men continue to cry 'the temple of the Lord, the temple of the Lord, the temple of the Lord,' the power and glory of ordinances may have passed away from them, and the kingdom may have been given to another people bringing forth the fruits thereof. Have we considered, then, whether we are altogether free from that condition of the Jews, or whether we incur the risk of approaching it? Have we, in all our congregations, a people whose senses are so exercised, that they come to ordinances as statedly as they return, not only with minds prepared to discern the stately goings of our God and King in the midst of the sanctuary, but with the full expectation that they will meet and commune with him there? Have we a people who stand in conscious agreement with their pastor as to the presence that is expected to glorify and to ennoble ordinances — who see a glory in the song of praise, which the great King condescends to inhabit (Psa. 22:3) — a glory in the prayer, where he comes forth to commune with us — a glory in the word, where he walks in majesty both in the solemn grandeur of the law, and in the winning grace of the gospel — a glory in baptism, where he comes nigh to seal a covenant engagement — and a glory in the supper, where the redeemed are brought into his banqueting house? Have we a people so intimately acquainted with the glory of ordinances that they are ripening for heaven in the use of them? While our worship differs from that of Rome particularly in the circumstance that it is an intelligent service from which the scenic is excluded, and every thing that man has made symbolical is swept away, have we a people so intelligently conversant with the various parts of worship, with the import of its symbols, and the design which they subserve, that they have nothing in common with the conclusion adopted by the millions of the Greek and Romish Churches, that ordinances operate upon them with the force and influence of a magic spell?[1] Have we a people who not only frequent ordinances for all the grace which they are fitted to impart, and which their own natures can receive, in a personal point of view, but who are also in conscious harmony with their spiritual guides as to the great aim of ordinances, who do not leave their pastor unaided, and whose unceasing prayers encircle him, whenever he ascends the pulpit, with a power not his own?

2. *Christ, the minister of the sanctuary, is present to conduct the whole communications of God to man, and also the whole worship of man to God.*

[1] It seems a certain law that, in proportion as men invent the symbolical in worship, it ceases to be intelligent, and that all the emblematic actions added to those which Christ himself has instituted only operate, as by retributive justice, in increasing men's ignorance. Thus, it is not only a usurpation of Christ's function and a disparagement to his wisdom, but a main source of ignorance. It is stated, with regret, by a Russian statesman, that the people of the Greek Church have not the remotest idea of the symbolical in their worship, of the lights which are kindled, and of the processions which strike their senses. Such a result is only the natural and inevitable consequence of will-worship.

He is the medium in both points of view. As he is, on the one hand, the channel of all those divine supplies, imparted to his people for the exercise of worship, so is he, on the other hand, the medium through which they offer all their returns of acceptable service.

That this point may be made more clear, let me here go back a step, and notice the essential elements that go to constitute, in a twofold respect, all spiritual worship. It must be held then that, in all religious homage acceptable to God, there is a reciprocal action between God and man. God first of all stands to us in the relation of a giver, before he is or can be a receiver from us. The worshipper must first of all be a partaker of the grace of God, and of the gift by grace, before he can present an offering; and when we do offer ought of worship to our heavenly Father, it is only of his own that we render to him. This action and return, by which God gives and man returns, or, in other words, by which God produces all and man acts all, must be considered as a first principle which lies at the foundation of all acceptable worship. Hence some divines, though not with great felicity, distinguish these two elements of worship into the *sacramental* — comprehending the word baptism and the holy supper, and the *sacrificial*[1] — comprehending thanksgiving,

[1] This distinction which owes its origin to one of Melancthon's expressions in his 'Apology,' was eagerly caught up a few years ago [i.e. a few years before 1856] and employed by many of the German divines. The distinction however may almost be said to have run its course.

praise, prayer, and confession of Christ with the mouth. But let it here suffice to say, without making artificial distinctions of this nature, that in every act of worship God is first a giver and then a receiver, or the bestower of the necessary grace before he is or can be the accepter of the offered service. Any other idea, however modified by words or gilded by deceptive phraseology, places the worship on a footing of legalism. The two constituent elements of worship, then, to be carefully distinguished from each other, are God's gracious donation, and then the due return to him; the latter of which can only be expressed in David's words — 'all things come of thee, and of thine own have we given thee' (1 Chron. 29:14).

Now this brings us to the action of Christ in both these points of view, and in both these relations. He acts from God to man and from man to God. He walks amid the seven golden candlesticks for this very end. He is a priest upon his throne amid the worship and the ordinances of his house for this end. As the minister of the sanctuary and of the true tabernacle which the Lord pitched and not man, he ministers from God to man as the channel of the whole divine supplies imparted for every act of worship, and from man to God as the one all-perfect High Priest who, in all our acts of praise or prayer, presents our persons faultless and our service acceptable before the presence of his Father with exceeding joy.

Thus, there is a twofold action of the Redeemer as he walks amid the golden candlesticks; and of this twofold action the Redeemer says expressly in one passage, 'I will declare thy name unto my brethren; in the midst of the church will I praise thee' (Heb. 2:12). On the one hand, he must be regarded as coming, in the exercise of gracious condescending love, to reveal by the power of the Spirit, the grace and truth of the Father, and to impart those heavenly gifts which the Father is waiting to bestow through the channel of his word and sacraments: for the dispensation of divine grace has always been administered through the medium of the word and emblems, and always will be, till the kingdom is delivered up to the Father. But, conversely, the Lord Jesus presents our worship acceptable by making it his own. We have thus the sublime and affecting thought that the living Saviour is praising the Father, through the mouth of his members on the earth. We see him condescending to make our desires, our supplications, our requests his own, and offering them up with the incense of his much merits, touched with a feeling of our infirmities. In those pleasant ordinances where the Christian never wearies, and which are replete with life and power, we must realize all this as going on, assured, that the Minister of the Sanctuary is negotiating between God and man, and between man and God, and that if the hidden world were unveiled, we should behold in vision all this which we are now permitted to apprehend by faith. He walks amid the golden candlesticks, covering our imperfections under that outspread righteousness which dresses heaven and earth in smiles, and brings back to us the sunshine of God's averted countenance; and O, should not the greatness of this hidden ministry prompt us the more highly to extol and honour him? At those ordinances, so replenished with the presence of the King of Glory, our vessels may be filled with all the fullness of God, just as a narrow shell is filled to its utmost capacity, as it lies in the ocean's depths. As Christ is there present to fill his mystic body with all the fullness of his life and with all the graces of his Spirit, we may safely conclude that, though the vessels are of various capacities, they shall all be full, if they do not, through the power of unbelief, and the excluding influence of worldly affections, forestall the communications which he comes to impart in the use of ordinances.

To all this view, however, the Tractarian notion of our day is diametrically opposed. It represents the church as an embodied Christ, and so confounds the relation between the two as to represent the action of the church as the continuation of the Redeemer's action. As if the church were a continued incarnation, they have come to confound Christ and his body, and to mistake union for identity, just as all Popish writers do who wish to clothe their opinions in an evangelical dress. That the church is, in a certain acceptation of the word, the organ of Christ, is an undoubted truth, for it is called his body. That Christ glorified in heaven may be said to continue his life on earth may be admitted in a similar sense. But that the church's action is to be accepted as a substitute for the action of Christ, or to be regarded as a continuation of his action, cannot be admitted, no not for an hour. It is one thing to hold on the ground of the mystic union, as Protestants do, that the church and ordinances are the channel through which the blessing is imparted, while the great High Priest is himself the Giver of the blessing, and an altogether different question to hold, according to the Romanist and semi-Romanist idea, that the person of the Lord is so identified with his body, that the action of the church is of itself a continuation of the meritorious or propitiatory work of Christ. That is tantamount to putting Christ aside and substituting the church in his room, as if the miracle of the incarnation was ever going on. It is to leave the Lord Jesus a mere inactive spectator in heaven. As opposed to that Romanist idea, whether more openly or covertly advanced, we must maintain the twofold position already advanced, (1) *First*, That the Lord Jesus comes into the midst of his people to give us all the Father's grace, and, (2) *Secondly*, That he offers up to the Father all our proper worship. He does both through the church, which, however, neither supersedes him so as to take his place, nor acts apart from him as independent.

If such a presence, then, inhabits ordinances and lends them their perpetual attraction, fragrance, and glory, our minds may be calm and settled as to the future. Whatever the world may say as to the waning influence of Christian truth on the minds of men, 'the power of his grace,' as Milton so well remarks, 'has not passed away with the primitive times as fond and faithless men imagine.'[1] The triumphant confidence with which the virgin, the daughter of Zion, was directed to laugh opposition to scorn (Isa. 37:22), should still be our mood of mind, and render us unmoved alike by the opposition of enemies, though a thousand-fold more virulent, and by the siren-voice of misjudging friends. 'Is not the Lord in Zion? Is not her King in her?' (Jer. 10:19). 'God is known in her palaces for a refuge' (Psa. 48:3).

One of the most frequent enquiries among thoughtful minds at home and abroad, in our day, is how shall public worship be replenished with such unfading interest, and with such attractive power, as shall not only win the ascendancy over the minds of men, but retain the necessary hold upon them. Various theories are advanced, according to the point of view from which the enquirer views the subject; various specifics are propounded, and in part attempted to be carried into operation. One of the most obvious features of our age, indeed, is that it teems with expedients of this nature, and that they are poured out in every quarter, and by men of every cast of mind with the most prolific and inexhaustible variety. All this indicates a wide-spread and general impression of a want, or of an aching void, which these expedients are meant to fill. But their most

[1] John Milton, *Animadversions upon the Remonstrants Defence* (London, 1641), Sec. 4.

strenuous advocates, alas! forgetting what is indicated by our text, only 'go from mountain to hill forgetting their resting-place.'

Thus, to instance one or two of the most prominent tendencies, some urge upon us that (1) *the revival of ancient forms and ecclesiastical observances* will restore to the church her hold upon multitudes who have broken loose from her, and make her again as powerful as when the Roman Empire gave way before the conquering power of the cross. The Tractarian builds all his confidence on the spell-like influence to be derived from ancient usages connected with a time when Christianity, as the strongest power that animates humanity, sent forth vibrations throughout the Roman world. But that is a delusive panacea. The exhausted soil that produces nothing better than an enthusiasm of this sort only tells of its poverty. It gives rise to no heroic deeds — it is the mere enthusiasm of a vacant admiration — it is an attempt to gain warmth at a painted fire — it is alien from personal intercourse with Christ, and from the living interests of men. We doubt not but that, in common with the worshipper of ancient forms, the wandering Bedouin of the desert, who pitches his tent amid the imposing ruins and splendid columns of Palmyra, dreams too of a mighty past which he can as little resuscitate as he can divine the sources of its greatness. It is said that Napoleon, on one occasion, when his fortunes had changed, and victory no longer waited on his nod, announced to those around him, 'the sun of Austerlitz is risen'; — but the return of that sun which brought round to him the memory of far other scenes, had no magic spell, no fatalistic power to turn the tide in the affairs of men. In like manner, however much men, in our day, may expect that the revival of measures once replenished with divine power may be repeated clothed with similar power, we may be sure the departed halo would not return, though the past were folly imitated, or almost re-produced with its many coloured shades. The spirit is gone, and who can call it back? But is not that the opposite of faith on him who walks in the midst of the seven golden candlesticks? And are we, in our relation to the word, merely to read the promises in the past tense, and to find their full significance only in a departed age and among other men? On the contrary, the living Head has not ceased to animate his church, nor has the living Spirit departed from his mission among men. If the stream of divine life has not dried up with those fresh times, if man's nature is still as susceptible of change, and if the living Lord, the true glory and power of ordinances, still walks in the midst of the seven golden candlesticks, we must look to him who in wise and glorious sovereignty makes all things new. 'Behold I make all things new' — and it is this alone that can make the church young again.

Others there are, again, who tell us that (2) *the pulpit is behind the age*, and their siren-voice would allure the church from her proper course and from her due function, in order to adjust her relation to literary men.

We bid literature all hail; and we add, that they who now are indifferent to the cultivation of literary tastes have forgotten the position into which the church is ushered by the course of history. In an age of so much culture, it affords a true delight to all right-minded men to meet with every one who is able, without forfeiting a spiritual tone, to usher in the Christian message in an attractive elegance and felicity of language to which men will listen. As Christianity is destined to glorify every thing, so literature, as one of the noblest vessels, should both contain the heavenly treasure and diffuse it, and while the spirit of Christianity disdains the affected, the unreal, the untrue, it honours all genuine literature. But it happens, unhappily for this specific, that it runs counter to the course pursued in the first grand triumphs of the Christian church, ushered as it was into the world amid the noontide blaze of Greek and Roman literature, and when the minds of men may be said to have been enervated by over culture or by an excess of culture. It is at once admitted that the literature of that day served a valuable purpose in providing a form or mould into which the new truth, that was spreading from Judea, could be poured. But so far from merely, or even mainly, calling into play those appliances that might win the literary minds of the age, the founder of the Christian faith and his disciples began at the very opposite point. The first disciples moved the social system, and turned round the opinion of their age, in the only way in which it ever has been changed. They preached the gospel to the poor: 'to the poor the gospel is preached.' They moved the highest minds only by beginning with those of little culture, and this process was repeated by the Reformers, by Whitefield, and by all who have ever moved opinion on its poles, and that which won them was the single fact that the sacred truth swayed an empire on the consciences of men. I say, it is an empire over conscience first, or over the man, and not over literary tastes alone. It is, besides, a striking fact that as men, and even literary men, advance in the divine life, they wish to win their way through the garniture of words to the kernel of solid spiritual truth; and literature is valued as a medium but despised as a substitute. And this just brings us back to our position, that the presence of Christ fills ordinances with all their attractive power, fragrance, and glory.

Another party in their endeavour to replenish ordinances with greater power, have advanced (3) *to novelty of doctrine*. For a sore and ulcerated state of religion, many have adopted the desperate expedient of new views, and conjured up a power which already threatens to overwhelm them. The temporary earnestness, with which these new opinions were associated, was thought, for a season, to be a passport to their general reception, and to supply that very lever power which was felt to be so desirable. But it soon appeared, from the result, that no convulsive efforts of nature, however earnest — no mere religiosity, however impassioned, can be a substitute for the hidden glory which breaks out in ordinances, and makes itself felt only by the presence of him who walks in the midst of the seven golden candlesticks. A greater security soon supervened wherever this expedient was adopted, whether in this country or in America; and in ordinances so denuded of all that satisfies the soul, there was found no attractive power to retain the minds of men.

A new scheme at present, indicating the same uneasy sense of want, is the attempt (4) *to unite the resources of art to the forms of worship*, a tendency not confined to a single country at this moment. That worship may form an affinity, to some extent, with art as a subservient element, provided the spirit is not enslaved by artistic forms, is not denied. But if this appeal to the imagination and senses is designed to be a substitute for spiritual unction, and to relieve a bareness which arises from another cause, the introduction of such elements into a once simple unadorned worship, is not a thing indifferent. To bedizen ordinances with the trappings of outward pomp, with instrumental music, liturgies, and theatrical show, especially where these things were never known, is not merely to set up showy forms which are jejune and tame, but something worse. All these, as a flag of distress or the confession that Ichabod is written on the ordinances, not only proclaim the aching void within, as the heart, no more the temple of the Spirit, seeks a substitute to make up for the want of God, but actually impose on the worshipper. When the true glory departed, popery imposed on men's minds by these empty forms, and churches, denuded of the sole glory of divine worship, the presence of the King, make every effort to present, like popery, some dazzling and imposing substitute. But our text points to the only glory and attractive power that ordinances ever had or ever can have.

3. *Christ is present as the holy scrutinizer of men's heart and conduct in the use of ordinances.*

So little are many aware of the great throne erected in ordinances, that they frequent those sacred spots just as they go to any other public meeting, and in the same common state of mind. Instead of feeling that the place is holy ground, and of acting with holy reverence, as Moses was directed to act at the bush, many never for a moment suppose, while they indulge a wandering fancy, that the jealousy of the Most High burns like fire in vindicating the sacredness of ordinances. The thought of a possible violation finds little, if any entrance into their mind. The aimless use of sacred things, the wandering thoughts, the natural conceptions of God by which his name is profaned, the common and unspiritual thoughts brought to praise, to prayer, and to the hearing of the word, bring down a blight on many a soul. A due sense of this sin, and a salutary fear of it may well be derived from the text, and from the words which the apostle employs in reference to the supper, 'for this cause many are weak and sickly among you, and many sleep' (1 Cor. 11:20).

In proof of the jealousy evinced by Christ as the holy scrutinizer of men's heart and conduct in the use of ordinances, I might point to very many evidences. But let it suffice to allude to the dread visitation that followed hard upon the profanation of ordinances in these oriental lands. Where are those seven churches? The glory is departed — the things that belonged to their peace have long been hid from their eyes; in some of them not even the name of Christian survives, in others but the name, and over wide districts the mosque stands on the ruins of the Christian church. On this branch of the subject however, time will not permit me to enlarge, and I shall merely indicate, that this description of Christ's walking in the midst of ordinances alludes emphatically, in the connection in which it stands, to the impressive truth, that the holy Saviour jealously guards their sacredness and purity.

In winding up this subject, I cannot but enquire, in pursuance of the main theme already indicated, how shall ordinances be replenished with a higher power, and glorified by evidences of the present King? That the Lord of glory is there we have already seen; that we are not to shut him up in heaven, nor view him as reluctant to commune with us, follows from his abiding presence and from the announcements he has made. As to those more marked occasions when he bestows revival, and when his arrows are sharp in the heart of the king's enemies, they are, beyond question, the result of a stupendous sovereignty. It is not man that first intends a revival, and then calls in the help of God to accomplish it. The great King appoints not only the work but also the instruments to be employed in it with a sovereignty, as marked as in the eternal decree of personal election, according to which, he has 'mercy on whom he will have mercy, and whom he will he hardeneth.'

But while this stupendous sovereignty, which it becomes us to acknowledge and adore, lies beyond the range of our disposal, there is another sphere that lies within the scope of the believer's duty. God is faithful to those promises which he has made; and it becomes us to consider, whether the church is over all her borders desirous to renew her youth, and to put away her unbelief as well as every barrier in the way of Christ's return to ordinances. Many there are, alas! who, whatever eagerness they may exhibit to meet with Christ in ordinances, and to find him at the Holy Supper, go away from him in secret, as soon as they are out of ordinances. In a dogmatic point of view, this is the mistake of all those churches which over-magnify or attach misplaced importance to the ordinance itself, and assign comparatively small importance to the state of mind belonging to the worshipper. But how can men expect to see the goings of the King in ordinances, if they do not bring the presence of the King along with them, if they are in earnest in ordinances and secure when absent from them, if desirous to be refreshed at those wells of comfort, but off their guard as soon as they depart?

But if evanescent earnestness and subsequent indifference explain, in part, the feebleness of the impressions made by ordinances in our day, and supply at least one reason why the word possesses so little power, another fact must needs be mentioned. God's people, in their secret and social wrestlings, stop too soon. Where do we find the body of the faithful united with their pastor in the sustained unfainting exercise of faith and prayer? Where do we find two or three united for a time, much less habitually, in waiting on the God of ordinances, and desirous to be replenished, up to their capacity, with the life and power of a present Saviour? Where do we find congregation after congregation united with their pastors in the eager desire to receive for themselves, and to see conferred on others, the whole enlightening, quickening, sanctifying grace which Christ is exalted to bestow? And yet, till this is done, we shall never see the text fulfilled, 'arise, shine, for thy light is come: for the glory of the Lord is risen upon thee.' United prayer, sustained waiting on the God of ordinances, together with a cordial desire to be completely occupied by the Spirit beyond the circle of public ordinances as well as in them, are not found among us to any adequate extent, and hence sermons fall but half way to men's hearts.

And yet, if living faith were exercised by the church in general on a Saviour present in the midst of ordinances — the faith that out of weakness is made strong — the faith that smiles at difficulties — the faith that grasps the promise as pledge enough for its accomplishment — the faith which is the echo of the promise and takes the word as fulfilment too, should we not find that God honours a faith that honours him? But O, where is that faith that puts the hand of God in motion?

But one thing mainly standing in the way is obviously this — the ministry, in the dispensation of ordinances, is not duly sustained by the people's prayers, at least in no proportion to the numbers of praying people in the land. Nor do congregations seem sufficiently to recognize this duty, or to understand that a minister is then only in his right position, and that ordinances can then only be replenished with their proper glory, when all the praying people, with united and affectionate co-operation, have been supporting the preacher with their prayers, and come together with a high expectancy to reap the fruit. Then only does the glory of the God of Israel shine through ordinances. Then only does a minister preach and pray with power in the great congregation, when he becomes the channel through which their prayers are answered. O, are we as people thus exercised? Are we as pastors seeking to enlist the spiritual members of the flock in such a work, and casting ourselves upon their sympathy to the full extent to which they would respond?

Fathers and brethren, let us seek to impress on others, and also on ourselves, what ordinances really are. When we shall see their glory from the margin of eternity, and reflect where we were permitted to stand from Sabbath to Sabbath, shall we not say what many say already, 'we have scarcely been half awake.' God has given us in recent days precious ministers. For such preaching as the land enjoys—for the words of grace uttered in every corner — for the bold aggressive character of our ministers, I give God thanks. But let us advance and not retreat. Let us seek to renew our youth. Let us *be men of prayer*. 'Prayer is the main work of a minister,' was the usual maxim of the well-known Hooker,[1] the Pilgrim Father. And when ministers come forth as Welsh[2] did from the bridegroom's presence — and that man of God spent a third part of his time in prayer — their words have an affecting influence and a penetrating power which cannot be explained by any other cause than by an impression from above. And for this end, let us seek to be ever in his society who walks in the midst of the seven golden candlesticks.

[1] Thomas Hooker (1586–1647) was a prominent Puritan colonial leader, who founded the Colony of Connecticut after dissenting with Puritan leaders in Massachusetts.—Ed.

[2] John Welsh (*c.* 1568–1622) was Church of Scotland minister of Ayr from 1600 until banished and exiled to France by King James VI & I in 1606. A powerful preacher, Welsh was reputed to have spent a third of his waking hours in prayer.—Ed.

6

The Improvement of a Revival Time[1]

Reader, have you ever reflected that it is a responsible thing *to live through* a period of Revival, and that it tests the religion of every member of the community? Your duties are made by your position, and you cannot shun them. Such a time leaves none among us as it found them. And the question proposed to even God's own children is, are we rising to the height of our high mission, or guilty of grieving the Spirit? Have you considered that Christ coming in the flesh, and his coming in the Spirit, divide and *separate* in a community, in a manner not unlike his coming 'with his fan in his hand to purge his floor?' When he came to Jerusalem, she did not know her time of visitation. And no one, whatever his condition or office, can exempt himself from certain duties connected with the fact, that we are living in a period when the kingdom of God is coming with *power*. Have you laid this to heart?

I cannot disconnect the present time of blessing from the sowing in tears which preceded. The harvest-time has come, but a long seed-time of preaching, expectation,

[1] *The Improvement of a Revival Time, New Year's Tract* (Edinburgh: James Taylor, *c.* 1860).—Ed.

and prayer, went before it. Seventeen years ago, there was a distinct anticipation among us that a time of Revival, greater than was enjoyed in 1839, was about to dawn. The seed has been scattered broad-cast over the land, and it has not been lost. The outpouring of the Spirit on America and Ireland has everywhere increased an expectation and confidence which have not been put to shame: the kingdom of God is coming. In our day, as we hear from one place after another, a mighty power is *breaking forth* from the kingdom of God, and with resistless force, sweeping over the community, bringing salvation to some, and imposing awe on others.

How is such a time to be improved? This is surely a question which no one may evade. Well would it have been for the Scribes and Pharisees, if they had come down from their prejudices and prepossessions to weigh this *practical* question, when the King came to Zion, meek and lowly, just and having salvation. Some will be offended in this time of spiritual power, just as of old many stumbled at that stumbling-stone, now made Head of the corner. His humble form; his unlettered disciples; his intercourse with sinners; his doctrines of grace; the *immediate forgiveness* of sins; the *suddenness* of conversion; as well as his uncompromising holiness, and his testifying of the world that its deeds are evil; made not a few stumble then, and will do so still. Many a Despiser will still 'behold, and wonder, and perish' (Acts 13:41).

Our design, in this little tract, is to point out some of those duties which devolve on all of us individually, and on the Church ecclesiastically, in a period when, beyond all question, Christ is coming in the power of his kingdom.

The churches have something to do in such a time as this. It cannot be denied that the praying people around us are, many of them, *waiting, as it were, to be led on*. A little while ago, the proper idea of co-operation was practically realized and carried out but by a very few: all was left to official action. For so great a change we give God thanks; and who does not long to see the ministry and people of this land embarking, with a united action, in this work of God? A ministry and people, with such a common aim, could not but exert the most happy mutual influence, acting faith on God for the *success*, and putting forth the gifts and capabilities with which the Church, as an organic body, is endowed. We are at a critical period. And as it is common, in a Revival-time, for the impenitent to *fear lest they be left*, the Christian may also *fear* lest the Spirit be withdrawn in consequence of our unbelief.

What part have private Christians to act in such a time? We do not mean that any dependence is to be placed on *means*, or any encouragement drawn from them. But the instrumentality called out must be endued with power from on high, and carry on its activity in personal communion with Christ. One of the most striking features of this Revival is, that the sympathies of the praying people and their action have been so much engaged in it. The narrative of Pentecost shows how instruments are first prepared, and then employed. Christian, ask yourself, Am I identifying myself with the *cause of Christ*, and making his honour my main concern? Am I 'living together with Christ' (1 Thess. 5:10), sharing in his triumphs, and offering myself willingly as an instrument by whom he may work? Am I acting faith on God for the success, and standing still, as it were, to see the salvation of God (Exod. 14:13)? Am I making advances on my own attainments, not measuring myself by myself, or by others?

Those first instruments prepared in Christ's immediate company, and then filled with the Spirit at Pentecost, show how we, in this day, are to be prepared. They waited for the 'promise of the Father'; and the truth became part of their inner being, a fire shut up in their bones. And what they saw in a light with which a stranger cannot intermeddle, they spoke without fear. Now, does the fear of man seal up my lips, or have I a word to speak for Christ? These first disciples, fitful and irresolute before Pentecost, no sooner received the Spirit, than they entered, with *unfaltering decision*, on the work of the Lord. They no more hesitated between the world and Christ, in a go-between existence, but went on in a career that knew no abatement, till they rested from their labours. Am I undecided, not established with grace, more disposed to conform to the world's views, and tastes, and ways, than to break with it and 'come out' (2 Cor. 6:17)? Or do I deceive myself, by vague romantic hopes of *some future decision*, which may never come?

In this season of Revival, the recent converts have an important part to act. Many eyes are turned to them. If they stand out as a good savour of Christ, his living epistles — with the Spirit of glory and of God resting on them; if, in other words, 'Christ liveth in' them, the effect on others is decisive. If they are kept humble, free from the rash conclusions, the censorious judgments, the ill-judged innovations into which a fiery zeal is apt to hurry them, greatly do they commend the work. If they betray, like Peter, a self-confidence in their superior love and devoted zeal, it will be well if they escape his fall. Young convert, we do not advert to this, to dull your spiritual edge or to quench your fervour by the cold cautions of experience. Rather we would stimulate you to maintain 'the beginning of your confidence' (Heb. 3:14), and the glow of 'first love' (Rev. 2:4), and to be as eager after conversion as before it. But remember, that for this end you must live *on Christ himself*, and stand fast in the liberty which he has given (Gal. 5:1). Emotional frames, excitement in public, will not supply the place of secret communion with the Lamb. This alone brings stability, and we may add, lowliness of mind. Look at the disciples under the breathing of the Spirit at Pentecost, and see how he consumed their dross, as the Spirit of burning. Though at an earlier day we find among them envy and jealousy, a desire of distinction, and a sustained contest, who should be the greatest, we hear of this no more when the Holy Spirit came! These feelings vanished in the heavenly serenity of love.

To those who are in anxiety about salvation, a time of Revival is peculiarly solemn. What momentous issues crowd into such a time! If the human mind, from its very constitution, cannot long remain in deep anxiety, and must find an outlet *some way*, how great is the danger of finding peace by a false way. If God has a present claim on that heart of yours, and cannot cease to demand the love and esteem of every heart capable of knowing him, will you rob God of his rightful property, and not yield upon the spot? Have you such a sense of your utterly lost condition, that you feel shut up to mercy, neither going to the law, nor in quest of evidences and feelings before you rely on Christ? You cannot too soon go beyond yourselves to the God-man as made under the law *for us*, and nailing the bond to his cross. But let me ask, whether you come to *give* or to *take*, to bring a price in your hand, or to receive salvation? They who believe to the saving of the soul, are such as simply 'look to Christ' (Isa. 45:22), 'come to him' (Matt. 11:28), 'flee for refuge' (Heb. 6:18), with a deep sense of want, and a full confidence in the sufficiency of his present salvation, which is accepted by the Father for all that receive him. Call up before your mind how the Lord Jesus received sinners in the days of his flesh, healing those who touched the hem of his garment, or cried to him as he passed by. He is as near to you, nay, nearer by his Spirit.

Nor, in speaking of the relation which various classes occupy to the Revival, must the formalist be omitted. It seems difficult, at first sight, to know how he can maintain his carnal equanimity, when God is so evidently coming out of his place. He concludes that, if any thing further is wanting, he needs only a little more earnestness to save himself. He conceives that he stands in a greatly better condition than those miserable outcasts who long abandoned the profession of religion, and are now taking the kingdom by violence. What if they are coming direct to the Saviour of sinners, and you, with all the privileges amid which you dwell, have no just sense of sin or of a Saviour? You are drawing something as an obscuring veil between you and that God who scrutinizes you; and forms, ordinances, and a connection with the Church, are made a *substitute* for a connection with Christ himself. How many are entering *the kingdom of heaven* before you!

Let me revert for a moment to the place which God's people, his remembrancers, occupy in connection with the progress of this great work, which causes joy in heaven, and diffuses gladness on earth. Be united in *prayer*, and give the Lord no rest, till greater things are done by his outstretched arm. 'It is of no use to preach,' said Nettleton, 'if the people do not pray.' But the prayer which opens heaven and brings down the Spirit, is not that feeble desire which ceases if it must encounter *delay*, or a *trial* of your patience; but that desire which will not go without the answer, and which asks on a scale not lower than God's 'riches in glory by Christ Jesus.' The prayer which breaks through the clouds, and which God owns, is that which grasps the *promise* as if it were the *accomplishment*: 'what things soever ye desire when ye pray *believe that ye receive them*, and ye shall have them' (Mark 11:24). And if you would harmonize with God in the object sought, let that be highest in your thoughts which is highest in the thoughts of God — his glory. Ordinances and efforts to promote the work of God are then only clothed with power, when the people of God, with a united and sustained co-operation, continue without ceasing in prayer (Acts 12:5).

The gospel has all 'the power of God' it ever had, (Rom. 1:16), — the same power as when it swept away the gods of ancient Rome. The same stream of divine life flows from Jesus of Nazareth: the same life-giving Spirit is equally mighty in his mission among men. And far from sinking in hope deferred, as if the freshness of early times were no more to be expected, events around us show that Christians have all the warrant they ever had to expect and pray. Disciples of Christ have to wait in the youthfulness of simple hope, *not for a spirit which they have not, but for more of the spirit which they have.* And let us, in order to testify of Christ aright, seek to be daily renewed in the spirit of our mind. Who can testify of the cross, if he does not daily stand fast in the liberty which it brings? Who can tell of Christ's abiding presence with his people, if he does not daily abide in communion with him, and in the enjoyment of his presence? Who can tell of the love of God, if he does not realize that God loves us as he loves his Son (John 17:23) — living under the present sense of an actual and full salvation? But if you do so live, then out of the abundance of the heart your mouth will speak. You will speak because you believe; and weary with forbearing, you will not be able to stay (Jer. 20:9).

7

Suitableness of Erskine's Writings to a Period of Religious Revivals[1]

IT has been thought that Ralph Erskine's practical works have elements specially adapted to the wants of a community under the influence of a religious Revival. In this feeling I participate and am happy to express it. A slight consideration of the spiritual necessities of such a time, and of the peculiar qualities of Erskine's Theology, will suffice to show that this is something more than a vague impression.

That a time of widespread revival has entered is evident to every spectator. And a theology adapted to it becomes a necessity to which no one can be indifferent. Men are living at this moment in an exciting period which will, no doubt, constitute an epoch in church history to which the subsequent enquirer will look back. Times these are, which prove like another Pentecost,

[1] An 'Introductory Notice' to Samuel McMillan's edition of *The Beauties of the Rev. Ralph Erskine* (Aberdeen, Edinburgh, London and Glasgow: A Fullerton and Co., *c.* 1860), pp. 31-8. Ralph Erskine (1685–1752) was a Church of Scotland minister from 1711 until 1737 when he joined the Associate Presbytery (Secession) Church. Ralph and younger brother Ebenezer were evangelical preachers of great power.—Ed.

that Jesus lives to dispense the Spirit; when breathless assemblies are hushed in a death-like stillness before the felt presence of the Lord, or the silence is only broken by an irrepressible sigh for mercy. Multitudes of men are looking on with mingled awe and wonder, or with an interest still more personal while a mighty power, of which they can neither tell the laws nor estimate the force, is breaking forth from the kingdom of God and sweeping *over* the community. And while the arrows of the King pierce many hearts, a widespread fear prevails lest others should be taken and they be left.

That a genuine work of the Spirit has appeared, in this great movement which is passing over many districts of Ireland and Scotland, is recognized by every one whose opinion is entitled to weight on a religious question. Nor will this conclusion be altered, though many things of a somewhat mixed character should arise in an exciting period of religious effervescence. Such a result would not be out of keeping with the precedents of history, whether we turn our attention to the Reformation or to the Puritan period.

These revivals are to be hailed as interpositions of the church's Everlasting Head. They do not arise when we attempt to conjure them. They are not in man's disposal, but in his power who has the government upon his shoulder. And a certain necessity for them, as well as a converging point in which they meet, can commonly be traced by the careful gleaner on the field of history. Thus, when a former Revival has spent its force; when elements of thought or action formerly supplied threaten to grow time-worn or effete; the ever-living Head under whose feet all centuries revolve, knows how to introduce a creative epoch, to supply a new impulse, or to construct into one consistent whole opinion previously broken and disjointed. These epochs are introduced for ends, the importance of which soon becomes apparent, and are harbingers of the time when all things shall be made new.

As to the economy of these Revivals, however, they are as far beyond our investigation as their production is beyond our power. They are the interposition of his hand who directs events to come and go at his pleasure. There are two extremes which we must guard against. There is, on the one hand, a theory of development which limits all advancement in the kingdom of God to the action of ordinary laws. And there is, on the other hand, the supposition that we have in a Revival an abrupt phenomenon, the immediate production of the Spirit without respect to previous labour. Both these notions are equally wide of the mark. They equally ignore important aspects of the kingdom of God.

As to the theory of development, it looks askance on revival. However variously modified, whether it supposes Christianity committed to its own natural course, or directs attention to a sacramental system which no extraordinary intervention is ever to invade, it sketches a Christianity which has no present corresponding to its past, as found in the Acts of the Apostles. It shuts out the action of the life-giving Head. In our day the great facts connected with these Revivals explode the theory in question. They supply the refutation by fact. And hence they who have allowed their minds to be swayed by this theory are at a loss to reconcile with it the fact of these revivals, that is, a movement which overleaps these ordinary rules and marches forward in its own career.

But neither are these Revivals the mushroom growth of a night. They can be traced in their connexion with previous labour. And those men wholly mistake their character who disconnect this harvest from the spring-time which went before, when devoted labourers, with long patience, committed the seed to the faithful bosom of the earth. They are a reaping time in the church's history. Do we act wisely to look at present results apart from the toilsome labour that preceded? Could we have reaped, if the field had never been sown? Not so does the Lord bid us view the connexion when, with the harvest full in view; he reminded the first disciples that other men had laboured and that they entered into their labours. One sows and another reaps: it is the joint-work of both: and certainly these Revivals are never to be disconnected from previous labour by some party. Rather they are the kingdom of God coming with power, after spreading for a season as the leaven. And a glance at the historic course of the kingdom of God will make this plain. An eminent historian of modern times remarks that the kingdom of God, after coming in a quiet unnoticed manner, spreading as the leaven or growing as the grain of mustard seed, next makes itself felt as a mighty power in humanity. And the day we live in is a verification of such a view. The sowing-time extended back for at least a generation. The present is a harvest, as is apparent from facts which are forcing themselves upon men's notice as moving-forces in the world's history. Though we are still too near the event to sketch its proportions and relative magnitude, which must be reserved to the careful inquirer in the field of history, this much may be affirmed, that so far as the Revival has yet gone, it is an unmixed good, having given rise neither to heresy on the one hand nor to sects on the other.

The design of our present remarks, however, is to call attention to the importance of connecting with this movement the circulation of sound doctrine. The important place that sound and spiritual truth occupies in the first rise of a religious movement, and in every thing bearing on its safe and right direction, must be self-evident. It might be a topic well worthy of elucidation in our times, what is that development of truth, that peculiar kind of preaching in unison with which the ministration of the Spirit is dispensed? That the Spirit is not given along with the enforcement of a legal morality, nor in attestation to doctrines not based on the humiliation of the Son of God, on the grace of God, and on the cross and righteousness of Christ, is put beyond doubt by the words of Scripture: 'Received ye the Spirit by the works of the law or by the hearing of faith?' (Gal. 3:2). Whatever explanation may be given of the connexion between this kind of doctrine and the gift of the Spirit, no doubt remains as to the fact that the resources of Christ's kingdom go along with that teaching, and with that only, which leans on the great facts of the incarnation, and on the person, work, and offices of Christ.

But the truth which originates a Revival is as necessary to sustain it. And in an epoch moved as ours is by an unprecedented religious impression, one of the first boons that can be conferred on the community is the diffusion of sound and spiritual views of truth. That the writings of Ralph Erskine, whether they are circulated entire or in the form of judicious selections, are fitted to meet the peculiar wants of this period of Revival, can be questioned by those only who are not familiar with their character and scope. They are replete with 'marrow-doctrine,' whether that expression may be taken in the limited sense formerly given to it in Scotland, or as descriptive of the central and most essential doctrines of the gospel. With these great truths Erskine's theology is mainly occupied. But it may be added that while he sets the doctrines of grace in a fresh and striking light, they are exhibited in connexion with a scheme of thought which gave a colour to Scottish theology in its best days. The federal theology is seen in Erskine at every turn in one of its happiest exhibitions. From this point of view he delineates the wider bearings and connexions of divine truth.

This federal scheme may be termed the concentrated essence of the Calvinistic system. But in the mind of our Bostons and Erskines it was gracefully associated with the freest and most unfettered announcement of the invitations of the gospel. This union is invaluable, and it was found in them in its perfection, resting on that scheme of thought which we have already mentioned, and the want of which is never supplied by any other compensation. But in these men both sides of truth enter into their rights. In the federal system, which Erskine knows to wield so skilfully, the high doctrines of Sovereign, special, efficacious grace on which the federal system rests are found in perfect harmony with the freest proclamation of the invitations of the gospel. If modern readers can feel at home in the antique form of these writings, they will find them to unite solidity and unction in no ordinary measure. They are not of the class of writings which merely regale the feelings without satisfying the judgment. I anticipate the best results from their circulation in the community in a period of Revival which has its own wants and demands a peculiar literature. In Erskine, while the great article of a standing or falling church is delineated from every point of view and in every variety of form, as a Luther would set it forth, we find also the fullness of Christ depicted as the source of all our holiness, much in the manner of John Owen. These writings adapt themselves peculiarly to a revival period from their unction, amplitude, and freshness, affording satisfaction in no ordinary way to the understanding and the heart.

8

Faith[1]

THE peculiar importance attached to faith in Scripture, and its relative position in Christian doctrine, become evident when it is viewed as that mental act upon which the whole application of redemption, on man's side, depends. The term (πίστις [*pistis*]) properly means *trust* on a personal Saviour, as opposed to man's native self-reliance; and the object of faith is not Christ's doctrine, nor his historic life as a mere pattern, but his glorified person, with whom the closest relation is formed by an act which is simply receptive, and raising the mind above the seen and temporal. That this is the proper meaning of the term faith, may be proved from the uniform usage of Scripture. Some have thought indeed that, in a considerable number of passages (e.g. Gal. 1:23; 1 Tim. 4:1; Jude 3), it must be taken in an objective sense, denoting the *doctrine* of the gospel. The best modern expositors, however, take all these passages in the ordinary sense, as containing the idea of trust; from which indeed we are not necessitated to depart in a single instance.

[1] 'Faith', in *The Imperial Bible Dictionary*, vol. 1, ed. Patrick Fairbairn (London: Blackie & Son, 1866), pp. 566-8.—Ed.

As to the position and importance of faith, it may be described as the organ or means by which redemption is appropriated. It thus presupposes Christ's finished work, of which it is simply receptive; and it is so closely connected with repentance that the one is never found without the other, and can never be in exercise without the other. The most essential light in which the subject can be placed then is, that faith is receptive and saves, not as involving obedience, but as receiving a gift.

The phrase, 'obedience of faith,' occurring in certain passages (Rom. 1:5; Acts 6:7), implies indeed an obediential element in the first act of faith, or a compliance with divine authority, even in the reception of the gift; for we are not, with some, to take the term 'faith' in these passages as equivalent to the 'doctrine' of the gospel, nor to view the obedience as that which faith produces. But while the gospel is a gift, there is a divine injunction to embrace it (1 John 3:22), involving in one and the same act the reception of a gift and the compliance with a divine command. While faith saves then, not as it contains an obediential element, but simply as it is receptive, there is an obedience of faith even in receiving the gift of righteousness.

That faith is simply receptive, may be evinced by all the passages where it is described in exercise, by the prepositions used with the verb or noun (as ἐπί [*epi*] and εἰς [*eis*]), and by the sensible representations under which it is set forth, such as 'a coming' (Matt. 11:28); 'a fleeing' (Heb. 6:18); 'a drinking' of the water of life (John 7:37).

We have first to consider faith in connection with the Pauline doctrine of justification. To show that everything is repudiated but faith alone, the apostle makes use of various forms of exclusion, such as (1) 'freely' (Rom. 3:21); (2) 'without works' (Rom. 4:6); (3) 'without the deeds of the law' (Rom. 3:28); (4) 'by his grace' (Rom. 3:21); (5) 'by grace through faith' (Eph. 2:8). Grace being represented as the exclusive source of justification, and the death of Christ as its material cause, faith is in this matter merely instrumental and receptive of the righteousness of God (Rom. 3:24). Nor has faith any other value beyond that of uniting us to its object, that we may be justified *in* him (Gal. 2:17).

But when the apostle Paul gives all prominence to faith in justification, must he be understood as also excluding works done after faith by those who are in a state of grace? That these works are all excluded from the justification of their persons is evident, because they follow justification; because the apostle repudiates every ground of glorying (Rom. 4:2); and because their justifying title is not only beyond themselves in Christ, but admits no addition of any kind. Carrying out the same mode of exclusion therefore as is set forth in Scripture, it may be affirmed (1) that it is faith that justifies, not repentance; (2) that it is faith, not love; (3) that it is faith, not works; (4) that it is faith, not holiness; (5) that it is faith merely as apprehending Christ, not as a grace of the Spirit.

Here it is necessary to explain how faith 'is imputed for,' or rather 'unto righteousness' (εἰς [*eis*], Rom. 4:3;

Gal. 3:6). That this does not result from the intrinsic quality of faith is self-evident. Just as little can it arise from any acceptation whereby an imperfect title is accepted for a perfect one; a supposition which the inflexible law and the character of the Judge forbid. What then is imputed unto righteousness? Grammatically construing the words, it is undoubtedly true that the act of believing stands as the nominative or subject of the affirmation. But then in that connection, and wherever we are said to be justified by faith, it must be added that, theologically, faith stands by metonymy for its object; that is, for the Lord our Righteousness, whom faith apprehends, and to whom it unites us. Thus, the party imputing is God, the ground of the imputation is the obedience of Christ, and the end contemplated is 'unto (εἰς [*eis*]) righteousness.' Faith then is not accepted as an imperfect substitute. The gospel has been widely corrupted by the supposition that in this imputation the act of faith is held sufficient for righteousness, and accounted to be what it is not. From the explanation just given it follows that the common phrase, 'the righteousness of Christ is imputed,' is the exact equivalent of that Scripture phrase.

While it thus appears that justification is by faith without the deeds of the law (Rom. 3:28), and that works or moral character neither constitute qualifications nor pave the way as preparations, it remains that we determine the character of justifying faith. This leads us to explain the seeming discrepancy between Paul and James. Paul affirms that it justifies without works, but presupposes that it is living faith. James, not calling in question the Pauline doctrine, repudiates a dead faith as devoid of justifying efficacy. The same subject is surveyed by both, without any contradiction, from a different point of view. But the truth in which they agree is, that faith is not a dead assent, but the act of a quickened soul, which possesses, like seed-corn, a germinating power. Originated by the Spirit of faith (2 Cor. 4:13), and overcoming the world by its very action (1 John 5:4), true faith is always living; but it justifies neither on account of the life nor of the fruits which are associated with it, but as it apprehends Christ. It must be added, in reference to the cause of faith, that it is itself the fruit of Christ's mediation (Phil. 1:29). Hence it is never represented as a legal condition on which men are thrown back, and which they are required to produce in their own strength, but as given to us, like every other blessing, by Christ.

It must be further observed, that while the sacred writers describe faith as a reliance on the personal Redeemer, they never fail to bring prominently into view that it is accompanied by a fellowship in *Christ's life*. The apostle John exhibits this most vividly. Though none of the aspects of the subject can be said to be wanting in any of the apostles, it is John that specially dwells on the thought that they who believe not only have fellowship in Christ's life, but receive him for this end. Paul, in like manner, is wont to pass from a description of justification by faith to the new life which is given *in* and *with* this faith (Rom. 6:1-11; Gal. 2:20); a life unfolding itself in *love* and *hope*, and ever advancing to larger measures of holiness. Nay, Paul is never content till he makes it plain, that the Redeemer whom faith embraces is himself the principle of all this new life living in the disciple by faith (Gal. 2:20).

Neither must it be omitted, that the apostles exhibit faith as implying a *change of nature*, and as having its root in the contrite heart, that is, the opposite of the life of sin. As that which constitutes the life of sin is in its deepest ground a course of self-reliance and self-contentment, the language of the sacred writers implies that faith is in its very nature a breaking with this life of sin — a renunciation of self-reliance for an objective propitiation, as Paul usually puts it — a longing for the divine or a new divine knowledge different from that of nature, as John puts it — but always involving a moral change.

It only remains that we advert to what has been termed the form of faith, which may be said to consist in *knowledge*, *assent* and *trust*. There must be necessary knowledge to apprehend correctly what Scripture reveals as to the way of salvation, and assent, whereby we accept as true what is announced, but ending in a trust, whereby the heavy-laden rest their weary souls on Christ. It is a reliance upon a person with a measure of confidence, not on a mere proposition (Eph. 3:12; Heb. 10:22; John 6:33).

But in connection with the trust which is the form of faith, the inquiry arises, Is assurance of the essence of faith in such a sense that a high degree of it is inseparable from its exercise? This requires to be touched with the utmost delicacy and caution. That a certain measure of assurance goes along with lively faith may be affirmed, but not in every case to the exclusion of all dubiety. Escaping from the doubting faith of Rome, the divines of the Reformation-period gave utterance to statements on the subject of assurance stronger than can well be vindicated; and many of the confessions of Protestantism partake of a similar character. But it is always safer to distinguish between faith and assurance, and to regard the latter as a reflex act, or the conclusion of an easy syllogism, as follows: — He that believes on Christ is justified and saved; but I believe: therefore, I am justified and saved. While care is taken to foster and not to discourage that personal appropriation of salvation which forms such a characteristic lineament of the Protestant church, yet it is always perilous to construct such a definition of faith as implies that its opposite consists in admitting a doubt of our personal salvation, for by such views the faithful are perplexed, and the formalists made more secure.

9

The True Preacher[1]

THE students assembled here today are in very various stages of their theological curriculum, some only beginning to make good their footing in this department, while others are in the position of looking back on the curriculum as lying behind them. My remarks will have special reference to the latter. That wide range of erudition and historic fact, of thought and investigation, which the nature of your studies has led you to survey, will often be recalled in your future years, and seen with a new significance amid the occupations of professional labour. It is to be hoped that you will not cease to be students when you commence as ministers, and that such a taste and passion for study have been acquired, as will make this to be a necessity of your natures.

Every true student will be the first to own that there are many topics of which he has but grazed the surface; that subjects at first deemed obvious, are now found to have infinite bearings; and that he passes from the

[1] Address to the students of theology, at the close of the New College, Edinburgh, Session on 27 April 1872. Published in *The Christian Treasury* (Edinburgh: Johnstone, Hunter, & Co., 1872), pp. 253-7.—Ed.

theological curriculum with a more vivid consciousness of the imperfection of human knowledge, than he ever apprehended when his studies began. It is not supposed by any of your teachers — though you have naturalized yourselves in the various departments of theological study — that you have had time to exhaust the discussion of the various doctrines, in their biblical authority, in their rationale and connections, and in their dogmatical, historical, polemical, and practical bearings. That remains as your life-work. And we take it for granted that though your future will not be a mere life of study, you will endeavour to combine two things not always found together: an ardent prosecution of study, and an incessant labour for the good of others, and that nothing will be permitted to extinguish the one, or to abate the other. We take for granted, too, that you will prove yourselves men not so much holding the truth, as held by the truth, held by it more than holding it. A man does not deserve the name of a theologian, who does not resolutely continue, to the utmost of his capacity, and with all the opportunity of leisure which Providence confers, to penetrate more fully into the truths which he has apprehended, to survey them in every relation and from every point of view, and to assimilate them to himself by the testimony of the Spirit, in their scriptural authority, as well as in their dogmatic, controversial, and practical aspects.

It is not to those points, however, that I wish, in this closing meeting, to limit your regards. I purpose to notice some of those elements which enter into a successful ministry, I mean, successful in the highest sense. Here it may be proper, at the outset, to say, that success does not lie within our resources or appliances in such a sense that it can either be commanded or made the subject of human calculation; that the increase is of God; and that the well-known line of [Martin] Luther's hymn finds a response on the part of every successful minister:

Mit unsrer Macht ist nichts gethan.[1]

But while that is one side of a great truth, it is not to be denied, that it has also a human side, and that a minister must needs have an organic aptitude for his office, or be a fit instrument. This last expression recalls to me what is told of the great medieval preacher Tauler,[2] who, after being ordained, became aware that he did not truly know the gospel, and who, after imposing retirement and silence on himself for two years, came forth again in a wholly new spirit; so much so, that on the first occasion of appearing in public, his sermon on the 'Bride of Christ,' was accompanied with all the profound awakening and transforming effects of

[1] Literally, 'With our (own) power nothing is done.' This is the first line of the second verse of Luther's hymn '*Ein Feste Burg ist unser Gott*' ('A Mighty Fortress is our God') (1529). The line is usually translated: 'Did we in our own strength confide… (Our striving would be losing)' (1853).—Ed.

[2] Johannes Tauler (*c.* 1300–61) was a German mystic, a Catholic preacher and a theologian.—Ed.

a great revival; upon which his friend, who had been what Aquila was to Apollos, the means of leading him into deeper views, remarked: 'you see what God can accomplish with a good instrument.' Yes. There must be the good instrument appropriately furnished with a personal organic adaptation for the work which is to be done. And among other things comprehended in this, such as personal consecration, dependence on God, incessant prayer, and the like, it is commonly found that it is the man who is imbued with the greatest desire for fruit who most plentifully reaps it. Not only so, the impediments or obstructions that stand in the way must, as far as possible, be put aside; and we may notice some of these obstructions.

1. *Nothing more contributes to render the gospel unfruitful than a system of reserve in setting forth the grand distinctive doctrines of the gospel.*

This has begun to prevail to a large extent, and may be traced partly to a theological bias, partly to a desire to be on good terms with the spirit of the age.

The first question, and the most momentous is: on what footing does the preacher take men up? How does he regard their relation to the Judge of all the earth, and what is the specific which he brings home to them as adequate to meet the case? A great degree of favour is at present shown to a theology which has very little to say of the enormity and guilt of sin; and a great deal to say as to a sort of life, which, for aught we know from the statements which are made, may exist in man's nature irrespective of regeneration, and be nothing more than an aesthetic and moral culture, or a highly developed civilization. And, if the pulpit enforces only this, and gives but an uncertain sound on ruin, redemption, and regeneration, can the impression be other than shallow and evanescent? In the mirror held up to the hearer, the sinner cannot discern his true character or recognize himself. There is nothing to bring him into the divine presence or to bring home the pointed address, 'thou art the man.' The preacher may think himself laboriously busy in enforcing ethical principles and moral duty, he may call forth a sensational enthusiasm by pictorial representations of exciting scenes, and by dramatized delineations of character, recalling with a tasteful effort the elegances of phrase and the mannerisms which certain literary men have brought into repute; but the sermons have not the weight or influence of preaching, because they never appeal to conscience, the master faculty of man's nature, nor bring men as sinners into the presence of the living God. In all this, what have we but petty efforts to bring in mere training or educating influences to the exclusion of the lofty authority of God?

On the contrary, for the scope at which the preacher aims nothing can be named as more important than the precision with which he must habitually draw the line of demarcation between law and gospel. This was, in truth, the great achievement of the Reformation, which, after the long torpor of ages, called preaching into full activity, and gave it the place which it occupied in primitive times. Without this distinction, which lays stress on man's relation to God, preaching loses its edge and force. And the necessity of keeping it alive in men's minds is at once apparent, when we reflect that the article of justification cannot be maintained without it; that all the points of doctrine must be referred to one or other of these heads; that the entire discharge of material duty must proceed on this distinction; and that in the absence of it, there arises a great confusion and dislocation of theological doctrine as well as a distress of mind and an anxiety of conscience which nothing can relieve. The law is enforced on the impenitent, and the gospel commended to the contrite, and they aid each other in the most eminent degree. The Reformation made this distinction familiar to all men as a household word, and gave it the prominence that belongs to it in the centre of theological doctrine. Thus [Martin] Luther says, '*qui bene novit discernere legem ab evangelio is gratias agat Deo, et sciat se esse theologum.*'[1]

But as the church receded from the freshness and liberty of Reformation times, the distinction was much obscured, as Luther apprehended it would be. Amid Rationalism and Moderatism there was no place for

[1] Literally: 'Whoever knows well how to distinguish the gospel from the law should give thanks to God and know that he is a real theologian.' See *Luther's Works*, ed. Jaroslav Pelikan, trans. Jaroslav Pelikan, vol. 26, Lectures on Galatians, Chapters 1-4 (St Louis, Missouri: Concordia Publishing House, 1963), p. 115.—Ed.

the distinction. Nay, it may soon be obscured, when the preacher assumes the safety of the mixed multitude which composes his flock, or when he takes for granted that he has but to edify them, much in the same way as a physician commits the mistake of prescribing nourishment and tonics to a patient without detecting his fatal disease. To avoid this risk, the only security is to give no uncertain sound upon the great doctrines of Christianity — the deep-seated ruin of mankind, and their vast guilt: the Deity, the mission, the atoning work of the Lord; the necessity of regeneration by the Holy Spirit; the need of forgiving grace; the assurance of salvation; the plan and tenor of the covenant of grace; that every mind may be aroused from security, and directed to turn from the error of its ways. My object in adducing this is to show that the preacher, who acts upon a system of reserve, inevitably forfeits ministerial success in the highest sense, and especially when he fails to seize the central doctrines of Christianity, and to make them bear on man's relation to the Judge of all.

Here the question may be raised: Has any connection been established by divine appointment between the exercise of saving power and the preaching of redemption by the cross? It is a momentous question, too little pondered by preachers, but capable of a distinct answer. We must distinguish. On the one hand, as has been explained, God never puts his blessings into the hands of others in such a sense that they can dispose of them at their discretion. On the other hand, a connection is established between the preaching of reconciliation by the cross and the exercise of divine power, at least to an extent that cannot be affirmed of any other type of doctrine. Here we are neither treading on the margin of mystery, nor treading insecurely, for we have the guidance of the divine word. Thus, when Paul declares, 'We preach Christ crucified, etc., the power of God,' we have a statement which explicitly affirms that divine power goes associated with the proclamation of the atonement, but will not be associated with a style of teaching which substitutes any other theme. In the same way the apostle says (Gal. 3:2), 'This only would I learn of you, received ye the Spirit by the works of the law, or by the hearing of faith' (or better, by the preaching of faith, *ακοη πιστεως* [*akoē pisteōs*]); a statement intimating that the Spirit had been received by the Galatians, not in connection with a doctrine which laid stress on ritual observances, or a mere moral code, but which enforced redemption by the death of Christ received by faith. To human view, indeed, no obvious link can be perceived between this style of preaching and the transforming power of God. But a divine connection exists, as is there explicitly declared.

In illustration of this let me adduce a crucial test in the actual experience of one who tried both methods; one, too, who was incomparably the most eloquent preacher of this century. In his memorable address to the inhabitants of the parish of Kilmany, Dr Thomas Chalmers says, — 'And here I cannot but record the effect of an actual though undesigned experiment, which I prosecuted for upwards of twelve years among you. For the greater part of that time I could expatiate on the meanness of dishonesty, on the villainy of falsehood, on the despicable arts of calumny; in a word, upon all those deformities of character which awaken the natural indignation of the human heart against the pests and disturbers of human society. Now, could I, upon the strength of these warm expostulations, have got the thief to give up his stealing, and the evil speaker his censoriousness, and the liar his deviations from truth, I should have felt all the repose of one who had gotten his ultimate object. It never occurred to me that all this might have been done, and yet every soul of every hearer have remained in full alienation from God, and that even could I have established in the bosom of one who stole such a principle of abhorrence at the meanness of dishonesty, that he was prevailed upon to steal no more, he might still have retained a heart as completely unturned to God, and as totally unpossessed by a principle of love to him as before. In a word, though I might have made him a more upright and honourable man, I might have left him as destitute of the essence of religious principle as ever. But the interesting fact is, that during the whole of that period in which I made no attempt against the natural enmity of the mind to God, while I was inattentive to the way in which this enmity is dissolved, even by the free offer, on the one hand, and the believing acceptance on the other, of the gospel salvation; while Christ, through whose blood the sinner, who by nature stands afar off, is brought near to the heavenly Law-giver whom he has offended, was scarcely ever spoken of, or spoken of in such a way as stripped him of all the importance of his character and his offices — even at this time I certainly did press the reformations of honour and truth and integrity among my people; but I never once heard of any such reformations having been effected amongst them. If there was anything at all brought about in this way, it was more than ever I got any account of. I am not sensible that all the vehemence with which I urged the virtues and the proprieties of social life had the weight of a feather on the moral habits of my parishioners. And it was not till I got impressed by the utter alienation of the heart in all its desires and affections from God; it was not till reconciliation to him became the distinct and the prominent object of my ministerial exertions; it was not till I took the scriptural way of laying the method of reconciliation before them; it was not till the free offer of forgiveness through the blood of Christ was urged upon their acceptance, and the Holy Spirit given, through the channel of Christ's mediatorship, to all who ask him, was set before them as the unceasing object of their dependence and their prayers; it was not, in one word, till the contemplations of my people were turned to these great and essential elements in the business of a soul providing for its interest with God and the concerns of its eternity, that I ever heard of any of those subordinate reformations which I aforetime made the earnest, and the zealous, but I am afraid, at the same time, the ultimate object of my earlier ministrations. You servants whose scrupulous fidelity has now attracted the notice, and drawn forth in my hearing a delightful testimony from your masters what mischief you would have done had your zeal for doctrines and sacraments been accompanied by the sloth and remissness, and what, in the prevailing tone of moral relaxation, is counted the allowable purloining of your earlier days. But a sense of your heavenly Master's eye has brought another influence to bear upon you; and while you are thus striving to adorn the doctrine of God your Saviour in all things, you may, poor as you are, reclaim the great ones of the land to the acknowledgment of the faith. You have at least taught me, that to preach Christ is the only effective way of preaching morality in all its branches and out of your humble cottages have I gathered a lesson, which I pray God I may be enabled to carry, with all its simplicity, into a wider theatre, and to bring, with all the power of its subduing efficacy, upon the vices of a more crowded population.'[1]

2. *Want of success is sometimes due to this, that Scripture terms are too sparingly used, and appeals to Scripture authority as equivalent to divine authority, are unwarrantably withheld.*

[1] Thomas Chalmers' *Works*, vol. 12, pp. 41-4.

The last reflection will suffice to show how much a defect in this respect blunts the ministrations of the pulpit.

As to the sparing use of Scripture language many are here wrong on system. Following Foster's one-sided counsels, or from theories still worse, many abstain from Scripture phrases, as if this were out of keeping with modern taste! Thus they put a change of manners for conversion to God, pious feeling in place of faith in Christ, amendment for regeneration by the Spirit, a new conduct for repentance, and the like, as if the style of Scripture must be modernized to adapt it to modern culture. This is consummate folly in every point of view. That there may have been overdoing in the quotation of Scripture, is granted. That it is uncouth to intersperse unduly the figurative style and the oriental garb of life and action when these have no application to western nations, may frankly be admitted. But the language of the divine word is a divinely constructed instrument for arresting the mind and opening an avenue to the human heart; and it would be foolish and hazardous to discontinue the use of it.

I also mentioned the defect of appeal to scriptural authority as equivalent to divine authority. There may be nothing in statement or matter that runs counter to the divine word, and yet the ministrations may not lean on Scripture or appeal to its authority. The connection may be a loose one, I mean the ultimate appeal may not be to God's authority. A preacher, who knows his position as a duly commissioned ambassador acting in the name of Christ, feels that he has not sufficiently honoured Scripture, if he has occupied men's attention with his own argumentation, and referred little to the divine utterances of Scripture, as adduced in the light of God's countenance, and applied to the present relations of life among us. Nay, the hearers expect to be brought before a higher presence; they feel a want they know not what when this is little done, they recognize a majesty and power in that mode of preaching which places men in the open light of God's presence, and compels them to listen to his authoritative declarations.

3. *Want of success is often to be traced to a defect in enforcing the obligations of Christian ethics on regenerate men.*

Our previous remarks were meant to show that the preacher aims too low who stops short of conversion. But when conversion is attained, a new vista opens to our view, and every duty is seen 'to be the natural outcome of the new life.'

On this point I cannot expatiate at length. Let me merely say, that everything will stagnate unless full prominence is given to Christian character, Christian experience, and Christian ethics, as well as Christian doctrine. They cannot long exist apart. Doctrine will not retain its freshness without life, nor life continue without doctrine. The great point at all times in Christian morals is, that ethical action does not go before reconciliation, but follows it, and that the entire character of the action is vitiated by reversing this order.

I feel, however, I have lingered on these topics too long; and with a few personal counsels, compressed into the briefest compass, I conclude. I say then:

(1) *Expound the divine word consecutively, and in its connections, as well as preach on separate texts.* If you do the one, leave not the other undone. The method I recommend carries with it peculiar advantages. It is accompanied with a self-evidencing power of the most important kind; and besides, it relieves the youthful labourer of a fear which often haunts him, that he will talk out his matter and be exhausted. Of course he may, if he preaches only on random texts, used as a motto for a topic, but never if he continues faithfully to interpret and expound the word in its connections, and brings it to bear on the relations of life. I pity a minister who never enriches his mind by continuous exposition; and I pity a congregation that has never been trained to survey and to apply a single book of Scripture. We condemn the pericope-system or lesson-system in the Lutheran and Anglican churches, as a most defective style of teaching. But the system of selecting loose texts is not much better. The people never see the connections, the organic structure of the word of God.

(2) *Familiarize your minds, as students and preachers, with the experience and habits of successful labourers in*

the vineyard. Be familiar with the life and labours of a Welsh,[1] a Whitefield,[2] a Bunyan,[3] a Brainerd,[4] a Nettleton,[5] and a whole galaxy of others, whose biographies were written to inspire the zeal of those who should come after them. Many undervalue biography of this kind, when they might have got a great impulse from it. It was this that peculiarly inflamed the piety of Neander[6] as he traced the stream of divine life flowing from Christ through all the centuries. Not only so, biography teaches the value of hard study for the work of the ministry, and the importance of a thorough preparation for it. A sentence or two from the letters of

[1] John Welsh (*c.* 1568–1622) was Church of Scotland minister of Ayr from 1600 until banished and exiled to France by King James VI & I in 1606. A powerful preacher, Welsh was reputed to have spent a third of his waking hours in prayer.—Ed.

[2] George Whitefield (1714–70) was an outstanding English preacher and evangelist who was mightily used by the Lord both in revivals in the United Kingdom and in the United States of America.—Ed.

[3] John Bunyan (1628–88) was a renowned English Baptist preacher, particularly well-known as author of *The Pilgrim's Progress* (1678) and other outstanding works of experiential Christianity.—Ed.

[4] David Brainerd (1718–47) was a missionary to the native Indians in North America, supported by the Society in Scotland for Propagating Christian Knowledge.—Ed.

[5] Asahel Nettleton (1783–1844) was an American theologian and evangelist greatly used in the 'Second Great Awakening' in America in the early part of the nineteenth century. He was a firm Calvinist in his theology. It was said that as many as 30,000 people were converted through his preaching.—Ed.

[6] Johann August Wilhelm Neander (1789–1850) was a German theologian and church historian.—Ed.

Dr James Alexander,[1] one of the most accomplished and saintly ministers in recent times in America, will show how he viewed this matter: 'Biography,' says he, 'has always been my favourite reading; in this I include all such developments of manners and mind as one finds in correspondence, in anecdotes, as well as formed characters. No kind of study so excites my enthusiasm, one example is to me more than discourses innumerable.' And he adds, 'I am sure that no works have had so much influence on my religious feelings as those which give the lives of pious men.'[2]

(3) *Let me add self-examination and prayer*. He who does not place his heart and actions daily before God, will have many faults, all too obvious to others, though hidden from himself, and certainly will want humility and integrity before God. The devoted puritan Harris[3] was wont to say, 'I have three Books, the Bible, my people, and myself.'

And I add prayer, as that by which all other activity is fitly carried on. The student's chamber and the

[1] James Waddel Alexander (1804–59) was an American Presbyterian minister and theologian who followed in the footsteps of his father, Rev. Archibald Alexander. He was Professor of Ecclesiastical History and Church Government at Princeton Theological Seminary, 1849–51.—Ed.

[2] John Hall (Ed.), *Forty Years' Familiar Letters of James W. Alexander*, vol. 1 (New York: C. Scribner, 1860), p. 85.—Ed.

[3] Robert Harris (1581–1658) was an English clergyman, known as a Puritan preacher, member of the Westminster Assembly, and President of Trinity College, Oxford.—Ed.

pastor's study should be his oratory as well as his sphere of mental effort, and its walls should bear witness to the one as well as to the other. 'There,' said an American to an English traveller, 'There is the pulpit where Payson[1] prayed'; and it conveyed a world of meaning as to the marked and prominent feature of that memorable man. You are familiar with John Welsh's praying, that model minister, perhaps the greatest of our Scottish pastors. 'Prayer,' said Hooker,[2] the eminent pilgrim father, the pillar of the New England colony, 'prayer is the main work of a minister, and that by which he must carry on all the rest.'

But I conclude, and now, in my own name and in that of all my esteemed colleagues, I say farewell. The blessing of the Lord be upon you; may you diligently labour in your day, and may we all of us meet on the right hand of the Judge, when the toils and labours of earth are ended, bringing our sheaves with us. We commend you to God and to the word of his grace, which is able to build you up and to give you an inheritance among them that are sanctified.

[1] Edward Payson (1783–1827) was an American Congregational preacher.—Ed.

[2] Thomas Hooker (1586–1647) was a prominent Puritan colonial leader, who founded the Colony of Connecticut after dissenting with Puritan leaders in Massachusetts.—Ed.

10

The Faithful Labourer's Reward in Heaven[1]

> *And they that be wise [or, better, they that are instructors] shall shine as the brightness of the firmament; and they that turn many to righteousness [better, who justify many] as the stars for ever and ever.*—Daniel 12:3

DEAR FRIENDS, — I select this text as highly appropriate amid the deep and overpowering sorrow spread not only over this city, but far beyond this city, by the removal of the preacher to whose instructions you all listened with delight, and whose voice we shall hear no more. With the acute sense of loss which is so widely felt, you need also to be reminded that in the instrument which God raised up and singularly fitted for his work, you possessed a great gift; and that in now surveying his career, we have the most certain monuments that

[1] A sermon preached in the Free West Church, Aberdeen, on Sabbath, 5 May 1872, following the passing of the Rev. Alex D Davidson, late minister of that congregation and published. Alexander Dyce Davidson (1807–72) was Church of Scotland minister in Aberdeen from 1832. He adhered to the Free Church in 1843 and became minister of the Free West Church in that city. He was renowned as an evangelical preacher in the city.—Ed.

he neither lived nor laboured in vain. In the great day many will rise up and call him blessed, as the text intimates in reference to successful ministers generally. Let us proceed to direct attention to the import of the text we have selected.

In the first division of the book of Daniel, contained in the first six chapters, the prophet describes the wonderful works of God which took place in his own time, and in which he bore a conspicuous part. The second division, extending over the six following chapters, brings under our notice a series of revelations as to the future history of the Church in the world. These communications, made to Daniel by the angel of the Lord from time to time, were intended to sustain him and to sustain the Church of which he was the representative by most encouraging promises of divine aid, and by pledges of deliverance from the calamities which should emerge in the course of history, both before and subsequent to the coming of the Messiah in the flesh. The last-mentioned danger, at the close of the previous chapter, is referred by most interpreters, and correctly, to the rise of Antichrist and to his final overthrow. The same history is continued into the first verse of the present chapter, which might, therefore, have been more fitly attached to the previous chapter. The allusion (Dan. 12:1) is to that time of trouble such as never was since there was a nation to that same time, — when 'Zion in her anguish with Babylon must cope.'

The revelation thus made to the prophet next passes without a break or indication of an interval from the fall of Antichrist to the day of final recompense, the resurrection day, much in the same way as John in the Apocalypse links these two events together. Next, we have described to us the different lot awarded to the righteous and the wicked — the one awaking to everlasting life, the other to shame and everlasting contempt. Next in order, the oracle proceeds to delineate the different degrees of glory with which God, in the exercise of his grace, will reward faithful teachers and successful labourers: 'And they that be wise (or teachers of others) shall shine as the brightness of the firmament, and they that turn many to righteousness (or who justify many) as the stars for ever and ever.'

Now the general theme or proposition here brought before us is, that a great reward is reserved in glory for true instructors or teachers in the Church of Christ, and for all successful winners of souls. That is the proposition and, according to the tenor of the text, it may be taken up in the three following points:

1. Here are divinely recognized teachers of the Church.

2. They are said instrumentally to turn many to righteousness, or to justify many.

3. They receive hereafter a great reward, an exceeding weight of glory.

And while we speak of these points, may that Almighty Spirit who alone can give efficacy to the word spoken be shed on us abundantly, that God's people may be edified, and that the dead may hear the voice of the Son of God and live.

1. *We have a divinely recognized order of teachers*. The word here rendered *wise* may be taken in the active sense to signify *instructors* or *teachers*; and the latter signification is much more appropriate in this case, whether we take the parallelism into account or the general import of the two clauses (compare Dan. 11:33). The priests and Levites were the standing teachers of the Old Economy: the priests' lips kept knowledge: and to these was added, from time to time, an order of prophets to bring about the spiritual elements of the Old Testament, to correct abuses, and to foretell that great event for the production of which all time was travailing. The New Economy has also its order of teachers: — first, apostles, secondarily, prophets, next, evangelists (1 Cor. 12:28) — who as commissioned for an extraordinary work have been all withdrawn from the scene. But the Church is still committed to pastors and teachers for the work of the ministry, for the edifying of the body of Christ (Eph. 4:11).

Here let me recall their mode of preparation for their function, and those names of office by which the Holy Spirit indicates their commission. As to their *preparation*, they are first made Christians or true disciples, and then prepared to be labourers in the vineyard. They first live, and then work. Though the gifts called into exercise have, in every case, their basis in mental or natural endowments, which were concreated with the man, these may often lie concealed from the eyes of others, and even from the consciousness of the possessor, till they are evoked and stirred into action by the entrance of the life of God into the soul. The Lord, the Church's ever-living Head, from whom all these endowments emanate, was well acquainted with the peculiar mental conformation, with which his servants were created, and had appointed the service to which they could be made available before it dawned upon their own minds. To draw an illustration from the career of him whose loss we mourn. Little did he think during those youthful years when he indulged the classical and literary enthusiasm which formed him to be the accomplished scholar, while acquiring the culture and refinement which his native city fully supplied, and attaching himself by sympathies, congenial tastes, and partialities amounting to a passion, to everything that may be said to belong to the inmost life of Aberdeen, that he was all unawares preparing to speak to its very heart, to touch its chords at every point, and thus effect the great destiny of his life — to turn the current of opinion toward Evangelical religion. If he was proud of Aberdeen, and Aberdeen in turn became proud of him, the design of him who had the arrangement of final causes in his hand was to fit an instrument for its appointed use — that the offering up of the Gentiles might be acceptable, being sanctified by the Holy Spirit (Rom. 15:16). The distribution of gifts in their manifold and beautiful variety is a daily proof that

Jesus lives as the dispenser of the Spirit, and that he acts in the preparation of the instruments before he works with instruments fitted for their allotted work. This is brought under our notice in the most impressive manner when we look at the preparation of the first disciples. They were already Christians before Pentecost, but their gifts were undeveloped. When the Spirit was given on the day of Pentecost, they were raised to an unwonted elevation, and had new conceptions of the spirituality of Christ's kingdom. And that is but an example of what is ever to be anew expected, and ever anew reproduced by waiting on the Lord, who gives to those who wait on him brighter discoveries of his person, and stirs up their gifts to greater efficiency.

As to the names of office to which I referred as indicating the ministerial commission, they are various.

(1) The term here used — *teachers*, or *instructors* — is derived from the relation in which they stand to the Church. And in the same light various other designations must be understood, such as *shepherds* to take heed to the flock; *labourers* to reap fruit to life eternal; and *builders* to raise up the fabric of the spiritual temple, by building one stone after another on the good foundation. But while these official names have relation to the Church, others are derived —

(2) From the relation in which *ministers* stand to the Lord himself. To adduce one or two of these, — we find them designated *friends of the Bridegroom*, a name which may be counted honour enough when the

world heaps upon them obloquy and scorn. It may be regarded, indeed, as but an indifferent sign, if in a world which deeply hated Christ, and which is still very much the same, a minister excites neither fear nor hatred on the part of those who are of the world. They are also termed *ministers of the word*, because they not only keep the word of God uncorrupted and unadulterated, but speak it with the weight of one who has a *thus saith the Lord* to proclaim. And closely allied to this is another title — that of *ambassadors* — because they come forth to their fellow-men on the behalf of God, and beseech them in Christ's stead to be reconciled to God. And if importance attaches to an embassy from an earthly court, what momentous issues crowd into an embassy from the court of heaven, from God to man!

I refer to this the rather because all levelling sects, both in former and present times, think that they do well to ridicule it as an absurd assumption if a minister speaks in the name of Christ, and declares his message as one of Christ's ambassadors. They represent this as playing the apostle, and seek to explode it as a preposterous claim. Their objection proceeds on grounds which would invalidate the divine right of the ministry, and leave the poor occupant of the office to discharge its duties in his own name, or in that of his employers. And nothing can more effectually tend to paralyze the effect of preaching than a theory which precludes the possibility of speaking with authority. On the contrary, we must make men hear the word of the Lord; and without this the speaker may be an orator, a vigorous reasoner, or an erudite expounder, but not a preacher. We must run the matter up to authority; and without this we do not preach. Though the ordinary preacher is not like apostles and prophets — the immediate recipient of a revelation, — his incumbent duty is to speak with the authority of one who has a 'thus saith the Lord' to utter. The difference between discussion or philosophical disquisition and preaching, in the proper import of the word, lies here. When the preacher identifies himself with revelation by an appeal to authority, and makes men hear it as from the mouth of God, they listen to something far beyond the wisdom, reasoning, or disquisition of man. This was a memorable peculiarity of him whose ministry is now closed among you. I never listened to those solemn expositions or appeals which returned always to the one point of making men realize their relation to the Judge of all the earth, without the feeling — There is a man who has a message from God.

2. *They are said to turn many to righteousness, or, instrumentally, to justify many*. The term *justify* must be taken here, as elsewhere, in its forensic sense; that is, as descriptive of the sinner's acceptance before God. But how can ministers be said to justify? The meaning cannot be that they have an arbitrary power or discretion to give men the remission or absolution of sins; for, in the first place, no man can forgive sins but God only; and, next, God never puts the dispensation of his

blessings out of his own hand. The meaning can only amount to this, that, while preaching a free salvation by the cross of Christ, they are used to justify men ministerially or instrumentally. That result is accomplished as they offer justification to penitent sinners, and point out the true way of salvation by faith alone, without the works of the law. Nor is this the only passage where preachers are so described. They are said to turn the Gentiles from darkness to light (Acts 26:18); to save themselves and them that hear them (1 Tim. 4:6); to present the Church as a chaste virgin to Christ to whom they have espoused her (1 Cor. 11:2); and to beget men through the gospel (1 Cor. 4:15). This style of language will be understood by comparing it with similar statements. Thus, they who convert a sinner from the error of his ways are said to save a soul from death and to hide a multitude of sins (James 5:19), which can only mean that they are the instruments of bringing him to the fountain opened for sin and for all uncleanness. The clause does not mean, that they conceal his many infirmities, because, coming after a statement that they save a soul from death, it must have a cognate import. And all this is effected only by the word which they preach, and which is the channel of divine power. To preach is to convey a message the most momentous that human lips can utter, — a message which, according as it is accepted or refused, decides man's destiny for ever. And to gain the end which preaching is meant to accomplish, it must come from the heart of ministers under a feeling of the deepest dependence on God.

They have no power of themselves to effect so great a result as turning many to righteousness, and must regard themselves as rather passive than active in the whole transaction; and therein lies the secret of their strength. [Martin] Luther may be adduced as an instance how a man, amid the unchaining of the spiritual forces which issue forth from the kingdom of God, felt himself to be nothing more than a helpless instrument in the hand of the Most High. Though in one sense intensely active, he, in another sense, comes before us as a man who stood still and saw the salvation of God. And the same thing holds true of all successful labourers. They work, and yet they look on, while God works. The effects produced by the gospel through the lapse of centuries have been accomplished by what Milton terms 'the unresistible might of weakness.' Hence it is that we find united in their action the greatest apparent opposites, — weakness and strength, emptiness and sufficiency, limitation and the boundless resources of omnipotence; the earthen vessel ready to go to pieces at the slightest pressure, and the excellency of power; an unimposing agency, and the mightiest force that stirs humanity; — in a word, a worm linked to omnipotence, yet thrashing the mountains and beating them small (Isa. 41:16). Nothing remains to man but the instrumentality.

Another mode of putting this, but amounting to the same thing, is to connect these results simply with the word. Thus, the gospel is called the power of God unto salvation (Rom. 1:16), implying that it not only has its origin with God, but becomes the channel through which the power of God displays itself. When speaking of the force put forth by the word, the apostle says: 'The word of God is not bound' (2 Tim. 2:9); and again he speaks of it as the sword of the Spirit, intimating that the Spirit wields the word as his sword (Eph. 6:17). The word is called *the power of God*, because it is the instrument by which men born dead in sin are raised to spiritual life, and because an almighty supernatural power goes along with it. But it is not with every sort of preaching that we find this accompanying power. That result is found to follow only when preaching is based on Christ crucified as the one ground of a sinner's hope, and when it sets forth the justifying grace of God as received by faith alone. The proclamation of free grace, as based on the great facts of the gospel, has produced from age to age, and will continue to produce till the end of time, in one locality or another, the great results of a new relation toward God, and the fruits of a sanctified life. For in such a case God inhabits the word, and the Spirit comes in it with saving power, as with the rushing mighty wind.

This was peculiarly characteristic of the preaching of our departed friend, and to this must be traced the singular power and saving efficacy, which, at an eventful period in the history of Aberdeen, went associated with his ministry. He preached *Christ crucified*. He opened up to men's gaze, as few preachers have been found to do, the whole doctrine of the covenant of grace, exhibiting, as in a bird's-eye view, the economy of God's plan of grace, from its commencement to its final consummation. He unrolled the map of God's procedure, and exhibited to the admiring view of spiritual minds the mingled wisdom and grace of that remedial plan on which man's hopes must be built for eternity. The whole scheme of saving grace was sketched in its great outlines; and in tracing, as you were privileged to do, law and grace, promise and fulfilment, plan and execution, his hearers acquired a full view of the manifold grace which projected the whole. When the magnificent outline of the scheme of salvation, as he was wont to sketch it, passed in review, embracing the counsel of God from its rise in a past eternity onward to the winding up of all things in the eternity to come, you can recall how you gained in comprehensiveness of view by the sublime and heart-affecting panorama submitted to your minds. My habitual impression during the four years that I and my family enjoyed his ministrations was, that nowhere could you find a nobler preacher, nowhere a more ample, varied, and all-sided exhibition of the gospel of the grace of God.

Nor was his ministry unaccompanied with a large amount of that saving power to which the text alludes. He turned many to righteousness. This will appear, whether you look at the cases of individual conversion with which you are familiar, or at the transforming influence exercised by his ministry on the general community. As to the former, I have personally conversed with one here and one there, who date their first impressions to his early ministry. I have heard testimonies of the most touching and affecting kind, to the power of his sermons, at a time when the doctrines of saving grace had to make their way, amid much opposition, to the recognition which they at length achieved. Thus, one friend in Edinburgh — who owes all to his ministry — writes to me two days ago: 'His preaching (first in Belmont Street,[1] and afterwards in West Parish Church, St Nicholas) was deeply searching and convincing. His powerful, clear-sighted intellect enabled him to grasp the truth with a firm hand, and he delighted to clothe it in the most simple language he could find, in order to make it intelligible to all classes of his hearers, who eagerly came to learn at his mouth the Lord's way of saving sinners. Many were brought to spiritual life through his precious ministry previous to the Disruption,[2] to which period these recollections more especially refer. A course of lectures on the Shorter Catechism, delivered from the pulpit about the same time, was blessed to many a soul in opening up systematically the great scheme of salvation. A sermon which

[1] The South Church (Church of Scotland) was situated in Belmont Street, Aberdeen.—Ed.

[2] A major Disruption took place in the Church of Scotland in 1843 in which the Free Church of Scotland emerged as a separate denomination. For details see Thomas Brown, *Annals of the Disruption* (Edinburgh: Macniven and Wallace, 1893).—Ed.

he preached before the Synod in 1839, on *the work of the Holy Spirit*, and then printed, aroused many from the death-like slumber into which the Church had fallen, and excited much discussion.'

But, besides these instances of individual conversion on the part of considerable numbers, there was a general result in connection with his ministry which warrants me to say that it formed an epoch in the history of Aberdeen. He rendered very much the same service in the seat of the northern University that Dr Chalmers[1] did in Glasgow, and Dr Andrew Thomson[2] and Dr Gordon[3] in Edinburgh. These men contributed largely to turn the current of opinion. They made evangelical religion respected and venerated where it had been previously despised. In the case of Aberdeen, as in the other cities just named, there were pioneers who went before the decisive change which may be said to have been effected here in the decennium from 1832 to 1842. Had I time to

[1] Thomas Chalmers (1780–1847) was a minister in the Church of Scotland from 1803. He became leader of the evangelicals in the Church and a leading light in the movements that led to the Disruption in 1843 and the consequent formation of the Free Church of Scotland. A renowned preacher and writer, Chalmers was one of the leading Scotsmen of his day.—Ed.

[2] Andrew Mitchell Thomson (1779–1831) was an outstanding evangelical preacher in the Church of Scotland, especially influential as minister of St George's Church in Edinburgh (1814–31).—Ed.

[3] Robert Gordon (1786–1853) was a Church of Scotland minister and influential as an evangelical preacher, especially in Edinburgh both before and after the Disruption in 1843. He entered the Free Church of Scotland at the Disruption.—Ed.

delineate the important preparatory work performed by a Kidd[1] and a Leith,[2] or the co-operation of a Murray[3] and a Foote,[4] a Tweedie,[5] a Stewart,[6] and others that might be named, it could easily be made to appear that they largely aided in bringing about this momentous change, and that they rendered the most essential service. But it is not the less true that the great spiritual and intellectual influence which turned the tide stood indissolubly

[1] James Kidd (1761–1834) was born in Ireland. He was appointed to the Chair of Oriental Languages at Marischal College, Aberdeen, in 1793. From 1801 he was also minister of Gilcomston Church of Scotland congregation in the city.—Ed.

[2] William Leith (1802–32), an Aberdonian, was minister of the South Church, Aberdeen, 1829–32.—Ed.

[3] John Murray (1784–1861) was minister of Trinity Chapel (Church of Scotland) in Aberdeen from 1816. In 1843 he adhered to the Free Church of Scotland and became minister of the North Free Church congregation in Aberdeen.—Ed.

[4] James Foote (1781–1856) was ordained in 1809. In 1825 he became minister of the North Church in Aberdeen (Church of Scotland). In 1843 he adhered to the Free Church and became minister in the East Free Church, Aberdeen.—Ed.

[5] William King Tweedie (1803–63) was minister of Aberdeen South congregation (Church of Scotland) from 1836. In 1843 he was translated to Tolbooth Church, Edinburgh. He then entered the Free Church in 1843 with the entire Kirk Session and most of the congregation, forming Tolbooth Free Church, Edinburgh.—Ed.

[6] James Stewart (1813–46) became minister of Aberdeen South Congregation (Church of Scotland) in 1842. The following year he adhered to the Free Church of Scotland and ministered in the Free South Church (Aberdeen) up till his passing three years later. Many years later George Smeaton provided a prefatory note to a volume of Stewart's 'Discourses' (see the listing of Smeaton's 'Published Writings' at the end of this volume, section 3, number 2).—Ed.

connected with him who has recently passed away from the midst of you; for the high culture and commanding pulpit gifts of that single-minded and humble servant of his heavenly Master could neither be depreciated nor ignored by any one. That was the great service rendered to this University seat and to the north of Scotland by him whom we today so much miss. That is his peculiar claim to the lasting gratitude of his townsmen. And if church history is faithful to its function of recording the labours of those who have influenced the movements of the kingdom of God, this work will not be forgotten. But at all events it will not be forgotten in heaven. His calm but regulated zeal, his fidelity and decision that would neither succumb to the anti-evangelical spirit of the age, when it cost something to be a preacher of the cross, nor be drawn aside from his path, and all fully recorded, and will ere long be read out from the Lamb's book of remembrance to an assembled universe. This brings to notice: —

3. *These teachers and winners of souls receive a reward.* They 'shall shine as the brightness of the firmament, and as the stars, for ever and ever.' The recognition awaiting successful labourers is nowhere more emphatically and touchingly expressed than in these words to Daniel; and they were presented to his mind, and to our minds, in and by him, that we may be induced by such a motive to surmount the discouragements and toils attaching to our earthly service. This shows the value which God

sets on assiduous toil in winning souls, and also proves, beyond the possibility of doubt, that the doctrine of rewards is fully compatible with salvation by free grace.

I say, it shows the value which God sets on assiduous and successful labour. This is in the sight of God great price, because that state of mind argues glowing zeal for the Divine glory, an appreciation of the great ransom by which souls are redeemed, and a compassionate love for souls, as well as a due estimate of their value. Times and economies, which are manifold and various, are here alike. Not only a Noah, a preacher of righteousness in the time of God's long suffering, and a Moses, faithful as a servant in all his house — not only the martyrs who shed their blood for Christ, and loved not their lives for his sake, but sincere teachers of all times, and in every variety of scene — shall be partakers of an exceeding weight of glory. This honour have all his saints (Psa. 149:9); and it may well sustain them, however irksome their post — however heavy their work — however great the obloquy they may be called to bear. He who puts honour on their ministry here — who invests their words with power, and gives them as their joy and crown, a company of justified and converted men, will consummate their reward at the coming of our Lord Jesus Christ.

The doctrine of rewards is thus compatible with salvation by grace. It is not a reward of merit; for merit we have none. We may say in the words of the hymn, 'My merit is destruction, a child of wrath am I.' But so vigilant is God to connect a reward of grace, a gracious recompense with every service, however small, which may be done in his name, that we are assured by Christ that not a cup of cold water given in the name of a disciple shall lose its reward.

That the two things are compatible is evident. While God bestows acceptance and eternal life simply on the ground of Christ's obedience finished on the cross, it is farther affirmed that God is not unrighteous to forget any work of faith or labour of love which is shown towards his name (Heb. 6:10). Moreover, the description which Christ has given of the Judgment is in the highest degree significant. He introduces a company of his redeemed servants expressing their astonishment that they should be represented as ministering to his necessities and visiting him in prison. They were more conscious of their infirmities and inconsistencies than of their services. But the faults are all forgotten, and only the services are mentioned, and they are surprised beyond measure at the favourable construction put upon offices of benevolence offered to the saints which their Lord accepts as done to himself — 'Ye did it unto me.' There you see the gracious reward which the Lord bestows.

But there are not only rewards but *various degrees* of reward and various degrees of glory. The weight of glory is according to the grateful service done. On the one hand all believers stand on the same level so far as they are justified and adopted. Here there are no degrees for one is not more justified than another. The right to heaven is the same in all believers; one has not more, and another less. Not only so: every vessel will be full, and enjoy complete felicity. But these facts are consistent with degrees of glory. This point may be established by many considerations. The Holy Scriptures explicitly teach it in numerous passages; and the nature of the case may convince us of its truth. Thus, two persons pass into the eternal world — the one a trophy of divine grace upon his death-bed, the other a shining example of Christian piety, and a successful labourer in the cause of Christ. Their vessels may be full of felicity in both cases, but the one is of larger capacity than the other from the nature of the case.

The *present life*, in a word, stands in close connection with that which is to come, not only as it affords men a day of grace in which they may obtain a title to the heavenly felicity, but also as it is a time of preparation in which men and women are formed to a capacity for heavenly occupations, or made meet to be partakers of the inheritance of the saints in light. And in this view every word spoken, every deed done, every thought cherished and entertained, according to its character, as spiritual or carnal, is of infinite moment to all eternity. All service rendered, all knowledge gained, all progress made, all usefulness in the way of impressing others, must be viewed as gain for eternity. And on the other hand, every sin committed, every neglect of duty, every imperfection in knowledge or holiness, activity or usefulness, is something deducted from our crown and a loss for eternity. And what a motive does all this supply to stimulate us so to run that we may win the crown.

It only remains to say in conclusion, that the mournful event which has brought me here this day has saddened the members of our Church far and near. Hardly can I realize Aberdeen without the presence of Dr Davidson. But apart from the personal loss which I share along with you, his removal leaves our Church immensely poorer. He was a prince of preachers; and none of equal eminence, in active service, is left to fill his place. He was one of those, now greatly reduced in number, who made the Scottish pulpit conspicuous, one whose ministry elevated as well as educated the community. I shall not attempt to set down the incidents or tenor of his life. Nor is this necessary, as he grew up among you from his boyhood; and every member of his flock is more familiar with his antecedents than a stranger can pretend to be. I shall notice only one or two things which struck me as characteristic of the preacher.

(1) His pulpit preparations, in respect of form, were admirably constructed and marked by an elegant simplicity. The language was always clear and appropriate, and he never left us in doubt as to his meaning. The thoughts were sharply defined, and given out with a rare power of expression which was always felt to be felicitous. There never was a stronger statement than the truth would

bear; and the words and phrases were so natural and unaffected, that they could readily be comprehended by any congregation. One incident recalls his notion of the necessity of transparent language. I remember him on one occasion in company declaring his full belief that a man did not know what he could not express, and that one knew only what he could clearly utter.

(2) The spiritual element of man's nature was always the proper object of Dr Davidson's address. I never heard him merely *entertain* a congregation by appealing to the sensuous or aesthetic part of man's being. He spoke to the distinctively spiritual in man's nature, or to that by which the finite is linked to the infinite, commending the truth to every man's conscience in the sight of God. The subject-matter of the preacher was the same great truths which had been received into his own soul; and he seemed to say with Paul — 'Which things we preach.'

(3) The general tenor of his preaching, though it was singularly varied, may be described as objective preaching, with a constant reference to the interdependence of Christian doctrines. I say objective or doctrinal preaching, for he aimed at impression through instruction. He acted on the principle at all times, that the heart can be touched only through the intellect. But the enlightenment of the understanding was not regarded by him as a finality. Nor do I recall a single Sermon in which he did not endeavour, by some of those master strokes which he could use so skilfully, and which generally came unexpected, to reach the conscience, and

call it into action by some allusions to divine authority and law. And such was his sense of the interdependence of divine doctrines, that he touched them one after another very much as a skilful musician brings out the tones of his instrument.

(4) To all this was added a deep though undemonstrative zeal, which you could count upon in every thing that bore upon the honour of his Lord. It was never a zeal untempered or without knowledge.

(5) He was singularly felicitous in his use of Scripture quotation, and his prayers were instinct with it. There is a peculiar charm and fragrancy to pious minds in the happy use of Scripture language, such as we find in the skilful hands of an Ainsworth,[1] a Brown of Wamphray,[2] in the late Principal Lee,[3] and in him who has just

[1] Henry Ainsworth (1571–*c.* 1622) was a Puritan who became a separatist and was driven by persecution to Amsterdam in 1593 where he ministered to an English congregation. He was an outstanding biblical and linguistic scholar, especially in Hebrew and Old Testament studies. See Joel R Beeke & Randall J Pederson, *Meet the Puritans* (Grand Rapids, MI: Reformation Heritage Books, 2006), pp. 15-17.—Ed.

[2] John Brown (*c.* 1610–79) was Church of Scotland minister at Wamphray (1655–62) before being exiled to Rotterdam where he ministered to the Scots Church there (1663–77). He passed away in Rotterdam in 1679. He was a prolific writer of evangelical, reformed and polemical works.—Ed.

[3] John Lee (1779–1859) was a minister in the Church of Scotland and after 1812 held various professoriates in divinity, including the Principalship of the University of Edinburgh (1840–59) where he was Professor of Divinity after 1843. He was orthodox in his theology but a 'moderate' in church policy.—Ed.

passed away. It has not only a charm, but a power for which other substitutes are a sorry compensation. Not only so: it is always singularly blessed of God. Hence, in the 'Memoirs of Halyburton,'[1] it is observed by that eminent man, 'a due application of Scripture is best preaching; for confirming which it is remarkable that though God may make use of the words of man in letting in to the meaning of it, yet it is the Scripture-word by which he ordinarily conveys the comfort or advantage of whatever sort: it is this instrument of God's own framing that works the effect.'

One parting word to all. You have still a meeting with your Pastor, though you shall see his face no more here. You will meet at the great white throne to give account of all that you have heard during a long-protracted ministry of *forty years.* The converted among you to whom his message brought salvation will recall your days of privilege, and lay up his words in your memory. But the unsaved have a great responsibility. They were never dismissed without hearing the way of a sinner's acceptance, the method by which a sinner can be reconciled to God. A dread responsibility rests on every one who listened to such teaching, and put off the moment of decision to a more convenient season. Permit me to ask

[1] This refers to the memoirs of Rev. Thomas Halyburton (1674–1712) first published in 1714. These are effectively his spiritual autobiography published posthumously and it was an enduring influential volume.—Ed.

you, how you will be able to meet your teacher in the presence of that Lord, to whom you were so tenderly yet solemnly invited from day to day? Did he not tell proud self-righteous sinners in their distance and rebellion that the Lord of Glory was bending at their feet, and inviting them to accept his great salvation? What an awakening thought it must be to not a few that every sermon and every expostulation must be brought back to mind! You have to meet again, and to give in the mutual account; and every entreaty to accept Christ and flee from the wrath to come will be flashed back upon your memory in the light of the Judge's countenance. There will be no forgotten sermons on that day: they *can be recalled* from the tablets of memory, and they will be so recalled. O, let the recollection of them move you now to accept the great salvation!

II

The Scottish Theory of Ecclesiastical Establishments[1]

WITH much pleasure I accepted the kind invitation of your Committee when they requested me to address the Glasgow Conservative Association on the question of Ecclesiastical Establishments. Though by no means a politician, my sympathies beat warmly in favour of perpetuating the religious character of all our institutions, and particularly in favour of the national support of the Church. 'All for the Kirk and something less for the State,' is an old Scottish watchword with which I have much in common. And when I see the rise of combinations which menace the stability of the Church and the public recognition of the Christian faith, I do not hesitate to avow myself a Conservative, in the ecclesiastical acceptation of the term — a Conservative, that is, according to the tenor of the Revolution Settlement and the Treaty of Union; the maintenance of which in their spirit and letter is the incumbent duty of every intelligent man, and of every Scotsman worthy of the

[1] An address given to the Glasgow Conservative Association, April 13, 1875. Appendices in the original publication have been omitted.—Ed.

name. They are the palladium of our religious privileges. Mature experience and reflection have only confirmed my early prepossessions as to the paramount duty of doing what in us lies to uphold the Christian state in its integrity, and conserving those religious elements which, from the Reformation downwards, have been interwoven in the civil constitution of the country. The secular state — that is, the state with the Christian constituents of the State eliminated from it, is in the last degree repulsive to me.

I purpose in this address to expound the Scottish theory of Ecclesiastical Establishments, and then examine with more express reference to present relations, how far the theory is realized. It will be my duty in compressing this inquiry within the compass of a lecture to travel over a wide field, and yet to make due provision that in an equal measure past history and present fact shall enter into their rights. I use the expression *Scottish Theory*, because, unlike the Anglican and Continental theories which served other nations for the erection of their State Churches, as they unhappily call them, the Scottish theory, is not only of a unique character, but capable of ample vindication. The Scottish Church alone among the Churches of the Reformation asserted it in words, and laboured to reduce it to practice. I have often said that in the Scottish theory we have the ultimate truth on the whole subject of the relations between Church and State, the result of the prayerful investigations and earnest contendings of some of the clearest minds and loftiest characters that adorned the Christian Church during the last three centuries. It was asserted by all Scotsmen, in a former day; and it will be appreciated in our day, when it is again practically brought into operation. So fully did it commend itself to the Scottish mind that during the last Episcopal Establishment in Scotland, it was in every person's mouth; and Bishop Burnet[1] informs us that he and his friends were 'amazed to find a poor commonalty capable to argue upon points of government, and on the bounds to be set to the power of princes in matters of religion.' For maintaining such a theory the Scottish Church has been denounced by statesmen as rigid and impracticable. But she held it with a high self-consciousness, according to the dictates of a peculiar teaching and experience. It was felt to be a trust committed to her; and hence it came to be regarded as the condition of Establishment on her side.

It will be necessary, before proceeding farther, to lay down some positions of a more general nature as they are pre-supposed or come to light in every instance of Church Establishment. I shall do little more than state them as fundamental postulates, that I may the sooner come to what is more peculiarly Scottish. The propriety of Ecclesiastical Establishments may be advocated briefly as follows: —

[1] Scots-born Gilbert Burnet (1643–1715) was a philosopher, theologian and historian. He became Bishop of Salisbury and wrote a history of the Reformation of the Church of England in several volumes.—Ed.

The State, considered in its corporate character, is *a moral person*, with a moral standing and responsibility. It is not the creation of the so-called social compact or of the popular will, but a divine institution based on natural religion. It coheres by a moral and religious bond; and its rulers are the lieutenants of God. If the State is a moral person, capable of performing duty, of committing sin, and suffering punishment, which every one must own who traces the fate of nations according to the divine word, it follows that a nation, acting by its rulers, can accept Christianity and make a public profession of it as the national rule and guide. It had been held together previous to the recognition of Christianity by some form of religion however impure, without which it could not have existed. And the first duty of the civil ruler when brought in contact with Christianity and persuaded of its divine origin is to *receive the Bible as a revelation* in a national way. The immediate effect of this is that it constitutes the State a Christian State, and pledges it to purge out its previous religion in the same way as Pagan and Mahommedan nations constituted themselves, according to their false religions, or as the atheistic state was constituted, or rather attempted to be constituted, by the French Convention. A nation must have a religion, and the only question is, which it will adopt. And when Christianity comes to the nation, or to the family, it does not frown on either of these institutions, which also are divine in origin, but enters into them with an elevating purifying power, and sweetly coalesces with all that is purely human in both. These ordinances of God now became vessels by which Christianity is diffused.

The national recognition of the Bible as a revelation subjecting the nation to its authority, though a great step gained, does not exhaust the nation's duty, as widely diverging views prevail upon the right interpretation of the Bible. The State must by the necessity of the case *adopt a creed* which will commonly be prepared by the Church. The same duty that devolves upon the individual Christian confronts a Christian State, and it naturally appends the civil sanction to the Church's creed. It must distinguish between scripture truth and its perversion. The State, by the adoption of a creed, gives utterance to the self-consciousness of a Christian community. It confesses the Christianity it has adopted.

There are several spheres, and in the course of a nation's history there are manifold occasions when the Christian state makes itself felt. Many have long been in the habit of affirming that the normal and proper sphere of state-action in matters of religion is to summon the intermediate action of the Church, without which it cannot competently perform religious rites, and without which sacramental actions cannot duly be celebrated. So far that theory is undoubtedly correct. But there are many actions of a direct and immediate kind that the State must undertake not only when religion is publicly adopted or nationally reformed — and we see both occasions in the history of European nations — but in maintaining the relations of the State to every thing bearing on the purity of religion during the course of ages. Such an immediate mode of State action in reference to Christian education, Sabbath laws, and Christian marriage, is earnestly called for by many advocates of National Christianity in our day, and especially by a noble class of American Christian men who urge upon their country with equal zeal and ability the religious amendment of the constitution. My task will be to show, that in both spheres, there is legitimate scope for the action of a Christian State.

The nation, acting by its rulers, must needs adopt a creed, and so distinguish between truth and error in the confession which it makes. It must be Trinitarian or Unitarian, Protestant or Popish, Calvinistic or Arminian, by the necessity of the position. These diverging lines of profession cannot be ignored. More than that; the responsible rulers must proclaim a Christian constitution and adopt a legislation all through the nation's history upon the principles of revelation. A Christian State is competent to make the same confession of its faith that an individual makes. This is amply confirmed by Church history; for whether we turn our thoughts to nations recently converted from heathenism to Christianity, such as Tahiti and Madagascar, or to our own country emerging from the darkness of Popery, we find that nations have uniformly acted in this way, under the prompting of a Christian instinct. Thus, at the commencement of the Scottish Reformation in 1560, the ministers were requested to draw up and lay before Parliament a summary of the doctrine which they were prepared to maintain as agreeable to scripture. The preparation of that outline was committed to six ministers, including John Knox and the prominent preachers of the Reformation; and in the course of four days the Scottish Confession of Faith was completed and immediately presented. It was publicly read before the whole Parliament, and full permission afforded to object to it if valid objections could be offered. The ministers were present, if need be, to defend the summary which they had prepared, but no exception even in appearance was taken by any party. Knox accordingly declares, 'The true religion according to the word of God, was almost unanimously ratified by the three Estates of the realm at Edinburgh, the seventeenth day of July, the year of God 1560 years.' That was the nation by its rulers confessing the truth, — the national Confession of Faith. That was as it ought to be. The nations and kings that had long given their power to the beast were, in the conscious or unconscious fulfilment of prophecy, transferring that power to the service of him who is King of kings and Lord of lords. The State as an organized community, occupying a moral standing before God, confessed its faith by the adoption of a creed. And in reply to those who hint a doubt or hesitate dislike of all State-action in this form, I reply by demanding — Can we suppose a moral person without a religion or the adequate profession of its faith, more especially in decisive times like those of the Reformation, when such a course is imperatively required by a sense of duty both to God and men? The rulers were required in their official capacity to avow the truth; and the neglect of this would have been a flagrant abandonment of duty.

The next State-action is the recognition of the Church, which no Christian State can ignore. The previous steps may be called the civil establishment of Christianity; this is *the civil establishment of the Church*. The Church may not withdraw or isolate herself from the State which asks her co-operation. It must not be imagined that this is simply equivalent to the endowment of the Church, or that the one idea is absolutely coincident with the other. In point of fact, the Reformed Church of Scotland was Established when the rulers of the land in 1560 ratified the Protestant doctrine, and gave full permission to the Church to exercise her mode of worship, and develop her government without prohibition or impediment; while in reference to national aid or support she continued unendowed till 1567.

Many are taught to look askance or with a pious horror upon any alliance between Church and State, such as is involved in the idea of Establishment. They talk as if the support of the State was dear bought. They imagine that the gospel is strong enough without human aid; and they set forth that the Church becomes the creature of the State if she forms any connection with it. There not only may be, but there ought to be, an alliance between Church and State. The authority as well as model, for that connection between Church and State will be found in the provisions of the Jewish Establishment, the existence of which, by Divine appointment, is conclusive as to the lawfulness of this arrangement. Christian rulers, holding office in a State confessing Christianity, may warrantably imitate, in the spirit of the gospel, what the Supreme Ruler was pleased to institute for his ancient Church. It were profane to call that sinful. Some call it a presumption, and others adduce it as an argument against a civil Establishment, that during the apostolic age and for two full centuries afterwards, no trace occurs of any thing of this nature. The sentiment derived from this — and it is but a sentiment — is, that this silence may be accepted as a directory for the guidance of the Church in all subsequent times in her relations with nations. Had a nation existed which came over from the profession of heathenism to the Christian faith, the apostles would have found it necessary to adjust the relations between Church and State. But every one acquainted with scripture is aware that the application of great principles is developed in connection with historical occasions; and that throughout the scriptures we are furnished with principles, not points. It is obvious that the Church was to be erected amid the world's opposition, and the world was thereby furnished with a proof that human wisdom had not conceived it, and that human power could not subvert it. But to any reflecting mind, a memorable analogy presents itself on comparing the fortunes of the Jewish and Christian

Churches. They were both erected amid a continuous train of miracles to accredit the supernatural economy which gave them birth. But when miraculous aids were suspended, the ordinary aids of civil power in both cases were providentially substituted. Thus, the miraculous intervention which had delivered Israel from Egypt might again have been employed to rescue them from their Babylonian exile. But it was not so; the interposition of the Persian monarchs was used for this effect. And in like manner at the Reformation, when the aid of Christian rulers was enlisted, we see the same principle applied in the emancipation of the Christian Church in every country that embraced the Protestant Faith.

To those who view the Church as holy and designate the State as the world, it is natural to doubt whether Church and State can occupy friendly relations without serious injury to the cause of religion. But that notion springs from a false idea of the State. Far from injury, the civil establishment may be most helpful to the cause of religion. Establishment was intended to be as our Scottish forefathers expressed it — not privative but cumulative — not to deprive the Church of what she had, but to superadd the favour and aid which States can bestow. That the two powers allied and acting under one common Head to whose will they defer, can render mutual aid, is assumed. We may confidently assert a harmony between the two as we do between science and revelation, or between natural and revealed religion. Dr Thomas Chalmers has felicitously said: 'There might be an entire dependence on the State for things temporal, without even the shadow of a dependence in things ecclesiastical. Although the Church should receive its maintenance, and all its maintenance from the civil power, it follows not that it therefore receives its theology from the same quarter; or that this theology should acquire thereby the slightest taint or infusion of secularity.' They are not incapable of combining to a joint result, though different in origin and scope, in their means and instrumentalities; and where they do not stand in the passive attitude of suspicious juxtaposition or cold indifference, which is contrary to the supposition of alliance, their ends are analogous — the temporal interests and eternal welfare of their members. And the promotion of men's spiritual advantage redounds at the next remove to their temporal advantage as citizens. It has always been held in the Protestant Churches and correctly held, that the civil ruler owes manifold and various duties to the Church, and that he accordingly must possess corresponding rights. He has the right of Establishment, the right of Reformation when the Church has grown corrupt, and the right of inspection through all the Church's history in his dominions. The two parties must be faithful to the understood terms of alliance. Our main complaint at present is that Christian rulers act so little or do not act at all. Till the happy event of last session of Parliament[1] they have for

[1] This is a reference to the Church Patronage (Scotland) Act passed by Parliament in 1874. This Act abolished Patronage which had

nearly two centuries taken little or no direct action for the welfare of the Church, to stimulate her efforts, to promote her zeal and reformation, or to encourage her in the various ways which lie to hand for promoting the moral and religious welfare of the community.

The next State-action in behalf of the Church is her *endowment*. We have always maintained that the State, viewed as a moral person, is not less competent than an individual Christian, to offer free-will offerings to him who is the Prince of the kings of the earth. We are prepared to maintain that national funds, given from the national treasury would, if necessary, be competently applied to the purpose of religiously instructing the community. That position may be maintained on various grounds — on the ground of Christ's supremacy and the national subjection to him; on the ground that religion is necessary for the ends of government as well as for right morality; and on the ground of the necessity of preventing the nation from sinking into ignorance and irreligion through the lack of schools and churches.

In point of fact, however, the endowments of the Church, though they are guarded by the authority of the civil ruler, are to be traced to the donations and bequests of individuals for the support of religion. And in the case of the Scottish Church we are relieved from the necessity of discussing the abstract question. Her ministers are not a State-paid clergy. At the Reformation

---

been a serious disruptive issue for the Church in Scotland since the Patronage Act adopted in 1711.—Ed.

a vast amount of ecclesiastical property, the accumulations of a thousand years, and the gifts of pious donors in the cause of Christ, was seized and appropriated by the court and nobility during the confusion of that transition period. Many zealous for the reformed opinions were not less zealous for appropriating money, which only by sacrilege could be alienated from its proper object. That was a serious malversation; for, as Calvin remarks with his wonted felicity — 'What has once been devoted to Christ and the Church is not the property of the magistrate.' After the unmeasured and unscrupulous spoliation in which the court and nobility permitted themselves to indulge, a comparatively insignificant remnant was left. The thirds of benefices according to the arrangement adopted, were assigned to the maintenance of the ministers. That was henceforth reckoned the patrimony of the Church. What was thus allotted to the Church — a mere fragment of the vast amount or property consecrated to religious uses — is in no sense of the word national property any more than a proprietor's estate is national property. The one may be wrested from the owner as well as the other, but in both cases it would be robbery and spoliation. The ministers of the Established Church are not salaried by the State: what they receive is their own. The words of the late Dr Thomas M'Crie,[1] in referring to these funds,

[1] Thomas M'Crie (1772–1835) was a Secession minister and an able Church historian and author. His biographies of Scottish Reformers John Knox (1811) and Andrew Melville (1819) were both acclaimed and

are worthy of quotation: 'If the system of some modern theorists had been adopted, if all laws relating to the Church had at once been swept away, *the ecclesiastical property totally secularized*, and a universal freedom in matters of religion proclaimed, the consequences would have been that many parts of the country would have been thrown destitute of religious instruction and worship; ignorance and crime and atheism would have spread through the land; and within a short time Popish superstition and tyranny would have regained that power which had been wrested from them with such difficulty and at the expense of so much toil and blood. The folly of such a course would scarcely have been less than that of abolishing all public institutions for education and the promoting of learning through the kingdom, and of leaving the object of these to be gained entirely by individual exertion or voluntary association; a measure which would be preposterous and, hurtful at any time, but which, at the period under consideration, would have been productive of ruinous and irremediable mischief.'

This brings me to *the distinctively Scottish theory* of Church Establishments. Many of the topics above delineated are common to all establishments of the Christian Church in various lands. What we have now to notice is peculiar to the Scottish theory. It is commonly assumed by those who have reasoned themselves into

---

influential pieces of work. His sympathies were entirely conservative and Reformed.—Ed.

an attitude of hostility to every form of connection between Church and State, that we must needs accept along with Establishment all those State-Church principles and theories which go associated with the most ill-assorted alliances that can be named, such as those of the English and Continental Churches. But it is not so nor is the Church a mere appendage of the State, existing by its favour and passing into dissolution by its frown. The existence of the Church is one thing, and her civil Establishment another. The Church is no more the appendage or creature of the State when she consents; on right terms, to receive the invaluable boon of a free establishment and an adequate endowment, than the bride in uniting herself freely and with full consent to a consort for life, deserves to be so regarded. The Scottish Church from the first, in entering into alliance with the State, retained a large amount of reserved rights which she held in virtue of the intrinsic jurisdiction imparted by her Lord, and which, if demanded of her, she would not forego nor surrender at the dictation of the State. She retained as an inherent prerogative or inalienable right her independence in spiritual things; and this gave a colour to her whole theory of Establishment, as it also puts into her hand the key of the position on the whole question of Establishment which is now fiercely discussed.

For holding this peculiar theory she has been represented by many as cherishing an illusion, and as retaining a fine unrealized idealism which never could be a reality. She has been described by a German writer as if she clung to an abstraction, and as if it were preposterous to think of a union with the State, and yet insist on the enormous reservations implied in the principle that the Church must remain spiritually free, and her flocks have liberty to choose their pastors. To all these representations the one reply is that this was the Scottish principle which she alone held among the Churches of the Reformation, and from which she never saw cause to depart. It was always held to be the duty of the civil ruler to recognize the true religion, and to support the Christian Church without claiming any jurisdiction in it, or attempting to supersede her distinct government.

A few words will suffice to explain the origin of this peculiarity, — and why it was so tenaciously adhered to on the part of the Scottish Reformers and their successors in Scotland. Of the Protestant Churches the last formed with one exception was that of Scotland. And the Reformers, when they took the necessary steps to digest the doctrines and consolidate the government of the national Church, had before them the defects and advantages of the other Churches of the Reformation. They knew that the princes who had been employed in the overthrow of Popery and in giving the national ratification to the Reformed faith, had in most countries introduced a sort of ecclesiastical supremacy for which scripture gave no warrant; that the German princes bore the title of Chief Bishop; that several Swiss cantons gave magistrates undue authority in what pertained to the external matters of religion and the government of the Church; that the English king, Henry VIII, had gone so far as to assume the title of Head of the Church; and that the common doctrine in England among statesmen and ecclesiastics was that the monarch was, under Christ, sole Head of the Church and supreme in ecclesiastical affairs. Our Reformers were put upon their guard. That the Church should be Established and yet free was the theory for which the Scottish Church was distinguished to her advantage among all the Churches of the Reformation; and from the days of Knox she has been summoned, by a succession of peculiar providences, to raise and to reiterate a noble testimony to that effect.

Many things — did time permit — might be adduced to show how essential in the eyes of the Scottish Church and of the Scottish nation was this peculiar testimony, and that on all sides it was consciously accepted as the condition of Establishment. Thus, when the Papal supremacy was annulled in 1560, not an attempt was made, such as had been made in England, to substitute the ecclesiastical supremacy of the Crown. The title, Head of the Church, applied to the sovereign, could never be endured. When an Episcopal Establishment was again and again set up on the fundamental principle that the king was supreme governor over all persons, and in all causes ecclesiastical, the dissatisfaction of the nation was such that this claim could not be continued. When on the occasion of the last Episcopal Establishment the ecclesiastical supremacy of the Crown was connected with the oath of allegiance at the restoration of Charles II, the ministers laid down their livings in multitudes sooner than swear it. But the testimony supplied by the rescinding of the Act of Supremacy at the revolution in 1690 is absolutely conclusive as to this point — that it was incompatible with the Scottish theory of Establishment. It is said in the Act rescinding it 'that the royal supremacy is inconsistent with the Establishment of Church government now desired.' The following is the Act containing the Declaration of the Scottish Parliament itself after the vain attempts of 120 years to maintain the supremacy: — 'Our Sovereign Lord and Lady, the King and Queen's Majesties, taking into their consideration, that by the Second Article of the Grievances presented to their Majesties by the Estates of this kingdom, it is declared that the First Act of the Second Parliament of King Charles the Second, entitled *Act Asserting His Majesty's Supremacy over all persons and in all causes ecclesiastical*,[1] is inconsistent with the Establishment of the Church government now desired, and ought to be abrogated: therefore their Majesties, with advice and consent of the Estates of Parliament, do hereby abrogate, rescind, and annul the foresaid Act, and declares the same in the whole heads, articles, and clauses thereof, to be of no force or effect in all time coming.' And in keeping with this the Prime Minister in the debates of last session declared that

[1] Act Asserting His Majesty's Supremacy over all persons and in all causes ecclesiastical. At Edinburgh, 16 November, 1669.—Ed.

English notions were not to be applied to the peculiarities of the Scottish Church, because the Queen is not head of the Church of Scotland.

On the prominent place occupied by the idea of independence in all the contendings of the Scottish Church, I cannot do better than quote the words of the late Dr William Cunningham at the commemoration of the Glasgow Assembly of 1638: — 'The Voluntaries talk on this matter,' says Dr Cunningham, 'as if the Established Church had nothing to do with this great principle of the Church's independence — as if they had a monopoly of this great and glorious truth, and as if we had no right to assert it and no right to act upon it. But this truth is contained in God's word, and God has made his word common property. Our Standards have contained these principles from the earliest periods — they held a place there before the Secession and before Voluntaryism existed; and I am persuaded that they will still hold their place when both the Secession and Voluntaryism shall have come to an end. I should like to know what portion of the Christian Church has more interest in this truth, or a better right to proclaim it; and I should like to know what Church has done so much, or half so much, to assert and maintain it, as the Established Church of Scotland. It is in the writings of the men of the Glasgow [1638] and the Westminster Assembly [1643–49] that we are to look for the fullest and clearest explanation of the doctrine of the Church's independence — it is to their exertions that we owe its triumph over the British Isles; and it is to these men we are to look as the most learned and devoted champions of this great and important principle. The Church of Scotland introduced sound views on this principle, even among the English Presbyterians; for they were generally willing to acknowledge the king as supreme governor in all causes, ecclesiastical as well as civil. The Scots would allow him to be supreme over all persons, but not over all causes ecclesiastical. I trust that on these grounds the Church of Scotland will continue to maintain, as she has done for ages, the spiritual independence of the Church of Christ, who is her only Head, while at the same time she asserts with equal zeal and diligence the obligation which is imposed on civil rulers, to aim at promoting the cause of Christ; and contends, in opposition to Voluntary objections, that, an alliance between Church and State does not necessarily involve the subjection of either the one or the other. We also contend, that except in the abomination of lay patronage, which I hope will soon be swept away, our Church has successfully maintained and secured her independence — having full liberty secured by law to proclaim the whole truth of God, to perform all the duties which Christ imposed on his Church, and to administer all the ordinances which he has appointed and which he has promised to bless.'

A question of pressing importance here presents itself: Can we affirm, in the light of recent legislation, that the Scottish theory which we have been describing is in any considerable measure realized? Yes: the unexpected has happened. Any lingering hope I cherished as to the resuscitation of the old and venerated constitution of the Scottish Church had well-nigh faded away from my mind. Such was the intensity of my affection for the old historic Church of Scotland that I often said with Thomas M'Crie: 'I would go seven times to the top of her highest mountain to look out for the harbinger of her relief.' It has come, and I am filled with joy and gratitude to him who is Lord of all. I hope the Church will have combined faithfulness and wisdom to use it aright. Nor has the harassing conflict which we maintained upwards of thirty years ago with the civil courts, and which issued in our separation or ejection from the pale of the Establishment been in vain. It has been overruled in the inscrutably mysterious Providence of God, to win for the Church the legislative recognition of her liberties. It has tended in a variety of ways to which I shall not more specially refer, to show the necessity and safety of passing the Act which has reversed the captivity of the Scottish Church, and is destined, whether men like it or not, to have a most important influence on Scotsmen and Scotland for ages to come.

A few words will serve to prove that the Established Church is replaced in all the privileges and immunities secured by the Revolution Settlement. And if this can be made evident, the conclusion at which we must arrive is, that she stands on a platform of freedom with the freest, with this additional advantage that it is a constitutionally-secured and legally-protected freedom. And a clear exhibition of this is imperatively called for in the interests of truth, and in opposition to the unmeasured and persistent misrepresentations of those who ought to know better. In the first place, it cannot be denied that, the yoke of patronage which was riveted on the Church for 160 years, and caused one secession and disruption after another, is totally removed. The man who calls this in question is not to be reasoned with, but pitied. As little can it be denied, according to the terms of the Act, that every question arising in connection with the settlement of ministers is to be decided finally and conclusively by the Church courts, and that the possibility of appeal is thus precluded.

But though this is conceded, as it must be by intelligent men, it is contended by certain parties eager to gain the ear of the community, that the adverse decisions of the civil courts professedly based upon the Act of Queen Anne,[1] which no longer exists, can still be used as legal precedents to warrant the same unlimited right of interference which was previously exercised to the Church's injury. It is not so. The Church now stands on Scottish ground. She has got back her old constitution to which

[1] Church Patronage (Scotland) Act, 1711. The decisions in the civil courts alluded to here refers to various issues arising in the ten years before the Disruption of 1843. There were crucial decisions in court actions involving the Church in Auchterarder (1838–43), Lethendy (1839), and Strathbogie (Marnock) (1839–43). See, Francis Lyall, *Of Presbyters and Kings* (Aberdeen: Aberdeen University Press, 1980), especially Chapter 3.—Ed.

the faith of treaties was pledged without a fragment of the treacherous legislation superinduced upon it and subverting it by the Act of Anne. The civil courts which pushed the binding and astricting clause of the Act 1592[1] to an extreme unwarranted by the other provisions of the constitution, are now precluded from interference. That is the true, the only independence of the Church in the eye of the civil law — when the State by her own action shuts out her courts from the ecclesiastical province; that is, from interfering in spiritual things; and beyond all doubt that is now secured.

But here it is incumbent on me to obviate a twofold objection originating in mistake or in exaggerated statement.

1. Outside the pale of the Establishment the general impression was, and still is, that at the time of the Disruption [1843] the Terms of Establishment were altered, and that new and irrevocable conditions were imposed. I shared in that conviction, and it does not seem to me that the party with which I acted in that momentous movement could have arrived at any other conclusion. This conviction is recorded in the documents which are the constitution of the Church which we formed separate from the State. An appeal was made to the State to alter the law, of which the interpretation was now found to be intolerable; and when the State was silent or declined to act, the only inference we could

[1] Act for abolisheing of the actis contrair the trew religioun, 1592, c.8. (See: www.legislation.gov.uk/aosp/1592/8/paragraph/p1).—Ed.

draw was that the condition on which we could retain the benefits of the Establishment was the interpretation given by the courts, and that this was irreversible. But while that sufficed to determine our duty and ejected us, it did not mean that these relations must for ever remain, like the laws of the Medes and Persians, unalterable. That construction which we put, and could not but put, on the conditions of Establishment, was not absolute. It was capable of modification when the relations were changed. It was not unalterable in the event of a new state of things, or of the restoration of the previous connection between Church and State, such as has anew entered into history. To suppose the opposite is to confound the judicial and legislative functions. In point of fact, during the whole period of the collision which issued in the Disruption, the State did nothing. She abstained from doing, and acted the part of a spectator when a remedy was possible. Though in an ethical point of view I do not exculpate the State, yet, in a legislative sense, it did no more than abstain from action. She left things to take their course, the issue of which could not be doubtful. One must succumb to the other; and in that unequal conflict the weaker must give way. But it is an inexcusable confounding of spheres essentially distinct, to make the legislative and the judicial identical. The State as such imposed no new conditions of Establishment, though her declinature to act left no alternative to the Scottish clergy. But the obnoxious law is now removed, and collision cannot occur again.

2. Another objection is, that spiritual independence in the abstract is not conceded to the Church. This I answer by demanding, Does not the Confession of Faith, to which our theologians have deferred from the days of Henderson, Gillespie, and Rutherford,[1] set forth the rounded outline of the doctrine of the Church's independence? Does it say nothing when it asserts the sole Headship of Christ (chapter 25:6); when it declares the distinct Government instituted by him in the hand of church-officers (chapter 30:1); when it postulates the existence of ecclesiastical as well as civil powers (chapter 20:4); when it marks out an ample sphere for the action and determinations of synods and councils (chapter 31:3)? It must be allowed that all this doctrine of the Confession is ratified by the civil sanction because the Confession is itself so ratified; consequently, that independence is secured to the Church by Revolution Settlement, by the ratification of the Confession,[2] and by the Treaty of Union, without the hazard of any intervening and obstructing influence. The true doctrine of independence is that of the Confession of Faith, in

[1] Alexander Henderson (1583–1646), George Gillespie (1613–48) and Samuel Rutherford (1600–61) were prominent Presbyterian ministers in Scotland in the seventeenth century. They were all members of the Westminster Assembly of divines (1643–49). For biographical detail see the relevant entries in the *Dictionary of Scottish Church History & Theology* (Edinburgh: T&T Clark, 1993).—Ed.

[2] See, The Confession of Faith Ratification Act, 1690. This Act of Parliament is the key to the Revolution Settlement in relation to Church and State.—Ed.

other words, the doctrine of co-ordinate jurisdiction, or of the distinct government of the Church; and we will not permit a new interpretation to be given to it on the part of those whose obvious aim is to render an Establishment impossible. Thus, to give an instance of what it may be necessary to oppose, the Dissenters, in replying to the friendly address by ministers of the Church of Scotland, before the Disruption, took up the following arbitrary theory of independence. 'The Church, as an Established Church,' said they, 'has no power to review or to alter the Standard-books without the authority of the power by which they are legalized? *Is this freedom? Is this independence?*' To which I answer, That is an attempt to insinuate an ultramontane independence[1] — an independence which I do not accept and never desire to see in any Church; established or non-established, an independence, of attained doctrine, and of a Church's constitution — a dishonesty, a tyranny. The only independence worthy of the name is liberty to be loyal to Christ, *freedom from civil control,* to act according to the Standards, and constitution of the Church, and not in violation of them.

It only remains to inquire after the exposition already given what duty devolves on the Scottish Churches

[1] *Ultramontane* originally referred to advocacy of supreme papal authority in matters of faith and discipline. In this context, the reference is to the exercise of centralized civil authority over against local independence, in matters of faith and discipline.—Ed.

which owed their rise to the Establishment[1] — though separated from her? As they collected numbers and resources by the profession of adherence to her doctrine, worship, discipline, and government — and as they justified their origin by appealing to a reforming General Assembly from within, or demanding a restoration of her violated constitution from without, an explanation is required, if they resolve to stand on a platform essentially changed. Had they continued moored to their early principles, it would not be hard, at the present favourable juncture in Scottish history, to re-adjust ecclesiastical relations on the old foundations.

But for union in one organisation the Churches plainly are not ripe. Much has yet to intervene. And after my experience of the utter failure of a projected scheme of Union,[2] which looked fair at the commencement, but only scattered mischief and disaster the further it proceeded, I and many like-minded, will look with wary circumspection on humanly concocted schemes of union to which men are not naturally led by events in history and openings in Providence. From all I have experienced and read on the subject of ecclesiastical

[1] This refers to the various Secession Churches of the eighteenth century and to the Free Church of Scotland which arose from the Disruption of 1843.—Ed.

[2] This refers to the first Union controversy that plunged the Free Church into controversy from 1863 to 1873. The issue related to moves for union between the Free Church and other non-established Presbyterian Churches which arose from various Secessions in the eighteenth century.—Ed.

union, my firm conviction is, that unless the Churches negotiating with this end in view go back to their starting-point and imbibe the principles, aims, and objects of their early days, or when they took their rise, there never can be union either satisfactory or lasting. There only can they unite. It may be that another generation, impatient of the ecclesiastical broils, and petty jealousies now in the ascendant, may take the matter into its own hand, and effect a union on the old foundation of the historic Church of Scotland. To that all my inclinations tend; and admiring as I have ever done from youth that admirable constitution, I have no objection to it in principle, if it were fully understood that the Standards of the Church of Scotland are to be carried out in their spirit and provisions. But the Churches as Churches are not ripe.

Meantime they might have joint-action to a common end. There might be, as in the relations of the United States, a *confederation* of the Churches, leaving the organization of the several bodies, as it is at present. Were a confederation of the Scottish Presbyterian Churches wisely carried out, the happiest results might come out of it. They each contributed to educate the Scottish mind, as they each represent an idea; and in prayerfully and kindly prosecuting what is practicable in the meantime, they might, ere long, be prepared for further adjustments. Need I say how much better such a course of action would be than the combination of two Churches to subvert and crush the third?

This brings me to examine that other alternative with which I can have no sympathy — the cry for *disestablishment.* This project is advocated in some quarters, as if by cruel mockery, in the interest of union, and as the way to union. Men have surely unlearned all their philosophy or knowledge of mankind who speak in terms so incoherent. The scheme of disestablishment is argued by some as a corollary from the voluntary position that the power competent to worldly kingdoms is wholly temporal, respecting only the secular interests of society — a position not warranted by a single text of scripture, and which every text condemns. It is argued again, though most illogically by the Free churchman, whose ordination vows bind him inflexibly to the Establishment principle, on the ground that the present Establishment is liable to grave objection. But from the Free Church principle, which asserts the obligation of national Christianity and the duty of rulers to true religion and the Church, no rational being can draw any other inference but this, that the ecclesiastical Establishment where it is faulty and defective through the rust of ages, ought to be corrected and reformed. But to test the latter style of argument, we have only to demand what is to be substituted for the present Establishment and wait for a reply. The simple fact that no substitute is even named is conclusive as to the significance and scope of every portion of that plea.

The remarks of the late Hugh Miller[1] on a proposal of this nature made in 1847, are so appropriate and forcible that I cannot but make room for them: — 'It earnestly urges them, if they wish effectually to prevent the endowment of Popery, to join the Voluntaries in a vigorous attack on all the existing Establishments of the empire. Now, this advice I deem so singularly unwise and dangerous that on no account could I be induced to second it in the *Witness.* Whether right or wrong in my convictions, I am at least thoroughly convinced that it would have the effect, if acted upon, of placing *the great Protestant front of the empire in a fatally false position*, and would, besides, be peculiarly injurious to the Free Church.

(1) In the first place, a war with the Establishments would have the inevitable effect of cutting off the earnest Protestantism of our own body from the earnest Protestantism of the English and Irish Churches; and be it remembered that in these Churches, notwithstanding their signal faultiness as Establishments, there are very many truly excellent men who are doing what the Voluntaries have long since forgotten to do — honestly maintaining a consistent protest against Popery.

(2) In the second place, it would have the effect of arraying on the side of Popish endowment a numerous

[1] Hugh Miller (1802–56) was a journalist and amateur geologist from Cromarty in Scotland. He was actively engaged in the controversies out of which the Free Church of Scotland emerged as a separate Presbyterian denomination in 1843.—Ed.

class who now stand neutral, men who — like the ministers of the Scottish Establishment, and the men clerical and lay of a corresponding character in England and Ireland — have a large secular stake involved in the question, and who much rather than that Establishment should fall altogether were they to find them assailed in the mass, would unite in calling in to their assistance and support the seven millions of Popish Ireland.

(3) In the third place we have, I think, direct evidence that though *the war against Popery is* in its effects on those who prosecute it *an eminently safe war, the war against Establishments is not*; never, at least, was the Church more spiritual than when she was warring against Popery — never did any Church in any controversy become more thoroughly secular than the Voluntaries of Scotland when warring against Establishments.

(4) In the fourth place while the *war against Popery would be strictly constitutional, the war against Establishments would not*; it would of necessity endanger with the assailed institutions not a few precious remnants of the Revolution Settlement in which no class have a larger stake than we; and it is, besides, a grave question whether the Free Church would not lose immensely more by *forfeiting the esteem of all solid men hostile to a position so decidedly revolutionary* than she could possibly gain through any consequent accession to the number of her allies from the ranks of the restless and the dissatisfied.

(5) In the fifth place, such a war as the Doctor desiderates would justly lay our Church open if waged ere the present generation passed away, to *a charge of gross and suspicious inconsistency*; seeing he recommends it should be a war carried on not simply on mere considerations of expediency, which may lead at various times to various courses of conduct, but also on a strictly religious principle, a principle which, if sound at all, must have been as much so ten years ago during the heat of the Voluntary controversy, as it is now; and seeing further that though since that time the Scottish Establishment has been revolutionized and degraded, no change has taken place in the constitution and government of the English and Irish Establishments, both of which were, in the course of the controversy, strenuously defended.

(6) And in the sixth and last place, I deem it all too obvious that the Voluntaries would not as a body be heartily our allies in the conflict.'

The crusade against Establishments, whether we think of its renewal in present circumstances, or weigh the merits of the agitation at any time, deserves the sternest reprobation. As to the circumstances in which the cry is now raised, the meaning must be — That the freer an Established Church becomes, so much the greater is the argument for its destruction. Why is this? Is it because the sects must have a vested right in the corruptions of the Establishment that they may continue to appeal to them as arguments for separation? or is it a dread lest the Establishment should have a fair field and full scope, and commend itself as a better method? There are two or three grounds on which I condemn in the strongest terms the present crusade as wild and mischievous; and of course it will be understood that my allusions are to the principles, not to the men.

1. *It proposes to substitute a non-religious state* — that is, a state purely secular, without a religion and without a creed — for the Christian state, which, as all historians allow, is the fountain of modern culture and refinement. The Confession of Faith would be expunged in Scotland, and the Thirty-nine Articles in England as the national creed — a creed which has brought a blessing on the Empire. No man can be permitted to deny this issue on the allegation that he means it not. He may not intend in its corporate character the State shall be infidel, but it is not a question of intentions. He subjects himself to the inexorable logic of a class of principles which are wild and irreligious, and he will be swept before them like chaff before the wind. From their very nature they are a universal act rescissory as to the laws which regulate religious education, the observance of the Sabbath, the purity of marriage, and the religious character of all our institutions; and what is this but the official infidelity of an atheistic State? Never till the dawn of the French Revolution[1] did this theory gain much attention or influence. For though we find it among the Anabaptists, the Quakers, and the untaught

[1] The French Revolution took place between 1789 and 1799.—Ed.

fanatical sects of the Commonwealth time — men who regarded the State as belonging to the empire of the evil power — it never menaced the institutions of the Christian state till the fury and impiety of the French Revolution insinuated themselves into other nations. The heathen philosophers, Plato and Cicero, speak with a deeper view of the religious character of States than Voluntary divines commonly evince. We are naturally led to enquire, What description of person must be the ideal ruler of the Voluntary theory, if that theory should ever be reduced to practice in any unhappy country? The answer can only be, that in order to be *a model ruler* he must needs be *a bad man* — a man denuded of the fear of God, for whom all religions are alike, and none worthy of encouragement.

2. *This movement would neutralize the oath sworn by Sovereign and Parliament to the Constitution.* In a word, it proposes what amounts to the most revolting perjury. And the audacity of the proposal to subvert the British Constitution in its choicest and most sacred part should be enough to render it innocuous to all reflecting men. How Christian ministers, or any man not dieted in revolutionary violence, can cherish projects simply destructive without any thing constructive, or welcome that scene of universal perjury civil and ecclesiastical, surpasses my conception.

3. *This disestablishment movement proposes the wholesale confiscation of Church property, and would be, if it succeeded, the consecration of sacrilege.* There is such a

thing as sacrilege, when property, devoted to God, and held to be the Church's patrimony, is alienated to a secular purpose by the State, or seized by avaricious men. The words of the Second Book of Discipline, prepared under the direction of Andrew Melville,[1] emphatically declare: — 'To take any of this patrimony by unlawful means, and convert it to the particular and profane use of any person, we hold it a detestable sacrilege before God!' If we consult the views of the Reformers — Martin Luther, John Calvin, Martin Bucer, Jerome Zanchius — or any of the more copious expounders of the eighth commandment, we find the alienation of the Church's patrimony, which they sometimes call the patrimony of Christ, denounced as the chief or culminating sin against that precept of the decalogue. It was the sin of Achan. Men in our day, however, not knowing what they say nor whereof they affirm, harangue with the utmost coolness on that sacrilegious project of surrendering the Church's annual income of £300,000, which just means, when stripped of the tawdry declamation, putting it into the pockets of the proprietors, who do not want it. That would amount to a very large capital sum; and I may say that this, along with glebe-lands, manses, garden ground, and unexhausted

[1] Andrew Melville (1545–1622) was a successor to John Knox in furthering the cause of Reformation and Presbyterianism in Scotland. The *Second Book of Discipline* was completed and adopted by the church in Scotland in 1578.—Ed.

teinds,[1] would form a capital sum of between nine and ten millions sterling. That is the Church's patrimony, and she holds it by a title equal to that by which any noble holds his lands. She holds it by a sacred tenure, if men will treat the subject aright. I will not believe that Scotsmen will be guilty of the consummate folly and infatuation of throwing all that property away for the sake of airing a mischievous and irreligious theory. If so, I will despair of my Scottish fellow-countrymen. For my part, I will defend, as far as in me lies, the sacredness of those endowments which were set apart by pious ancestors as the Church's patrimony, and which for three centuries have been protected by the law of the land, as the means of providing religious instruction to the people of the various parishes.

As to the revival of the Voluntary agitation in the present day for the overthrow of ecclesiastical Establishments, it recalls to me the early days of my ministry, when a similar agitation convulsed the country. The question was then discussed with the utmost keenness and singular power. The subject was new; the arguments were fresh, such as they cannot be again. Men were a little taken by surprise when they found themselves surrounded by an unlooked-for outburst of Anti-Reformation and revolutionary principles which, it soon appeared, had long been smouldering in secret,

[1] *Teinds* is the name given in Scotland to tithes or strictly to that part of the estates of the laity which is liable to be assessed for the stipend of the clergy of the established church.—Ed.

though the existence of them was known only to a few. It so happened that at the time when the agitation became violent, and assumed rather formidable dimensions, men occupying the foremost place as orators, historians, and controversialists, and justly regarded as among the ablest whom the country ever produced, were ready to confront it. The literature to which the discussion gave rise from the hand of Dr Thomas Chalmers, Dr Thomas M'Crie, Dr William Cunningham, Dr James Gibson,[1] and others, still exists and can be consulted to advantage. Much of it may be, and should be reproduced, to meet the present necessity. The doctrine of Establishments was examined in every light in which it could be placed. It was canvassed on grounds of scripture and on grounds of expediency; surveyed by the light of history and by the results of experience; weighed by their tendency to affect the interests of the Church, and to promote the welfare of the nation. Men took their sides, and the conclusions to which they came cannot be reversed.

When we trace the issue of the controversy historically, it does not admit of doubt, that after a ten years' arduous effort — from AD 1830 to 1840, during which time it burned most fiercely — the agitation for disestablishment egregiously failed to convince the reason or to satisfy the conscience of the nation. They who lived

[1] See the relevant entries for these nineteenth century Scottish Presbyterian divines in the *Dictionary of Scottish Church History & Theology*, 1993.—Ed.

as I did through the period, and can recall almost every part of it and every movement, are well aware that the Voluntary agitators had the worst of the argument; that far from winning the assent of the community, they discredited their cause by extravagant opinions as to the relation of the civil magistrate to religion in any form, and that the positions which the representatives of the party took up were deemed unworthy of sober and reverent expositors of scripture. Their countrymen felt that they had failed; and that in their extreme views as to the purely secular character of states, they were not in harmony with the dictates of either natural or revealed religion. Men of long views, moreover, who were in the habit of putting principles and their fruits together, reflected that the country had had the opportunity for upwards of a century of surveying what had been accomplished by Nonconformity, both in England and Scotland. They saw that it had manifested a considerable amount of an ungenerous, selfish, and narrow spirit; and they were satisfied that when tried by its fruits, as every system must consent to be, it bore no comparison to the lofty, heroic, uncompromising, and self-sacrificing Christianity of the representative men — the Scottish worthies — who adorned the Established Church during both the first and second Reformations.[1] Nor was the type of the Voluntary Nonconformists of that day in any one respect superior, if equal, to the

[1] Respectively taken as 1560 and 1638.—Ed.

men who ministered in the Scottish Establishment. There might be much of the self-complacent sect-life; but there was nothing of the noble effort of the Scottish witnesses of an earlier day, to bring a Covenanted nation as an offering to the Lord.

What may be the effect of the revived agitation it would be premature to say. For my own part I anticipate that it will have still less success; partly because the arguments have not the former novelty; partly because exceptions taken to practical corruptions and abuses, and to the *personnel* of the Establishment have little weight when the undeniable fact remains that the old constitution of the Establishment is restored. The constitution under which she acts is that defined by herself, and errors of administration are incident to every system.

Sir, I have done. On an occasion such as this, I might perhaps take leave to send my congratulations to the Established Church of Scotland, and add a hope that her courts and members will serve themselves heirs to their inheritance of liberty. The Church is free and independent: let her breathe that freedom, and *declare herself*, as other Churches expect she will, *in possession of that independence*. No lingering remains of a servile spirit, often the accompaniment and ill effect of having been in servitude, will, I trust, be found adhering to her.

But while I rejoice in the restored constitution of the old historic Church of Scotland, no less importance attaches to the spirit which is to animate it. And feeling her corporate identity with the Church of past times, she ought to enter on a new career with gratitude, humility, and full confession of sins. I shall not refer to the sin of ejecting the Seceders, and those who became the Church of the Relief, nor to the sin of ejecting us — for had the Moderate party gone along with us, there would have been no Disruption, and a powerful Evangelical Church would have been rejoicing in the liberty now given at last. I refer to the sin of past unfaithfulness, of legal preaching, and of that perversion of the gospel known as Moderatism, which ran counter to all that was peculiar to the gospel as a dispensation of grace, and displayed a secular disposition of mind. For that long period, which I well remember, there ought to be deep humiliation on the part of the Church with an effort to purge out the old leaven. The old Moderate type may be extinct, while its spirit has migrated and is active in new forms. And the modern type of doctrine — with its superficial views of sin and law — of the substitution of Christ, imputed righteousness, and the new birth — may be working equal havoc and ruin. I remember the happy day when Evangelical doctrine triumphed, when Thomas Chalmers, the greatest pulpit orator of this century, thundered with Demosthenic power in this city, and when Andrew Thomson and Robert Gordon in Edinburgh made any other doctrine than the gospel of God's grace to be discountenanced. I hope to see similar days return to the Establishment.

Nor should the Established Church be unduly solicitous about heterogeneous unions unless they are honourably and naturally brought about. Better than these will be the revival of the true worship and doctrine, of the true zeal and activity of her early days. She is put back to her old constitution; let her imbibe the spirit of the Scottish worship without the sensational innovations and appliances of the present superficial age. Happy will it be if the Church is faithful to her standards, and true to her traditions. On many accounts she is exposed to the temptation of looking to English ritualism and English modes of worship, and thinking it well to take a sort of mimetic attitude, or the place of a parasitic plant. By this she will only gain harm and loss. She has no occasion to be ashamed of her past, or to apologize for her Scottish individuality, if only the evangelical spirit is eagerly and zealously diffused through all the peculiarities that past history has stamped upon her as distinctively her own. The Church, if true to her divine Head, has nothing to fear. She will, by devotedness and faith and prayer collect her energies, and be able to meet her enemies in the gate. She has already again and again overcome by the blood of the Lamb and the word of her testimony.

12

A Faithful Minister of Christ[1]

Who is for you a faithful minister of Christ.
—Colossians 1:7

Dear Friends, I have selected this text as suitable to the occasion. The death of your beloved pastor, and the wide-spread sense of loss in the removal of such a man, make thousands and tens of thousands mourn along with you. His decease makes the Church poorer. The memory of his consistent, manly, inflexible career, amid a vacillating age, makes us sadly to realize what we have lost. Another outstanding figure in the ranks of those who, at the Disruption, testified for great truths has passed away from the midst of us — one on whom his brethren leant in the day of trial with full confidence, and who never failed them. Wherever the true ecclesiastical principles

[1] A Sermon preached in Free St Matthew's Church, Bath Street, Glasgow, on the occasion of the death of the Rev. Samuel Miller, D.D., on the forenoon of Sabbath, 10 July, 1881. Samuel Miller (1810–81) was ordained in the Church of Scotland at Monifieth in 1835. He entered the Free Church at the Disruption (1843) and in 1844 was translated to Free St Matthew's, Glasgow, from which he 'retired' in 1875, continuing as senior minister until his passing in 1881. In the controversies of the day he was invariably on the conservative, or constitutionalist, side.—Ed.

of the Scottish branch of the Protestant Church were asserted, wherever the deepest aspirations and genuine sentiments of scriptural religion were to be maintained, you were safe in counting on him. Alas! we shall hear his voice and see his well-known form no more. But he shall stand in his lot at the end of the days.

Brethren, this epistle, from which the text is taken, was addressed to a congregation that had been planted some years before in Colosse, a city of some importance not far from Laodicea and Hierapolis. It is usually supposed, from the allusion at the beginning of the second chapter, that the apostle Paul was not the immediate founder of that Church. During three years residence at Ephesus the apostle had the opportunity of meeting many from the surrounding districts, so that all who dwelt in Asia heard the word, and Epaphras, to whom honourable testimony is borne in the text, appears to have been the founder of this Church, which flourished brightly for a time, and, like the other Apostolic churches, was ere long menaced with erroneous doctrines.

The arch-enemy, who never lets a pure church continue long without sowing tares in it, inflated them with a desire for higher knowledge, and false teachers alleged a connection with a spirit-world very different from that which Scripture opens to our view. They boasted of science, falsely so called, and seem to have been the precursors of a tendency which developed into the Gnostic errors, and put to hazard the way of salvation by Jesus Christ. As to their views, we trace in the Epistle two or three points of their system. Their teaching erred in reference to the person and office of Christ: — First, they had no true idea of Christ's divine person as supplying all the objective knowledge of God which it is possible for us to reach; second, they dilated on an order of angels which the apostle denounces as a voluntary humility and worshipping of angels (chapter 2:18). Instead of Christ's sole mediatorship, they brought in a host of mediators between them and the One Mediator between God and man, indulging a prurient love of transcendental science which lay beyond their ken, and left the question of sin and redemption in the background.

In refutation of these views, which tended to lower Christ and exalt the angels, the apostle points to the Eternal Son by whom all things were created that are in heaven, and that are in earth, visible and invisible, whether they be thrones or dominions, principalities or powers; extolling Christ as the Creator, the first begotten from the dead, in all things bearing the pre-eminence (chapter 1:18). He renders it clear that other mediators are superfluous, and can have no existence. He warns the Colossians against being spoiled by philosophy and vain deceit (chapter 2:8). The asceticism, which went along with these pretentious claims to higher knowledge, he exposes as contrary to the true spirituality and liberty of the gospel, which repudiates the bondage of such maxims as they applied to the distinctions of meats and drinks 'touch not, taste not, handle not' (chapter 2:21).

In opposition to these views the apostle brings out (1) the dignity and glory of the Lord Jesus. He gives a positive statement of his Supreme Deity and Mediatorial office, showing that Christ is the Head, and that the Church is his body. (2) He throws his apostolic shield over the doctrine, teaching, and pastoral fidelity of Epaphras, whose hands were weakened, and he sends Tychicus, who would confirm the truth against the seductive arts and erroneous views of those false teachers to whom the epistle alludes. The epistle seems to have been written during Paul's imprisonment of two years in Rome.

I wish you to notice his commendation of Epaphras — 'A faithful minister of Christ.'

With regard to the names of office for the Christian minister, some are delivered from the relation in which the pastor stands to the Church, and others from the relation in which he stands to the Lord himself. As to the official names which have relation to the Church we find that they are called teachers, shepherds, ministers, labourers, builders, building stone upon stone on the one foundation, which is Christ. As to the names which are applied to them from their relation to Christ, they are designated friends of the Bridegroom, preachers, servants, stewards of the mysteries of the kingdom, ambassadors coming forth to their fellow-men, on behalf of God, and beseeching them in Christ's stead to be reconciled to God. I refer to these designations, the rather because many in former and recent times think they do well to deny that a minister speaks with authority.

Several titles of ministers adduced in this epistle will serve better than any more general reflections to exhibit the nature of the ministerial commission. Of these we shall mention the following three taken from this first chapter, namely, 'ministers of Christ' (verse 7); second, 'ministers of the Church' (verse 25); third, 'ministers of the word' (verse 23), and, while we speak of these points in order, may that Almighty Spirit, who alone can give efficiency to the word spoken, be poured out on us abundantly.

1. *First of all then, according to this order, one title descriptive of their commission is 'ministers of Christ.'*

The idea of being Christ's property and of being sent by him is the most common in the prophetic and apostolic Scriptures. It pervades the oracles of God, it lends to the Lord's servants all that lofty superiority to worldly influences which they display. The thought 'the Lord hath sent me and will not abandon his commissioned servant,' supplies an intrepidity in the discharge of duty and a promptitude to confront the world's opposition, which puts them for the most part above temptation to accommodation and compromise of any kind. What we trace in apostles and martyrs is seen in men called to the ordinary work of the ministry. It was this that fitted John Knox to confront a hostile Court and made him a conspicuously faithful minister, neither to be seduced by its allurements nor frightened by its frown.

But along with the thought that ministers are called and sent, there is associated the further conviction that they are but instruments in a higher hand. Nothing is man's but the labour. The tendency to self-complacency is swallowed up in a feeling of dependence, which is the secret of their strength, and in a salutary fear, lest he 'who resisteth the proud but giveth grace to the humble' should cease to use the instrument any longer; and to bring Paul to this dependence, he was often reduced to such straits that he despaired even of life, that he might learn not to trust in himself but in God 'who raiseth the dead' (2 Cor. 1:8, 9).

One additional explanation is required. The commission involved in this title does not imply that God puts those blessings which constitute ministerial success out of his hand, or deposits them in the hand of his ministers. They cannot at will impart conversion or pardon. They cannot confer the spirit or dispense regeneration at their discretion. These blessings are not committed to men but retained in the hand of God, and given by him, through whom he will and to whom he will; and it becomes the ministers of Christ to acquiesce in this, and to proclaim it. They are servants, not lords. They are preachers, not dispensers of salvation. They proclaim the salvation, they cannot give it.

And yet there is one point in the order of connection between the preaching which God prescribes and the blessing which God bestows, to which we do well to advert. It is the preaching of Christ crucified that is expressly called 'the power of God' (1 Cor. 1:24): not the inculcation of a mere ethical system, not religious forms or ritualism, not mere sentiment or philosophy, but the preaching of Christ crucified is the power of God.

It is one important thought constantly adduced by Christ when speaking of his servants, that they are to follow him. Thus he says, 'If any man will come after me let him deny himself and take up his cross and follow me' (Matt. 14:34); and again, 'If any man serve me, let him follow me; and where I am, there shall also my servant be' (John 12:26). From these directions it is clear that they are to follow his example as a teacher, to follow him in bearing their cross, to follow him by drinking into the same spirit with him.

(1) I say, first, *they are to follow his example as a teacher.* The method he adopted in teaching; the order and nature of the truth in public instruction, the expansion of it in the narrower circle of his apostles, are all significant. He sought to bring men to stand in the presence and under the eye of the Holy Law-giver. This is evident to every attentive reader of his history, whether we recall the preaching of repentance with which his ministry began, or the Sermon on the Mount. A few words will show the importance of following the Great Teacher in his method, especially in the case of those who find it hard to take in abstract truth, but are susceptible of an appeal to moral sensibilities. Nor is this of less importance in

the case of men in the transition state to unbelief. A sceptic, rejecting the grounds on which Christianity rests, is often reached by awakening his moral nature, by an exposition of the purity and holiness of the moral law, by exhibiting the distinction between good and evil, right and wrong, in the light of the divine perfections.

(2) Then I say secondly, *they follow him in taking up their cross* (Matt. 16:34), his disciples served him and followed him in his course of self-denial, however different their work might be from his. 'If any man serve me let him follow me,' that is, 'if any man shall be my disciple in the full acceptation of the term, let him prepare himself for something very different from a life of carnal ease.'

What does the Lord mean by taking up our cross, or bearing our cross? The origin of the figure may be traced to the Roman custom of compelling the party sentenced to crucifixion to bear his cross to the place of execution. This, be it noticed, is the disciple's cross, not Christ's cross. Christ's cross as the surety of sinners was unique. His substitution could be shared by none. His satisfaction was his own peculiar work. This cross that we speak of is the Christian's cross. But it must be borne in mind that he undergoes it simply as he is a follower of Christ and for no other cause. 'He fills up,' as the apostle expresses it, 'what is behind of the sufferings of Christ,' and they who suffer with him shall also be glorified together; they are co-sufferers, and finally co-glorified — no cross, no crown.

When it is called the disciple's cross the words imply that every disciple is summoned to bear a cross peculiar to that individual. It is not another's; every one receives his own. As every Christian has a peculiar portion of earthly goods, more or less, as to the Great Disposer seems meet, and as every one has his own peculiar history assigned to him, so each receives his cross, and it becomes him to say, 'This is my allotted history, and it is sent for the two-fold purpose of glorifying Christ by my sincerity, and of weaning me from undue attachment to transitory things; it is mine and I must bear it; shall I decline to lay upon my shoulders what was destined for me by my Father from of old? what will it avail to discover a froward reluctance to comply with what is sent?' The Christian's cross has this peculiarity, that it must be spontaneously assumed. In other sufferings a man exercises no choice, he is involved in sickness, calamity, adversity, apart from any discretion of his own. But in the bearing of his cross he is a consenting party, though he cannot recede if he would be faithful to his Lord. Thus Moses acted when he abandoned the splendours of the palace and the court of Pharaoh, esteeming the reproach of Christ greater riches than all the treasures of Egypt.

(3) But again, thirdly, *they follow him by drinking into the same spirit with him; and by looking to his example*. What is that example? Brethren, while majesty or complete greatness in all its parts is the impression made upon us, it is of a kind so absolutely new and

so unprecedented, that every mind devoid of a spiritual sense is insensible to the glory of Christ's character. But let me more particularly evolve one or two of the distinguishing features of Christ's moral perfection: —

(i) First, his greatness was in condescension. He laboured not to rise aloft. He was the lowly one and the abased. His public was not the stage of human opinion, but the eye of an omnipresent Father, before whom all human distinctions are little, nay, utterly contemptible. Humility is the basis of the Christian system and the true foundation of all Christian ethics; and agreeably to this peculiarity of Christ's religion, his dignity was veiled in abasement, and found its expression in the words, 'I am among you as one that serveth.'

(ii) Again, there was no disturbance of the calm equanimity which had its everlasting temple in his soul as in his native element. Nothing moved him from his path or disturbed his calm self-control, and he describes the inner harmony of his feelings when he says, 'Peace I leave with you, my peace I give unto you.' Nor was the harmony to which we have adverted disturbed in the opposite conditions of action and suffering. We see on the one hand how he solicited in Gethsemane the company of his disciples, as if he had a nature which asked for human sympathy, and which was consoled by that sympathy when it was enjoyed; and, on the other hand, how he was independent of it, when he told the daughters of Jerusalem, 'Weep not for me,' and showed, at every step, that he was the giver, not the receiver, of aid and sympathy.

(iii) But we must still further notice the principle which regulated the entire life of Christ, 'My meat and my drink is to do the will of him that sent me, and to finish his work.'

As man he must also be viewed as the image of God, and that image is found in the perfect knowledge of God, in unspotted holiness; in purity of heart, in unswerving conformity of life to the divine will, in a living example which displays the loveliest of all moral scenes, and which shines in him in order that it may be conveyed to us. And to this allusion is made when we are said to 'behold as in a glass the glory of the Lord, and to be changed into the same image.' We could have no idea of the created image of God as impressed on Adam if we did not see it living, moving, breathing in Christ. But in him all is made plain. John Owen, the great Puritan writer, remarks that it is a foolish thing to talk of the imitation of Christ: till we have a new sense and relish for divine things and see a glory in the things themselves. But, on the other hand, when we do, in this spirit, habitually dwell in his society, and see his glory like the first disciples, when we have a fellowship with him in all the scenes which he irradiated with his presence here, when the Church holds converse with him as if we formed part of that little company who went in and out along with him and listened to the gracious words that proceeded out of his mouth, when the followers of Christ really gaze on all those beams of glory which shine from his Person and animate our souls, when we habitually inquire how the redeemer acted in similar scenes, and you will find that there is something analogous in them to every position in which Providence will place us; when we ponder his meekness and lowliness, his self-consuming zeal, his patience in bearing the contradiction of sinners, his tears over the lost, his long-suffering with the wayward ambition of his followers, his spending whole nights alone in prayer, his silence under insults, and his sympathy with those who needed it, the unshaken friendship and tenderest affection that ever beat in a human heart as displayed in the bosom of the family of Bethany, we have a picture which the world cannot do without. And on that divinely creative pattern which is life-giving and communicative of strength, and therefore unlike all others, the Church must fix her gaze till every feature and lineament of his image is renewed upon our souls. And there it will shine till time merge in the glories of eternity to vivify, ennoble, elevate, and conform us to what he himself is.

2. *But not only is it said that a minister is a minister of Christ — a faithful minister of Christ — he is also, secondly, called a minister of the Church.*

The sacred title descriptive of the minister's commissions is 'minister of the Church' (Col. 1:24, 25). They promote the Church's welfare with the most affectionate concern, and at any cost; and hence says the apostle — 'I endure all things for the elect's sake, that they also obtain the salvation which is in Christ Jesus with eternal glory' (2 Tim. 2:10). The Church is dear to every minister, because it has been bought with the precious blood of Christ, as of a lamb without blemish and without spot. The apostle accordingly, while directing the elders of Ephesus to take heed to the flock, enforces the precept by the consideration that Christ purchased the Church with his own blood. To be permitted to minister to the Church and promote her welfare is deemed a privilege by all who drink into the same spirit with the Lord who loved the Church and gave himself for her.

But while the pastor comforts the feeble-minded, warns the unruly, speaks consolation to the troubled, he receives seven-fold into his own bosom, or is comforted by the mutual faith called into exercise. This will always hold good unless cold formality and hackneyed officialism have settled down on men's minds. The sense of connection with the Church lends elevation to the character. We can give no quarter to the paralysing thought that the support of Christ's Church is cast upon us in such a sense that we have rather to support it with our puny efforts and defences than be supported by it. On the contrary, the resources of the kingdom of God are upon the scene to bear up the minister. All who ever effectually promoted the cause of Christ, accordingly, were wont to regard themselves rather as passive instruments than active movers in the onward march of the kingdom of God. This comes to light in the words of Luther, Whitefield, and others who felt that the kingdom of heaven rather apprehended them and caught them up as well as sustained them to act their part in its triumphal march. They spoke as men well aware that they had rather to stand still and see the salvation of God than originate the movement, and felt that they were moved by a mightier Hand. But such is their love for the Church that they say, 'If I forget thee, O Jerusalem, let my right hand forget its cunning; if I do not remember thee, let my tongue cleave to the roof of my mouth, if I prefer not Jerusalem above my chief joy' (Psa. 137:5, 6).

3. *They are termed not only ministers of Christ and ministers of the Church, they are next called ministers of the word.*

This title intimates that the word is of paramount authority, and that the pastor's main business is to expound that word, and to enforce its authority. The loss of power in the Church compared with former days may be traced in a large measure to the fact that there is little appeal to inspired authority. There is a vague substitution of human opinion in place of that which is divine. The word of God must be heard authoritatively as from God, and where that is wanting men are not sufficiently brought into the presence of God, and before the bar of God as sinners. All powerful preaching is run up to the authority of the oracles of God.

It was said by an eminent Christian philosopher, Wynpersse, of Holland,[1] when setting forth the distinc-

[1] Dionysius van de Wynpersse (1724–1808) was an eighteenth-century Christian philosopher-theologian in the Netherlands.—Ed.

tion between mere disquisition and the proclamation of the gospel message, 'I attend to a preacher when he says "I will prove the point under discussion from the nature of the thing"; I attend still more when he says, "experience also teaches it"; but in the Church of God it is indispensably necessary to have something more. I expect that he shall further explicitly declare what has been testified respecting it by Moses, David, or one of the prophets, — by our Lord Jesus Christ, or some of his apostles. Then only have I heard the word of God.' Thus, did a great man of philosophic mind contrast preaching with the philosopher's peculiar walk of disquisition.

In a word, the preacher must run the matter up to authority. He must make men hear the word of God, and without this he does not gain the end of preaching, which is to bring men's minds into subjection to the obedience of Christ. Though the ordinary preacher is not like apostles and prophets, the immediate recipient of revelation, yet as the expounder of words which have perpetual validity, and under a realizing sense of having received his commission from the same Lord, with a charge to proclaim the same message, he feels warranted to speak with the authority of one who utters a 'thus saith the Lord.' And the hearers are well aware of the difference when they are thus addressed. They expect to be brought into a higher presence, and before a divine tribunal; they feel a want, though unable to describe what it is, when that is little done. They recognize a majesty, a power, a weight in that style of preaching which places them in the full light of God's presence, and compels them to attend to an authoritative declaration of law and gospel. Then only do they listen to the oracles of God and not to the guesses and opinions the wisdom and disquisitions, of their fellow-men.

The line of demarcation must be carefully drawn between law and gospel, a distinction which was once familiar as a household word in the Protestant Church. The entire discharge of ministerial duty proceeds on that distinction, and every point of doctrine refers to one or other of these heads. If it is not made apparent that the law commands and the gospel gives; that the law speaks terror as the ministration of wrath, and that the gospel speaks comfort as the ministration of righteousness, the utmost confusion and dislocation of theological doctrine ensues. Where distress of mind or anxiety of conscience exists, nothing relieves it. The proclamation of the gospel embraces the grand central truths to which the Church always confessed, the missive solid truths to which men's minds always turn for comfort. The deep-seated ruin of mankind and their vast guilt, the necessity of regeneration, the Deity, the mission, the atoning work of the Lord, the need of forgiving grace, the assurance of salvation, the mission and work of the Holy Spirit, the Comforter, the plan and tenor of the Covenant of Grace must stand prominently forth to view.

The preacher who acts upon a system of reserve, who fails to exhibit the truths bearing upon man's relation to the Judge of all is invariably blighted and forfeits the success which he perhaps expected. If the pulpit gives an uncertain sound as to the great articles of the ruin and remedy, Redemption and Regeneration, the impressions will be superficial, and little fruit will be reaped. In the dim mirror which is held up the sinner cannot recognize himself, nor be aroused by the appeal 'Thou art the man.' Preachers adapting themselves to the caprices of modern culture are often silent on the claims, extent, and spirituality of the divine law, as if men were no longer comforted by them. They ignore the vicarious sacrifice and atoning blood of Christ. They put amendment in place of repentance, pious feeling instead of faith upon the Son of God, they substitute Christian sentiment and culture for conversion to God, as if man were not a fallen being. Amusing the mind by historic pictures or dramatized delineation of character, they abandon the appeal to conscience and no longer strive to bring men before God's tribunal. Not to speak of the want of faithfulness involved in this, such a method shuts the avenue to the heart.

If the pastor feels that he is a minister of the word he will subject his mind to it. Does a text drop as the honeycomb with the sweetness of redeeming love and mercy? — the preacher while desirous to show its relation to the context and its connection with the system of divine truth will not deprive it of its peculiar character. Does a text echo with the terrors of the law? — the preacher while pointing to the method by which these terrors are disarmed will not remove its stern severity. Does a text propound the inscrutable mysteries of the gospel such as the Trinity, the Sonship of Christ, the Incarnation, and the mission of the Comforter? — the preacher, while anxious to make it practical, will not feel warranted to evacuate it of the inscrutable. Does a text enforce good works and their reward at last? The preacher will feel that it is not his part to evade the questions presented to him under the dread of not making all consistent with the gospel of the grace of God. The Scripture harmonizes itself in every mind, if it be expounded all round.

Dear friends, it only remains to say that the mournful event which has brought me here today has saddened the Church in no common way. Dr Miller, whom we mourn, was one of those who made the Scottish pulpit a power; a minister in that three-fold sense, a minister of Christ, a minister of the Church, and a minister of the word. Born in the manse of Eassie in March, 1810, he had passed his seventy-first year. Responding to his father's wish that he should study for the ministry, he early discovered remarkable aptness and decision. When he came under the transforming power of divine grace he became a noble witness and advocate of Scriptural Calvinistic doctrine. Being appointed minister of Monifieth in 1835 he remained till the Disruption (1843) an able and consistent preacher of evangelical doctrine. The intellectual power and unction of his ministrations, as I well remember, were remarkable and highly appreciated in Dundee and in all that district till the Disruption. In 1844 he was chosen minister of Free St Matthew's, Glasgow, and here you have had the rare privilege for thirty-six years of enjoying his remarkable ministrations, which for their faithfulness, power, and biblical character, entail on you a great responsibility. He was a singularly complete man. With an imposing personality seconded by great mental powers and deep piety, his preaching came home with arresting influence to men's business and bosom, he was ready, aye ready, and in full possession of his powers which always commanded attention and respect. A son of the manse, he was acquainted, as few men of his day were, with the Scottish ecclesiastical life of this century in all its phases and prominent personalities. When listening to his descriptions of the men and timings, of the theological tendencies and currents of the period, given in the raciest and freshest descriptive style, I often wished they could be written down for general use. They were always put in the light in which a profoundly religious man views everything bearing on the kingdom of God, and on man's capacity for the inheritance of the saints in light. He always spoke as a man who deeply felt that service rendered or neglected was gain or loss for eternity.

I shall notice a few things which struck me as characteristic of the man: —

(1) First, he had a rare power of expression and a felicitous ease of utterance always at command. From

the clear and elegant simplicity of his language no one could fail to apprehend his meaning. With sharply defined thoughts, and a certain intensity of mind, his language was incisive, but never stronger than the truth would bear. His style was like the man.

(2) Second, he always addressed himself to the elements in man's nature which linked the finite to the infinite, the creature to his Maker, Law-giver, and Judge. He did not entertain a congregation by sensuous or pictorial descriptions to the neglect of direct appeals to the spiritual elements which are to find an echo in man's nature. He commended the truth to every man's conscience, and dilated on the grand doctrines which he had received into his own soul. But he was bent on reaching the entire man, the whole mind of the hearer. While objective doctrinal teaching was fully given to inform the understanding, and to make the impression which is fitly produced only by this channel, he never allowed his hearers to rest there till he reached their conscience by some of those allusions to the divine authority and law which he knew so well how to use.

(3) Third, he enforced doctrine and duty, justification and sanctification, in admirable proportion. No one could allege against him that the certain and indissoluble connection between justification and sanctification was not emphatically taught. He felt that a preacher aims too low who stops short of conversion. But when men are converted he deeply felt that every thing will stagnate, unless prominence is given to Christian character,

Christian experience, Christian ethics; that they cannot exist apart; that doctrine will not retain its freshness without life and conversely; and that Christian ethics infallibly follow, but do not precede peace with God.

(4) Fourth, add to all this a deep calm zeal which, while admitting whatever of good attached to any religious phenomenon, never bartered away certain truth for the uncertain possibility of advantage or spent its energy in restless bustle. His balanced mind and regulated zeal like an instinct kept him in the happy medium.

I admired many things in our departed friend, who deservedly filled a large place in the public eye. But there was none that attracted me more than his inflexible allegiance to truth and duty, and his ripe spirituality of mind. He entered with astonishing clearness of perception into the historic incidents and doctrines of Scripture, he identified himself with these many-coloured scenes on the principle that the new creature is the same in every age, and that the believer's relation to Christ is the same amid all the degrees of objective light. He lived over again the principles, aims, and motives of the several characters, and could at every turn distinguish grace from nature with singular precision. His first inquiry was how men would act, and ought to act, in given circumstances; and he brought out the principles from which they did act with marked accuracy, recognizing what was of God under every garb and every weakness. He exhibited the gospel in its application to men's life, and he owned nothing as true which had not enough of vital energy to throw a transforming influence over life.

Alas! we shall see his face no more. One parting word to all. You, his flock for whom he assiduously laboured as one that must give account, have yet to meet him at the great white throne, and to give in your account for the improvement made of a ministry of thirty-six years among you. The unsaved who withstood the entreaties and expostulations addressed to them have a vast responsibility. They who have put off the moment of decision to a more convenient season, have to meet that faithful minister of Christ in presence of their Judge. Where will you appear if you are still impenitent? What a thought is this to the self-righteous, the unconverted, the procrastinating hearer! O awake in time, before it is too late! Let the recollection of all that you heard during the ministry that is now over move you to repentance. Accept the great salvation, which it was the business of his life to commend. At that day, that awful day, his sermons and expostulations will be all recalled, and nothing will be forgotten — recalled from the book of God's remembrance, as well as your own memory.

13

The Confessing of Christ before Men, and the Promised Reward[1]

Whosoever therefore shall confess me before men, him will I confess also before my Father which is in heaven.
—Matthew 10:32

DEAR FRIENDS, — Amid the wide-spread grief and lamentation caused by the removal of the preacher to whom you listened with avidity for many years, and whose voice we shall hear no more it seems proper to fix attention on one of the most marked features of his public life. I have selected this text to remind you that he may, in a pre-eminent measure, be described as a witness of the truth, as a *confessor* who was never

[1] A sermon preached in Newington Free Church, Edinburgh, on the occasion of the passing of the Rev. James Begg, D.D., on the afternoon of Sabbath, October 7, 1883. James Begg (1808–83) became a Church of Scotland minister in 1830. In 1843 he adhered to the Free Church of Scotland. He was actively engaged in the controversies of the nineteenth century Church and society, invariably taking a conservative evangelical position. In 1835 he became minister in Liberton, Edinburgh. After the Disruption he became minister in Newington Free Church, where he spent the remainder of his ministry till his passing.—Ed.

ashamed of the gospel of Christ. He believed with the heart and *confessed* with the mouth: and a weighty responsibility rests on you, and on the society in which he moved, for the way in which you have pondered and accepted his testimony.

Throughout this chapter the Lord Jesus gave a solemn charge to the apostles, as he sent them out on their first missionary tour. He gave them detailed directions, as well as general principles and motives, for the discharge of their commission. They might be timid in view of imminent danger, and fail to confess their Lord, and in this text the Lord encourages and nerves them for their task — (1), by setting forth their duty, 'Whosoever shall confess me before men'; and (2), by describing the great reward, 'Him will I confess also before my Father.'

1. *They who were called by the Lord Jesus were charged to confess him before men.* They were boldly to confess him as the Son of God and as the Messiah, and his doctrine as divine doctrine. They received the apostolical commission for this very end. Well might they be filled with awe when they reflected what they had undertaken to perform. Thus Paul, referring at a later time to the sacred and momentous trust committed to him, says: 'To me, who am less than the least of all saints, is this grace given, that I should preach among the Gentiles the unsearchable riches of Christ' (Eph. 3:8). The apostles received a commission to be boldly executed in his name, — a commission to preach his gospel, and to

confess his name — a commission having for its scope to testify, in the name of a Three-One God, that all has been done that God held necessary to be done for the world's salvation; that men have only to come and receive, to believe and be saved, without money and without price; and that nothing but a Christ-rejecting unbelief now shuts men out from the possession of the Divine favour.

As to these first *confessors of the truth*, they were first made Christians or regenerate men, and then labourers in the cause of Christ; and so it is with ministers still. They are first made alive to God, and then work. *Though the gifts* which the Spirit calls into exercise *have their basis in mental or natural endowments* and often lie concealed from others and from themselves till they are stirred into action by the entrance of spiritual life, it must never be forgotten that the Lord Jesus, from whom all these endowments emanate, had appointed the service to which they could be made available, before the consciousness of possessing them had dawned on their own minds. This distribution of gifts, in their manifold and beautiful variety, is a daily proof that *the Lord Jesus lives* as the Dispenser of the Holy Spirit, and that he prepares his instruments as well as uses them. Thus the first disciples were Christians before Pentecost, though their gifts were undeveloped. But when the Holy Spirit was given at Pentecost, they were raised to an unwonted elevation, and to conceptions, such as they never knew before, of the spirituality of Christ's kingdom; and that is but an example of what is ever anew to be expected, as they wait on him who stirs gifts into greater efficiency and power.

The ordinary preacher is not the immediate Receiver of revelation; but when he identifies himself with the Revelation, and appeals to its authority, he makes men hear it as from the mouth of God, — a testimony infinitely more impressive than all the wisdom or reasoning of man.

The word of God must be adduced *so that it shall be heard authoritatively* from the mouth of the Lord; and wherever this is wanting, men are not sufficiently brought into the presence of God, and before the bar of God, as saints and sinners. It was happily said by a Christian philosopher: 'I attend to a preacher when he says: "I will prove the point to you from the nature of the thing." I attend still more when he adds, "Experience also teaches us." But in the Church it is indispensably necessary to have something more. I expect that he will explicitly declare what Moses, or David, or one of the prophets, — what our Lord Jesus Christ, or one of his apostles, testified respecting it: *then only have I heard the word of God.*' There you see how a highly philosophic mind distinguished preaching from his own peculiar walk of disquisition. *We* must run the matter up to authority. *We* must make men hear the word of God, and without this we do not gain the end of preaching.

The ultimate appeal must be to authority, and every preacher, as a commissioned ambassador, feels that he has not sufficiently honoured Scripture, or spoken in the name of him from whom he derives his commission, if he occupies attention with his own argumentation, and refers but little to the authority of God, to the divine utterances of Scripture, to the examples there recorded, as seen in the light of God's countenance, and applied to the present relations of life among us. The hearers expect to be brought before a higher presence: they feel a want, they know not what, when this is little done, or ineffectually performed; they recognize a majesty, power, and weight in that style of preaching which places them in the full light of God's presence, and compels them to attend to his authoritative declarations. Then only do they listen to the word of God, and not to the wisdom or disquisitions of man.

Office-bearers, extraordinary or ordinary, are nothing but ambassadors; and an ambassador, treating in the name of his king, has no arbitrary power of his own, no discretion beyond that which is conferred on him. In like manner, all the testimony of confessors *is founded* on the word of God, and their message has neither warrant nor validity apart from it.

If you would image in your minds a true servant of Christ, picture to yourselves a man who watches for souls as one that must give account, — who, with pastoral care, teaches the ignorant and them that are out of the way; who reclaims the erring and invites the desponding; who, with genuine sympathy, ministers to the wounded spirit, and to the distressed in circumstances, — who receives infants to the seal of the Covenant, and brings them under instruction at the proper age for the Lord's Supper, who blesses them in marriage, and comforts them in sickness, by directing them to the true source of consolation; who waits upon them on their death-beds, and follows the remains of those to whom many services affectionately bound him, to their last resting place. All this falls to his lot, and, so far as strength permits, all this is cheerfully performed by a true servant of Christ, as the noblest service to which human energies can be consecrated.

That *a great amount of time* is required for this he well knows; but he grudges not the time. That this must be chiefly done away from the eyes of others he also knows; and he is content, and desirous that it should be so, having no wish to win the applause of men for the discharge of functions, manifold and various, to be seen only by him who seeth in secret. The Holy Spirit has made him overseer over the flock, and he does all this as a homage to the Shepherd and Bishop of souls, who commissioned him to feed his sheep and lambs. He conveys a message the most momentous that human lips can utter — a message which, as it is accepted or rejected, decides man's destiny forever.

He proclaims the message of reconciliation, with the greatest power and effect when he is most in the *attitude of dependence* — when he prays with the greatest abasement when the proclamation of the gospel comes from one who cherishes an entire and absolute dependence on God. The result at which he aims is proportioned to the dependence which he cultivates during the time of preparation, in the announcement of the message, and after it has been delivered; and to maintain this dependence, to suppress anxiety, to exclude self-complacency, is a task of no easy attainment. *But it is this which, more than ought else, links him to Omnipotence.*

Such is the service of Christ's servants in confessing him before men. They avow their allegiance: they confess his authority as Lord of all, and this is associated with the following of the Lord Jesus in all his example — in his love and zeal, in his self-denial and prayerfulness.

2. *Consider the recompense of reward.* 'Him will I confess also before my Father who is in heaven.' The servants called to this arduous task — the martyrs who have shed their blood for Christ, and loved not their lives for his sake, the sincere disciples of all times, and in every variety of scene — shall be confessed before his Father, and be made partakers of an exceeding weight of glory. This honour have all the saints. It sustains them in continuing steadfast to the end, however heavy their work, however irksome their post, however great the obloquy which they may be called to bear. But when the Lord says, 'Him will I confess before my Father who is in heaven,' are we to understand that this recognition takes place immediately after death? In the highest sense the reward is reserved for the resurrection day, and will then be fully enjoyed. But as everything is developed

step by step, so is the reward awaiting them above. Scripture, for the most part, speaks as if the consummation of the Christian's felicity were kept in store for the saints on the day of their final resurrection; but it also holds out to us the most pleasant rest in God and spiritual refreshing immediately after death, without the fear of any trouble or invasion that can enter to disturb it. They find immediately after death the unspeakable deliverance of being freed from sin, and a perfect holiness which is never reached on earth, — and an increase in the life of God of which they had no conception here. Above all, they are '*with Christ*,' and in his immediate presence; as the apostle expresses it when he says, 'Having a desire to depart and to be *with Christ*, which is far better' (Phil. 1:23).

(1) *It must never be forgotten that Scripture holds out the prospect of this recognition at the resurrection as a special privilege.* But this is far from obscuring the assurance of happiness immediately after death. At the coming of the Lord with all his saints the advantages connected with a glorious and incorruptible body will be received for the first time. All the pleasures which 'new heavens and new earth' impart will then be fully known. All the honour and joy of a public recognition before assembled world will then be fully given. Those who are alive and remain till the coming of the Lord, and who shall never pass through the death and dissolution of the body which we have to encounter, will be changed in such a way as at once to put on the resurrection body, and be spectators

of the great and glorious works indicated by the phrase, 'the restitution of all things.'

(2) *The teaching of Scripture on the final glory of the redeemed leads us to conclude* that they shall 'be with Christ' in glorified bodies, 'according to the working of that mighty power whereby he is able to subdue all things to himself.' What the place may be, and what the nature of the place shall be, is not minutely revealed. The Scriptures inform us that it is the Father's House, and that the Lord Jesus will confess them before his Father.

The *first stage* of this felicity, I repeat, begins *at death*. The text has its incipient accomplishment the moment the Christian closes his eyes on the things of sense and time. When the earthly house of this tabernacle is dissolved, we have a building of God, a house not made with hands, eternal in the heavens: and the apostle says, 'We know this' (2 Cor. 5:1).

(3) *A difficulty is presented to some minds by the consideration of the fact that the soul is created to dwell in a material body*. They see that in the present state they have the knowledge and enjoyment of external material things only through the use of the bodily senses; and it seems to them *as if the soul could not truly possess the enjoyments* when deprived of the body. Some minds, exercised with these thoughts, have arrived at the unwarrantable conclusion, that at death the soul falls into an *unconsciousness or rest*, in which it is no longer sensible of time or outward things till the resurrection.

But, as soul and body are certainly distinct and can be separated, we cannot presume to limit or set bounds to that knowledge and enjoyment which the soul may have apart from the body. The opposite may be the truth. The separation from the body till a fit material organism is given at the resurrection day, may be the very way by which the soul is made capable of a knowledge of enjoyment, unknown before, impossible before. Certainly, Scripture makes it evident that the souls of the redeemed are at their death taken to be with Christ in his eternal felicity — taken from sorrow to joy, from conflict to rest, from time to eternity, from seeing through a glass darkly, to a condition when they shall know even also as they are known.

This comes out again and again in our Lord's words with peculiar clearness. He says, with an amplitude of meaning which we cannot fully comprehend, 'He that believeth in me shall never die,' 'shall never see death' — language which points to the continued enjoyment not only of mental life but of spiritual life, in an exercise more unimpeded and more active than was ever experienced before. Not only so: the Lord Jesus says, 'Father, I will that they also whom thou hast given me be with me where I am, that they may behold my glory which thou hast given me' (John 17:24). He meant that his people should be with him after his death, which was near at hand. When he says, 'Father I will that they also whom thou hast given me be with me,' he intimates that he was to be already there to be seen in his glory, and that he who died for them had an absolute right and claim to them — a greater right to take them home than we can have to retain them here.

Here I may allude to some enquiries or perplexities which are found to haunt the believing mind in certain moods or mental states. These it may be useful to remove, so far as the light furnished by revelation suffices to remove them.

(1) *It may be said, How do the spirits of the saved reach those glorious mansions?* How do they reach the place prepared for them? How do they evade the obstructions and difficulties of that strange and solitary path? It is enough that the Forerunner has for us entered — that he has gone to prepare a place for us, and that he takes us to be for ever with himself. It is enough to fall back on the word of him who has no difficulty in accomplishing all his promises to the letter: 'Where I am there shall also my servant be.' He who took the malefactor with him to Paradise, he who made Stephen feel that he was receiving the departing spirit, is possessed of all-sufficient resources to convey the ransomed spirit home.

But the Lord Jesus expressly tells us, moreover, *of ministering spirits.* In the parable of the rich man and Lazarus, we are informed that in the last necessity the departing spirit is safely conducted by angels to their blissful rest. *Much may be portrayed, doubtless, in figurative language*: but the entire parable has for its object to display the nature of the separate disembodied state; and we cannot doubt that it indicates at the hour of death the service of angels in the case of the meanest and most despised believer, the honour of an angelic convoy to those celestial mansions. O, welcome expectation! O! blessed thought on the bed of death! O, reassuring prospect! Angels are ready at Christ's command, wherever the saints expire, to bring the ransomed spirit home. They who ascended and descended on the Son of man in the days of his flesh — they who continually pass from heaven to earth, and from earth to heaven, know to bear, more quickly than thought itself, the emancipated spirit to the glorious abode prepared for it — to the society of Christ and the spirits of the just men made perfect. Conscious of human weakness, we are ready to imagine that the departing spirit might be filled with fear at the appearance of those glorious messengers of God. But their friendly and comforting presence takes all fears away. They make the way unspeakably pleasant, as well as short, the ardent and longing desire of the disembodied soul, that soon finds itself before the throne of God and the Lamb.

(2) *Another question is, What do they enjoy in their disembodied state?* More than they have ever tasted here. Paul, who enjoyed the highest consolations, and who said, 'I can do all things through Christ that strengtheneth me,' — expressed his deliberate judgment when he said, 'to depart and be with Christ is *far better*' (Phil. 1:23). He knew that to die was *gain*; that he would gain much that was hitherto unknown to him; that to be with Christ would *bring with it a* supply of glory,

holiness, and joy, such as had no place in his experience on earth. They have the most ecstatic joy.

That the mind may be moved by the meditation of eternal life, the Bible proposes a boundless compensation or over-payment for all the reproach and persecution encountered in the present life — in that hour when they pass from time into eternity. They are ushered out of great tribulation, which would of itself make them of all men most miserable, into a rest which is an infinite compensation for all they have endured — 'the rest that remains for the people of God.'

(3) *Above all, They enjoy the beatific vision.* The Lord their God, whom they now know only by faith, and in whom they here find much that is still incomprehensible, will then be fully known, for ever beheld, as well as intimately enjoyed. The beatific vision, consisting in the full display of all God's attributes as seen in Christ, who is the image of the invisible God, is a theme of the greatest moment, the discussion of which, when rightly handled, is highly sanctifying. It was largely descanted on by the scholastic divines in mediaeval times, though the expositions that emanated from them were unduly speculative. It was a favourite theme with John Howe, Richard Baxter, Thomas Shepard, and others of the Puritans,[1] whose theology was largely influenced by the study of the divine attributes, and who contemplated

[1] For biographical details of these divines see Beeke and Pederson, *Meet the Puritans* (Grand Rapids, MI: Reformation Heritage Books, 2006).—Ed.

the blessedness of the righteous in seeing God. It fills a large place in the writings of Jonathan Edwards, the basis of whose entire theology rests on the Divine attributes.

In what does the beatific vision consist? In an enraptured contemplation of the essential excellences, and attributes, and Trinitarian relations of God. But the invisible God, even in the bliss above, will not be discerned by eyes of sense. Though the organs of vision will be gratified, when the resurrection-body is restored, by gazing on the glorified humanity of Christ in the separate state, it would be assigning sense its usual undue pre-eminence, to imagine that the beatific vision will be solely enjoyed with eyes of sense. Even in the beatific vision Christ is still the image of the invisible God. The expression frequently used in Scripture, 'to see God,' denotes that our view of God will be direct and vivid, as well as posses the utmost certainty and clearness; and the creature, in the enjoyment of that vision, will become impeccable, reflecting that bright beauty and surpassing glory with which it holds transforming intercourse. It will be like him, for we shall see him as he is.

The blessedness of the beatific vision consists of contemplating the perfections of God, and the persons of the Trinity, in their unity and distinction. Such a view must be transporting to a creature, when it affords eternal satisfaction to God himself. When the light and splendour of all the divine perfections on which the mind fastens its unwearied gaze, *is seen in full-orbed glory*, the pure in heart will find in that view everything congenial to their nature. The views of God will not be gathered, as they now are gathered, from the works of his hands; for in the light above, the attributes themselves, and not their reflection on the works of his hand — will form the subject of our adoring contemplation. And every fresh look of which eternity prolongs the privilege will indefinitely expand the mind, as your reflections upon the effect of the beatific vision on the mental powers will at once convince you.

And on God's side the constant supplies of divine communications will never be interrupted. 'They shall hunger no more, neither thirst any more,' etc.: 'the Lamb that is in the midst of the throne shall feed them, and lead them to living fountains of water: and God the Lord shall wipe all tears from their eyes' (Rev. 7:17).

So careful is God to connect a reward of grace with every service, that Christ assures us 'not a cup of cold water given in the name of a disciple shall lose its reward.'

These two things are fully consistent: salvation by grace, and the full recognition of service done. God justifies his people on the ground of Christ's finished work alone; but it is emphatically affirmed that he is not unrighteous to forget your work of faith or labour of love shown toward his name (Heb. 6:10). *Take one illustration out of many.* The description which Christ has given of the judgment introduces a company of servants, expressing astonishment that they should be represented as ministering *to his necessities* and visiting *him* in prison: 'Lord, when saw we *thee* an hungered and fed *thee*, or thirsty and gave *thee* drink, when saw we *thee* sick or in prison and ministered to *thee*?' They were more conscious of infirmities and inconsistencies than of important services, and beyond measure surprised at the construction put on offices of benevolence offered to the saints, which their Lord accepts as having been done to himself: 'Ye did it unto me.' There you see how the Lord confesses them before his Father, and their gracious reward. Let me only further add that there are degrees of glory. All believers stand on the same level, so *far as they are justified and adopted*, for one is not more justified than another: one is not more adopted than another. The right to heaven is the same to all believers, for the righteousness of God is unto all and upon all them that believe (Rom. 3:22). But the *degrees of sanctification* are as manifold and various as there are individuals, and the same thing holds true of the degrees of glory: 'To sit on my right hand and on my left,' said Christ, 'is not Mine to give,' that is, by mere arbitrary donation: 'but it shall be given to those for whom it is prepared' (Matt. 19:23).

Brethren, it only remains for me to refer to *my esteemed and loved friend* for whom we mourn this day. Hardly can I realize the fact, that in all the departments of Church-work, where he was always a central figure, we shall see his face no more. In designating him a *witness and confessor*, for all that the Church has accepted as divine truth, I use what seems to me *the most appropriate term* to describe him. He was ever ready to confess the name of Christ, and to recognize his Lord's authority in those very relations and spheres of action from which the present mode is to exclude that name. Dr Begg, by his great personality, and by the historic place which he had taken in all the discussions of his times, was one of a class, now greatly fewer, who made his Church conspicuous, and who did much, by his religious advocacy of great questions, to educate as well as raise the tone of the community.

It were out of place, except in the most cursory way, to refer here to the incidents in his life with which his flock and the public are already familiar. Nor do I refer to him at all with the design to exalt the man, but only to extol and magnify the grace of God, by which he was what he was. I have little doubt that the Church, which mourns his loss, will embalm his memory among her most cherished recollections.

In the manse of New Monkland, his father — a true embodiment of the Scottish Churchman, and of the Covenanting spirit — trained his distinguished son in all that was dear to himself, especially to the almost unparalleled acquaintance with the Scriptures, and a full appreciation of Presbyterian principles. Sent at an early age to college, he soon discovered well-balanced mental powers of a superior order, quickness of apprehension, a mature judgment, and singular precision as well as readiness of expression. Licensed to preach the gospel when comparatively young, his native eloquence, united to an unswerving attachment to sound doctrine and evangelical views, and engrafted on a genial and generous disposition, threw around the youthful preacher a peculiar charm; the effect of which, as I well remember in my student-days, was as impressive as it was attractive. It was a sufficient proof of the appreciation in which he was held, that he became, in quick succession, assistant to Dr Buchanan,[1] associate of Dr Jones, minister of Maxwelltown, of Paisley, and of Liberton. The two men to whom our late friend profoundly deferred in the ecclesiastical sphere, and at whose torch he lighted his fire, were Dr Andrew Thomson and Dr Thomas Chalmers, who exercised the most decisive influence on his future life and labours. The relations between Dr Chalmers and him appeared on the one side in a sort of paternal complacency, and on the other, in an affectionate veneration, which moulded him into the fluent advocate, as well as receptive follower, in the promotion of views which were of national as well as ecclesiastical importance. The services which Dr Begg rendered, under the animating

[1] Smeaton is referring here to James Buchanan (1804–70), an outstanding Reformed Theologian of the nineteenth century. Buchanan was ordained to the ministry of the Church of Scotland at Roslin in 1827. James Begg was ordained in 1830 as associate of the Rev. Dr Thomas Snell Jones (1754–1837) at Maxwelltown, Dumfries. Begg had been an 'assistant' to James Buchanan at North Leith, to where Buchanan was translated in 1828. Buchanan, like Begg, adhered to the Free Church of Scotland in 1843.—Ed.

influence of Dr Chalmers, in the cause of Pauperism and Church extension, in the defence of national religion, and in the long and arduous non-intrusion controversy, ending in the memorable Disruption of the Scottish Church were very great, and tended, along with the concurrent Labours of many like-minded men, to evoke a zeal and an energy, a national sentiment, and an ecclesiastical enthusiasm, which nothing but the impulse of great minds in combination — under the accompanying influence of the Spirit of God — could possibly have created.

Our departed friend was my next neighbour at Liberton when I was minister of Morningside, in 1839 and 1840. It was then that I really knew Dr Begg. Much pleasant intercourse subsisted between us. I saw his noble aims, his affectionate, tender nature, his magnanimous spirit in denying himself for the Church which he loved, and his complete indifference to the censure and calumny which, like the prophet's mantle, was borne by him through all his life. He touched life at many points. He had an affinity, a many-sided point of attachment to minds which might be very differently constituted, but capable of meeting on some subjects of common interest. One obvious peculiarity, which could not fail to arrest the attention of all who were much in contact with him, was that his mind *gravitated to the practical and to what was capable of being realized*, while he bade away from him — as not only distracting but of little moment — all that was merely speculative and transcendental, and also all of which the logical result was doubtful.

When we turn to *the preaching* of our lamented friend, it was objective and doctrinal, discovering a clear perception of the mutual dependence of the several doctrines. His expository opening of the chapter read at every service, was in reality a condensed summary or lecture, and showed an analytic as well as synthetic power as rare as it was unpretentious. He uniformly acted on the principle that the heart is to be reached only through the understanding; and hence you never were subjected to the sensational and spasmodic style of producing an impression, often as evanescent as it is unmeaning. But while he always appealed to the intellect, few men produced a deeper impression by his appeals to Christ's authority as King, and by his skill in speaking to the conscience. He preached law and gospel with commanding power. He opened up to your minds, as few men have been found to do, the full doctrine of the Covenant of grace, exhibiting in all its outline that remedial plan on which men's hopes for eternity are built. He sketched the Trinitarian way of grace; and his hearers will recall how their views of truth *gained breadth, clearness, and amplitude*, as he unfolded the scheme of the divine procedure from its origin to its final consummation.

As an *ecclesiastic* Dr Begg had his marked peculiarity and definite sphere. He was the impersonation of the Scottish Churchman. The place which he occupied, *and which was everywhere allowed to him*, arose not only from his native vigour, and force of character, and pre-eminence as an accomplished and ready orator, but from his fidelity to convictions, which were based upon the supreme authority of Scripture. To his mind God is represented as coming to us in the Divine Word, and as clothed in the divine word. Hence, he held by the word as the reason and rule of action, without conferring with flesh and blood. If Martin Luther was wont to say: 'How difficult it is to stand before God without God's word,' we may say that, in altered circumstances, a similar heroism was uniformly evinced by our departed friend, who always spoke of the unaided reason of man, with all its arrogance and fancied power, as grovelling in its conceptions of truth and duty, and as little reliable, except in so far as it was ennobled and expanded by the revealed word of God.

But while Scripture, in his regard, was absolutely paramount, he never deemed the doctrinal affirmations of the Church or her past attainments as having no significance and no validity for the nineteenth century. He never thought or allowed it to be said, that our Lord's promise, 'My sheep hear my voice,' had in past ages failed of its accomplishment. He lived in his own age — as few men have ever done — with an open eye, an intense amount of interest, and a deep, calm zeal for the declarative glory of God. But he lived in the past as well as the present; and he stoutly resisted the tendency to sever the thread which connects us with the past, and would inaugurate a development which shall be wholly and absolutely new. Nay, he measured the present time, with its heady and high-minded self-complacency, by a previous time in which spiritual elements were more abundant, and submission to divine authority more profound; and he held that the landmarks of the past religious attainments in our native land were ever to be duly considered, and not lightly abandoned. He regarded the struggles for our Fathers as manifesting the presence and operations of the living Redeemer along the line of history, — as a school of instruction — as an evidence of the transforming power of Christianity, and as announcing much which we must have an ear to hear.

It would carry me beyond my limits to advert to the societies and enterprises, social, benevolent, and religious, into which his large and loving sympathies prompted him to enter. Around him may be grouped all the ecclesiastical notabilities of a bygone generation, prior to the Disruption and subsequent to that event. Around him may also be grouped all the Free Church Leaders, with whom he acted as founders of a new organisation, or carried on discussions when divergency of views emerged.

Let it suffice to say, that in the latter portion of his life three or four subjects largely occupied his thoughts — Popery, National Religion, the German School of Religious Thought, and Scriptural Worship. But I can do no more than name them.

One of the most pleasing incidents came out in connection with his last appearance on the sanctity of the Lord's day. I understand that he sent a message to the working men, by one who has their confidence, to guard the Lord's day as their fundamental position. 'Tell them,' said he, 'to begin with the Sabbath: that is their day, and no man can take it from them.'

I have only to add that our departed friend was one of those men whose rising in any epoch infuses a general confidence that they are moving in an orbit which is safe, and that a certain centripetal and centrifugal force operates upon them, from opposite sides, to preserve them from extremes. His lot was cast in an age which showed a great readiness to make concessions, adjustments, and compromises in the domain of proper doctrine; and in him we see one standing like a rock, inflexible and unmoved amid the billows which dashed on him from every side.

One parting word to you all. Follow him as he followed Christ, and only as he followed Christ. 'Whose faith follow,' says the apostle. The converted in the congregation, whom he regarded as his joy and crown of rejoicing, will meet him in the presence of the Lord at his coming. The unconverted in the congregation, and in this city and land, who often heard that manly and bold Confessor of the truth, have a great responsibility — How will you be able, in the great day of the Lord, to meet him in the presence of that Lord and Saviour to whom you were so urgently and tenderly invited, from day to day? O remember how times and opportunities pass away. *That voice you will hear no more.* And yet you have not done with those sermons, invitations, and appeals, which followed one another during that precious and long-protracted ministry. They will all be recalled in eternity to your woe and agony, if they fail, in your recollection of them, to influence and move you to accept the great salvation. O, may the Spirit of illumination yet descend on you, to melt you and subdue you. How often has he said, 'Come': 'Come, for all things are ready!' 'We beseech you, in Christ's stead, Be ye reconciled to God.'

The Published Writings of George Smeaton[1]

1. PRINTED SERMONS AND LECTURES

1. 'The Lord's jealousy against backsliders consistent with his unchanging love,' in *The Free Church Pulpit*, vol. 1 (Perth: James Dewar and Son, 1845), pp. 587-97.

2. *A witnessing church — a church baptized with the Holy Ghost* (Perth: James Dewar and Son, 1846). This sermon was also reproduced in *The Free Church Pulpit*, vol. 3 (Perth: James Dewar and Son, 1847) pp. 23-33.

3. *Necessary harmony between doctrine and spiritual life: being an introductory lecture, delivered on 9 November 1853 to the Free Church students attending the Divinity Hall at Aberdeen* (Aberdeen: A. Brown; Edinburgh: Johnstone & Hunter, 1853).

4. *Introductory lecture, winter 1853–54, on the origin, objects and necessity of the Association* [Aberdeen Reformation Society] (Aberdeen: Stevenson, 1853).

[1] This is taken from the editor's biography *George Smeaton: Learned Theologian and Biblical Scholar* (Darlington: Evangelical Press, 2007).

5. *Basis of Christian doctrine in divine fact: with particular reference to the modern realistic development of theology, being an introductory lecture, delivered at the opening of the Free Church divinity hall, Aberdeen, on Tuesday, 7 November 1854* (Aberdeen: A. Brown; Edinburgh: Johnstone & Hunter, 1854).

6. *'The real presence of Christ in the midst of his people,' a sermon [on Rev. 2:1] preached before the Free Provincial Synod of Aberdeen, on Tuesday, 8 April 1856* (Aberdeen: Davidson, 1856).

7. *Great Anti-Union Meeting in Glasgow, 25 October 1870: Speech of Rev. Professor Smeaton of Edinburgh* [Free Church Defence Association, Offices: 109 West George Street, Glasgow] (Glasgow: Dunn and Wright, 1870).

8. *'Union inadmissible on the basis proposed': being speeches delivered by members of the majority of ministers in the Free Presbytery of Edinburgh, on 8, 9 and 10 November 1870; with appendices* (Edinburgh: Duncan Grant, 1870), pp. 48-59.

9. *'The faithful labourer's reward in heaven,' sermon [on Dan. 12:3] preached in the Free West Church, Aberdeen, on Sabbath, 5 May 1872, being the Sabbath after the funeral of the Rev. Alex. D. Davidson, DD, late minister of that church* (Aberdeen: D. Wyllie & Son; A. & R. Milne; and John Smith, 1872), pp. 3-23.

10. 'A faithful minister of Christ [on Col. 1:7]' in *Sermons preached in Free St Matthew's Church, Bath Street, Glasgow, with special reference to the death of the Rev. Samuel Miller, DD, by the Rev. Professor Smeaton, DD,*

Edinburgh; the Rev. John Watson, MA, Sefton Park Church, Liverpool; and the Rev. Charles A. Salmond, MA, Free St Matthew's, Glasgow (Glasgow: John N. Mackinlay, 1881), pp. 5-17.

11. 'The confessing of Christ before men, and the promised reward [on Matt. 10:32]' in *Sermons preached in Newington Free Church, Edinburgh, on the occasion of the death of the Rev. James Begg, DD, by Rev. John Kennedy, DD, and the Rev. Professor George Smeaton, DD, on Sabbath, 7 October 1883* (Edinburgh: James Gemmell, 1883), pp. 19-32.

2. BOOKS AND PAMPHLETS

1. *The Improvement of a Revival Time*, New Year's tract (Edinburgh: James Taylor, *c.* 1860).
2. *The Doctrine of the Atonement as Taught by Christ Himself* (Edinburgh: T&T Clark, 1868; second edition, 1871). Reprinted: 1953 (Zondervan); 1991 (Banner of Truth Trust); 2001 (Sovereign Grace Publishers). Published in the 1970s in the USA by Sovereign Grace Publishers, bound in one volume with *The Doctrine of the Atonement as Taught by the Apostles.*
3. *Memoir of Alexander Thomson of Banchory* (Edinburgh: Edmonston and Douglas, 1869).
4. *The Doctrine of the Atonement as Taught by the Apostles* (Edinburgh: T&T Clark, 1870). Reprinted: 1957 (Zondervan); 1979 (Alpha); 1988 (Hendrickson);

1991 (Banner of Truth Trust); 2001 (Sovereign Grace Publishers).

5. *National Christianity and Scriptural Union* (Edinburgh: Johnstone, Hunter & Co., 1871).

6. *The New Scheme of Incorporation*, Free Church Tracts, no. 3 (Edinburgh, 1871).

7. *The Scottish Theory of Ecclesiastical Establishments and How Far the Theory is Realized. An address to the Glasgow Conservative Association, 13 April 1875* (Glasgow: Association's Rooms; Edinburgh: Lyon & Gemmell, 1875).

8. *The Doctrine of the Holy Spirit* (Edinburgh: T&T Clark, 1882). Reprinted: 1958 (twice); 1961 (Banner of Truth Trust). Second edition, 1889. Reprinted: 1974; 1980; 1988; 1997 (Banner of Truth Trust).

3. PREFACES AND INTRODUCTIONS

1. 'Suitableness of Erskine's writings to a period of religious revivals,' in *The Beauties of the Rev. Ralph Erskine*, Samuel McMillan, ed. (Aberdeen, Edinburgh, London and Glasgow: A. Fullerton and Co., n.d. [1860]), pp. 31-8.

2. Prefatory note to *Outlines of Discourses by the Late Rev. James Stewart, Aberdeen* (Edinburgh: Andrew Elliot, 1860).

3. Prefatory note to *Lord's Day*, by Johannes Gossner (London: T. Nelson and Sons, 1860).

4. Prefatory note to *Means and Methods to be Adopted for a Successful Ministry: Being an Introduction to Dr Spencer's 'Pastor's Sketches,'* by John Angell James (Birmingham: Hudson and Son, 1861).

5. Preface to *The Closer Walk, or, the Believer's Sanctification*, by Henry Darling, DD (Edinburgh: Andrew Elliot, 1862).

6. Preface to *Statement of the difference between the profession of the Reformed Church of Scotland, as adopted by the seceders, and the profession contained in the New Testimony and other Acts, lately adopted by the General Associate Synod: particularly on the power of the civil magistrate respecting religion, national reformation, etc., by the late Thomas M'Crie, DD (1807)* (Edinburgh: C. F. Lyon, 1871).

7. Introductory note to *On the inspiration of the Old and New Testaments: a chapter from Thomas Chalmers* (Edinburgh: Andrew Elliot, 1879).

8. Prefatory note to *The inspiration and circulation of the Bible*, by the Rev. William Fergusson (London: Elliot Stock, 1880).

9. Preface to *Memorials of the Late Miss Agnes Atken* (Edinburgh: James Taylor, 1882).

10. Preface to *Instrumental Music: A Consideration of the Arguments For and Against its Introduction into the Worship of the Free Church of Scotland*, by the Rev. John M'Ewan (Edinburgh: James Gemmell, 1883).

4. MAGAZINE ARTICLES

George Smeaton was editor of *The British and Foreign Evangelical Review*, in succession to William Cunningham, from 1860 to 1863. During that time and earlier he would have been responsible for many articles in the *Review.* Unfortunately, articles during that period were not attributed. The articles from the *Review* listed here have been picked up principally from notes in the appendix to the second edition of Smeaton's *The Doctrine of the Atonement as Taught by Christ Himself* (1871). In the case of articles listed in 3, 7, and 8 below, there is no more than a strong likelihood that these were from Smeaton's pen.

1. 'Immanuel: A discourse,' in *The Scottish Christian Herald* (vol. 2, second series, 4 Jan.–26 Dec. 1840), pp. 617-22.
2. 'Augustus Neander — His influence, system and various writings,' in *The British and Foreign Evangelical Review* (vol. 2, no. 6, Sept. 1853), pp. 701-39.
3. 'Old orthodoxy, new divinity and Unitarianism,' in *The British and Foreign Evangelical Review* (vol. 7, no. 23, Jan. 1858), pp. 168-99.
4. 'Anselm and his theory of the atonement,' in *The British and Foreign Evangelical Review* (vol. 8, no. 30, Oct. 1859), pp. 918-56.
5. 'The theory of an incarnation without a fall,' in *The British and Foreign Evangelical Review* (vol. 10, no. 35, Jan. 1861), pp. 80-96.
6. 'Oxford essayists,' in *The British and Foreign Evangelical Review* (vol. 10, no. 36, April 1861), pp. 407-30.

7. 'False theories of the atonement — McLeod Campbell and Baldwin Brown,' in *The British and Foreign Evangelical Review* (vol. 10, no. 37, July 1861), pp. 532-53.

8. 'Introduction to Romans,' in *The British and Foreign Evangelical Review* (vol. 10, no. 37, July 1861), pp. 607-23.

9. 'The Pauline doctrine of the righteousness of faith,' in *The British and Foreign Evangelical Review* (vol. 11, no. 39, Jan. 1862), pp. 192-206. The substance of this article was reproduced in expanded and amended form in Smeaton's *The Doctrine of the Atonement as Taught by the Apostles* (Edinburgh: T&T Clark, 1870), pp. 106-26.

10. 'Dr Cunningham's theological works,' in *The British and Foreign Evangelical Review* (vol. 11, no. 40, April 1862), pp. 480-4.

11. 'The atoning blood,' in *The Christian Treasury* (1 February 1871), pp. 73-75. From Professor Smeaton's able, learned, and exhaustive volume on the atonement (Edinburgh: T&T Clark, 1870).

12. 'The true preacher,' in *The Christian Treasury* (Edinburgh: Johnstone, Hunter, & Co., 1872), pp. 253-7.

13. 'Faith,' in *The Imperial Bible Dictionary* (London: Blackie & Son, 1866 [1864–6]), pp. 274-6.

5. SPECIAL STUDIES: WORKS BY OTHER AUTHORS

1. Homer Lehr Goddard, *The contribution of George Smeaton (1814–89) to theological thought* (PhD thesis, University of Edinburgh, 1960).

2. Norman Paul Madsen, *Atonement and pneumatology: A study in the theology of George Smeaton* (PhD thesis, University of St Andrews, 1974).

3. Malcolm Andrew Kinnear, 'George Smeaton and the development of the Calvinist view of the atonement,' in *Scottish New Testament scholarship and the atonement* (PhD thesis, University of Edinburgh, 1996), pp. 124-79.

4. Robert Mark Shillaker, *The federal pneumatology of George Smeaton (1814-89)* (PhD thesis, Highland Theological College, 2003).

OTHER BOOKS BY GEORGE SMEATON
PUBLISHED BY THE TRUST

The Apostles' Doctrine of the Atonement
568pp. cloth-bound, ISBN: 978 0 85151 599 1

Christ's Doctrine of the Atonement
520pp. cloth-bound, ISBN: 978 0 85151 600 4

The Doctrine of the Holy Spirit
400pp. cloth-bound, ISBN: 978 1 84871 704 6

'Page after page glows with the ardour of a preacher who is enamoured of his theme. ... The truth is so real to his own experience that he cares little for unprofitable controversies.' — C. H. SPURGEON

'Dr Smeaton was the master of a very clear and unobtrusive style of expression. ... He was as modest and unassuming as he was thorough and painstaking. A man can take his word in regard to any theme that he handles as soon as that of any writer on theological subjects.' — PRINCIPAL JOHN MACLEOD

BANNER *of* TRUTH

The Banner of Truth Trust originated in 1957 in London. The founders believed that much of the best literature of historic Christianity had been allowed to fall into oblivion and that, under God, its recovery could well lead not only to a strengthening of the church, but to true revival.

Interdenominational in vision, this publishing work is now international, and our lists include a number of contemporary authors, together with classics from the past. The translation of these books into many languages is encouraged.

A monthly magazine, *The Banner of Truth*, is also published, and further information about this, and all our other publications, may be found on our website, banneroftruth.org, or by contacting the offices below:

Head Office:
3 Murrayfield Road
Edinburgh
EH12 6EL
United Kingdom
Email: info@banneroftruth.co.uk

North America Office:
PO Box 621
Carlisle, PA 17013
United States of America
Email: info@banneroftruth.org